DATE			

Greece, Rome, and the Bill of Rights

Oklahoma Series in Classical Culture

Oklahoma Series in Classical Culture

Series Editor

A. J. Heisserer, *University of Oklahoma*

Advisory Board

Greece, Rome, and the Bill of Rights

SUSAN FORD WILTSHIRE

University of Oklahoma Press : Norman and London

to

ATW, Jr.

viro bono, civi bono, agricolae bono

By Susan Ford Wiltshire

(ed.) *The Usefulness of Classical Learning in the Eighteenth Century*
(University Park, Pa., 1976)
Public and Private in Vergil's Aeneid (Amherst, Mass., 1989)
Greece, Rome, and the Bill of Rights (Norman, 1992)

Library of Congress Cataloging-in-Publication Data
Wiltshire, Susan Ford, 1941–
    Greece, Rome, and the Bill of Rights / Susan Ford Wiltshire.—
1st ed.
        p.   cm. — (Oklahoma series in classical culture : v. 15)
    Includes bibliographical references and index.
    ISBN 0-8061-2464-4 (alk. paper)
        1. Human rights—Greece—History. 2. Human rights—Rome—History.
    3. United States—Constitutional law—Amendments—1st–10th.
    4. Natural law. 5. Comparative government.   I. Title. II. Series.
JC599.G728W55   1992   92-54142
323'.0938—dc20   CIP

Greece, Rome, and the Bill of Rights is Volume 15 of the Oklahoma Series
in Classical Culture.

Contents

Preface

THIS book began as part of a symposium on the classics and the United States Constitution, held at Boston University in 1989 in honor of Meyer Reinhold on his eightieth birthday. Professor Reinhold, principal founder of the study of the classical tradition in America, understands in a deeply personal way the relationship between scholarship and citizenship. *Greece, Rome, and the Bill of Rights*, like my original symposium paper, is meant as a tribute to this valued scholar and friend.

I could not have undertaken this project without the help of my colleague Thomas A. J. McGinn of the Department of Classical Studies at Vanderbilt University. I am grateful to Professor McGinn, a specialist in Roman law, for his expertise and enthusiasm for this endeavor.

Kimberly Wiar of the University of Oklahoma Press saw the possibilities for this book at the outset and was a trusted companion in the process of its completion.

The staff of the Vanderbilt Law Library, especially Mary Colosia and Howard Hood, offered patient help and hospitality to a stray classicist for many months. Other Vanderbilt colleagues who contributed bibliography and ideas were Robert H. Birkby, Robert Drews, Jean Porter, and

William H. Race. James Mathis, a classicist and lawyer, assisted in the early stages of research.

Michael Gagarin and the anonymous readers for the University of Oklahoma Press not only prevented errors but also enhanced the content of these pages with their thoughtful suggestions.

By happy coincidence I was summoned for jury service at the Metropolitan Davidson County Courthouse during the same weeks I was writing the chapter on the origins of juries. The seriousness with which my fellow jurors took their responsibilities confirmed my appreciation for the remarkable notion that ordinary citizens are properly entrusted with decisions affecting the lives of their peers. At the courthouse, too, I had occasion to witness firsthand the commitment to the Bill of Rights of my friends Judge Walter C. Kurtz, Chancellor Robert S. Brandt, and Clerk and Master Claudia C. Bonnyman.

Dean Jacque Voegeli of the Vanderbilt College of Arts and Science arranged a timely leave of absence for the completion of this work. Russell G. Hamilton, dean for graduate studies and research, provided funds from the Vanderbilt University Research Council for preparation of the manuscript. Robert Dale Sweeney read the drafts of the chapters with his practiced eye and good judgment, ruthlessly excising such jargon as "paradigm shift." Linda Narrow, a Nashville attorney, checked the legal references. David Coffta helped prepare the bibliographies. Anne Browning Lara, undaunted by recalcitrant computers, gracefully brought the manuscript into final order. I am grateful to them all.

My hope is that this book will contribute to a deeper understanding of the origins of the Bill of Rights and also to a greater appreciation of the importance of constitutional protections for both the individual and the common good.

SUSAN FORD WILTSHIRE

Nashville, Tennessee

Greece, Rome, and the Bill of Rights

Introduction

THE principle that a purpose of government is to protect the individual rights and minority opinions of its citizens is a recent development in human history. When the Bill of Rights became part of the United States Constitution on December 15, 1791, notions of human liberty and the civic status of individuals took a form unprecedented in the history of political governance. These principles were for the first time articulated in unmistakable terms and encoded in a nation's written constitution, enforceable by courts of law and subject to restatement only by the consent of the governed. The ideas and practices behind the Bill of Rights, however, have a very long history that it is the purpose of this book to explore.

In the Declaration of Independence, Thomas Jefferson referred confidently to the "Laws of Nature and of Nature's God" as the source of the "self-evident" truths that "all men are created equal" and are endowed "with certain unalienable rights." In this confidence Jefferson was elaborating ideas that had their origins more than two thousand years earlier in classical Greek philosophy. Eventually these ideas became attached to the practicalities of Roman law and thereby shaped the political institutions of the West. Almost all of the provisions of the Bill of Rights reflect civic practices first developed by the Greeks and Romans.

Alfred North Whitehead intuitively evoked these linkages with antiquity when he observed: "I know of only three times in the Western world when statesmen consciously took control of historic destinies: Periclean Athens, Rome under Augustus, and the founding of your American republic." In speaking of the framers of the Constitution, he added: "They were able statesmen, they had access to a body of good ideas; they incorporated these general principles into the instrument without trying to particularize too explicitly how they should be put into effect; and they were men of immense practical experience themselves."[1]

Theories of rights assume a dignity of persons and a status of individuals that did not exist in the classical world. In ancient Greece and Rome, the status of individuals was determined by their relationship to the state. In ancient Athens, where the state took priority, a private person living apart from public life was considered a nonentity. Both Plato and Aristotle are explicit about this. Plato says in the *Laws*: "Neither your own persons nor the estate are your own; both belong to your whole line, past and future, and still more absolutely do both lineage and estate belong to the community."[2] Aristotle confirms this principle in similar terms: "We must not regard a citizen as belonging just to himself: we must rather regard every citizen as belonging to the state."[3]

The slow transition from a state-defined to an individual-defined political identity was mediated by a belief in natural law.[4] The five chapters of Part One trace the evolution of political identity forward from Greek philosophy and Roman law through the Middle Ages to the eighteenth-century Enlightenment and the Bill of Rights.

Chapter 1 considers the origins of natural law in ancient Greece, culminating in the philosophy of Stoicism. Chiefly through Cicero, natural law became attached to Roman law and the belief in the *ius gentium,* or "law of nations." This provided the foundation for a Christian version of natural law and the Christian state in the medieval period, which is the inquiry of Chapter 2.

Chapter 3 looks to England and the evolution of common law, the other great source of American political thought. Attention is paid in this chapter, too, to the relationship between common law and the Roman law which prevailed on the Continent.

Chapter 4 carries the story of natural law into the Enlightenment, tracing the emergence of the individual into full status, now no longer contingent on definition by the state, in the thought of John Locke.

Part One concludes with a brief description in Chapter 5 of the framing of the Bill of Rights, its relation to the previously adopted Constitution, the ratification process, and some thoughts on its meaning.

With a reverse of perspective, the five chapters of Part Two survey antecedents for the various provisions of the Bill of Rights in Greek and Roman political thought and practice.

The freedoms most commonly associated with the Bill of Rights are those protected by the First Amendment: freedom from state-established religion and the freedoms of religious expression, speech, press, assembly, and petition. All of the First Amendment provisions except freedom of the press reflect issues that were in some measure concerns also in Athens or Rome. It is the purpose of Chapter 6 to explore these concerns.

Chapter 7 addresses early precedents for the Second and Third Amendment issues of armsbearing and the quartering of soldiers. In the heroic world of Homer's *Iliad*, the worth of individuals was determined by their skill in warfare. As civic life developed, armsbearing became more problematic. The Third Amendment recalls one of the many strategies by which Rome managed the peoples it conquered, that of conferring on favored cities the privilege of not having to quarter Roman soldiers.

Chapter 8 suggests a long lineage for Fourth Amendment protections against search and seizure. Apparently even older than the Twelve Tables of 451 B.C. was the protection against fraudulent search of one's home. In

Rome this ritual, known as *lance et licio*, defined the procedures by which such searches might be conducted.

The Fifth and Sixth Amendments provide protections for persons accused in criminal cases, while the Seventh protects litigants in civil cases. Chapter 9 considers the mechanisms in Roman law for bringing indictments and for protections against self-incrimination, together with the origins of trial by jury in Athens and Rome and its further development in English common law.

The final two amendments of the Bill of Rights raise issues considered in Chapter 1. The unenumerated rights addressed in the Ninth Amendment reflect the natural rights theories traceable to the Greeks. The reserve of powers to the states or the people in the Tenth Amendment recalls the Roman genius for administration of its large and diverse empire, especially through the arrangements established by Augustus. Because the Ninth and Tenth Amendments deal with structural issues, I depart from the practice of the preceding chapters by considering recent court cases that illustrate fundamental problems raised by these amendments.

My purpose in Part Two is not to suggest direct influence or to propose a cause-and-effect relationship between classical antiquity and the Bill of Rights. Part Two is rather a study in comparative politics, while Part One is an inquiry into the history of an idea.

In the Conclusion I address two questions growing out of this inquiry: what are the political implications of the Graeco-Roman heritage of the Bill of Rights, and how might such a long heritage affect our attitude toward the values it protects?

PART ONE

From Athens to America: The Evolution of the Idea of Rights

CHAPTER 1

The Origins:
Greek Philosophy
and Roman Law

*Democracy was cobbled together, thousands of
years ago, by the Athenians.*

CYNTHIA FARRAR

*Every nation's law, except our own, is crude and
almost laughable.*

CICERO

THE earliest origins of the Bill of Rights lie in
classical Athens, for it was the ancient Greeks who invented the revolutionary idea that human beings are capable of governing themselves through laws of their own
making. The Athenians, however, were better at the idea
than the practice of self-governance. It was the supreme
achievement of the Romans to create, over a period of a
thousand years, a system of law that would survive the
fall of the empire and form the basis of political and civic
organization in the West from that time forward.

The idea that individuals have inherent rights apart
from their relationship to the state is a later development,
but it could never have evolved if a belief in self-gover-

nance had not first been established by the Athenians and
the rule of law elaborated by the Romans.

The thread that connects all the episodes of this long
story is natural law. Growing out of Greek political theory, especially that of Aristotle, natural law became a
major tenet of Stoic philosophy during the Hellenistic age
and exerted profound influence over Roman legal doctrine. Natural law theory underwent several transformations before Jefferson claimed it as the basis of the
"unalienable rights" of Americans, but the idea was conceived in ancient Athens.

GREEK BEGINNINGS

The Greek alphabet was invented around the middle of
the eighth century B.C. It developed out of Phoenician
script but with the addition of a full set of vowels, which
made the Greek language relatively easy to read and therefore facilitated access to the laws by ordinary people.[1]
Because people could read the laws, they could participate
actively in carrying them out.[2]

The earliest surviving publicly inscribed law in Greece
is a stone inscription in the Cretan city of Dreros, meant
to prevent corruption of the political process for personal
gain, dating from the middle or late seventh century B.C.[3]
From that time forward, cities throughout the Greek
world began to promulgate written laws. These codes
were actual legislation governing the judicial life of the
community. The existence of written laws signals the
attitude that substantial numbers of citizens had the right
to know the law and to benefit from the fact that the laws
were public and fixed.[4]

Even in the early, predemocratic Greek cities, the assumption was that political business was public business
and that the laws, though perhaps somehow attributable
to the gods, were promulgated under the authority of the
city. The emergence of written laws in the early history
of the Greek city-states distinguishes them from the theocratic monarchies of the ancient Near East. Near Eastern
laws were meant not to inform the people but to inspire

reverence for the ruler or God. Michael Gagarin concludes that the public nature of Greek laws has no parallel in the law codes of the ancient Near East.[5]

The public spirit of community life in early Greece was furthered by substantive legislation, much of which strengthened the authority of the polis over its members. Conversely, one's identity was also determined by membership in the city. This was the case whether the political organization was democratic, aristocratic, oligarchic, or tyrannical. The power of the Greek polis increased at the expense of individual families throughout the archaic period, and the written laws, publicly displayed, served to strengthen not one group or party but all citizens by virtue of their membership in the polis.[6]

In classical Athens, political life was considered the proper business of all citizens. Professionalism was actively discouraged, and the legislative, executive, and judicial functions were exercised by commissions of citizens drawn by lot. Further, citizens were required by law to plead their own cases.[7] Consequently, there were no lawyers as such in classical Athens,[8] although litigation was so prevalent and the rotation of offices so frequent that R. J. Bonner calls Athens a "nation of lawyers."[9] Speech writers, orators, and advocates in certain situations formed the germ of the legal profession, but it was at Rome that law and lawyers would flourish.[10] Greek law itself, says one observer, "failed of fruition." Except for Greek maritime law, the legal science that would influence the world came from Rome.[11]

The great contribution of Greek law to the West was political philosophy. From a very early period the ancient Greeks thought reflectively about how human beings should govern themselves.

Prefatory to an idea of natural law is the notion of justice itself, that is, that right relations among human beings are subject to principles based on higher than ordinary claims. In tracing the evolution of justice from Homer through Plato, E. A. Havelock shows that although we find no *principle* of justice (*dikaiosune*) in Homer, there is "just action." The term *dike* for just action has a regulative function legally in the *Iliad* and morally in the *Odyssey*. Hesiod later formalized discourse about justice in ways that would lead to philosophy. Plato's contribution was to transform the problem of justice into an abstract concept and a normative principle.[12]

Among the Presocratics, Heraclitus (d. 478 B.C.) opened the way for a natural law theory when he wrote: "This world-order . . . did none of gods or men make, but it always was and is and shall be: an everliving fire, kindling in measures and going out in measures."[13] Kirk and Raven observe that the thought of Heraclitus seems "completely new," adding: "Practically all aspects of the world are explained systematically, in relation to a central discovery—that natural changes of all kinds are regular and balanced."[14] This line of thinking would be eclipsed by the anti-nature thought of the Eleatics and Plato, but would rise again with Aristotle.

A theory of justice raises questions concerning the basis of the laws framed to promote it. Are those laws arrived at simply by human consensus and convention? Or do they exist somehow in the very nature of the universe? The relationship between nature and convention, between *physis* and *nomos*, had been debated vigorously by Greek thinkers in the fifth century B.C. as a philosophical issue.[15] In the following century Aristotle took up in his *Politics* the legal implications of the problem.

Aristotle insists, first, that there is a distinction between laws that merely have been enacted, which may or may not be good laws, and those that have been enacted well, that is, enacted according to the higher law of nature. In the same context he distinguishes between laws that are best for the individuals for whom they are enacted and laws that are absolutely the best.[16] Thus, for Aristotle, natural law has an existence apart from the conventional or positive laws that human beings enact to deal with matters of everyday justice.

But how are we to arrive at knowledge of such higher laws? Aristotle does not answer that question directly. He could not rely on revelation from God as Aquinas later would do. He does hold, however, that the special capacity

of human beings is to exercise the mind in accordance
with rational principles and that first principles are apprehended partly by induction, partly by perception, and
partly by developing the habits of reason.[17] John Locke
quotes these words of Aristotle in his *Essays on the Law
of Nature* in support of his own formulation of natural
law.[18] Locke's reference suggests that Aristotle's doctrine
may properly be understood as one of the original sources
of natural law theory.[19]

In addition, Aristotle assumes that human beings are
born with a natural tendency to be good.[20] This tendency
requires habituation and right education, but an instinct
toward natural virtue enables human beings, aided by the
exercise of reason, to discern what is morally good and
just.

Aristotle died in 322 B.C., a year after his former student,
Alexander the Great. Alexander's conquests ended the
autonomy of the Greek city-state and the vigorous practice of self-rule that had evolved over several hundred
years. It is not surprising, therefore, that political theory
became more and more abstracted from actual political
life. While for Plato and Aristotle politics was still rooted
in the city-state, the philosophical schools that inherited
their legacy saw the world in more universal terms because by that time the Greeks exercised little political
control within the cities they actually inhabited.

THE CONTRIBUTION OF THE STOICS

Cosmopolitanism was the special characteristic of the
Stoic school, founded on a porch, or stoa, in Athens by
Zeno of Citium in about 300 B.C. No theory attributed to
the Stoics has been more influential than that of natural
law. The Stoic understanding of natural law is difficult to
delineate, however, in no small part because of the elusive
quality of the terms themselves.

Even to link the words nature and law—*physis* and
nomos—was a radical move, given the intense opposition
between them that had raged during the fifth century.
Law was seen as what human beings devise out of custom

and compromise. Nature, by contrast, was seen as fixed and unchanging. How, then, could there be a "law of nature"? Nevertheless, the evidence suggests that the Stoics deserve credit for articulating this hybrid doctrine, which earlier would have been seen as a contradiction in terms.

The Stoics, following Aristotle, believed that human beings are born with a self-awareness that leads them first toward self-preservation. From this follows a capacity to distinguish good from bad. Eventually this capacity to discern right from wrong leads toward development of laws of thought and ethics. These laws are seen to apply to all people at all times and in all places. Plutarch describes Zeno's cosmopolitan viewpoint as presented in Zeno's now-lost *Politeia*:

The *Politeia* of Zeno . . . is directed to this one main point, that our life should not be based on cities or peoples each with its view of right and wrong, but we should regard all men as our fellow-countrymen and fellow-citizens, and that there should be one life and one order, like that of a single flock on a common pasture feeding together under a common law. Zeno wrote this, sharing as it were a dream or picture of a philosophic, well-ordered society.[21]

This cosmopolitanism suited well the changed political circumstances of Hellenistic Greece after the conquests of Alexander, and Zeno's language here supports the understanding of a theory of universal law that would affirm such world citizenship. It is to be a law "common to all" (*ho nomos ho koinos*).

This law "common to all" is, for the Stoics, not a mere abstraction or theory. It describes the material universe as it really is. As A. A. Long puts it: "The foundations of logic for the Stoics are embodied in the universe at large. They are not merely a system, something constructed by the human mind." The universe is thus a rational structure of material constituents, the connections of which are the work of nature or god—typically called *logos* by the Stoics.[22]

What the Stoics did was to match language and thought with natural phenomena. They reject Plato's universals, which made no sense to them because universals lack objective existence. Universals provide a way to classify things, but they do not conform with the structure of reality. We observe particular objects in nature, Stoics would say, not universals.[23]

For the Stoics, nature is intelligent and directs everything. Nothing is outside its purview. If any chance were admitted to this scheme, or if any event fell outside the scope of nature's power, then the world could not be understood as entirely subject to natural law. It is fundamental to Stoicism, however, that everything should be understandable in this way. Furthermore, this world is the best of all possible worlds, since divine providence organizes it so that each part is in complete harmony with the whole.[24]

The popular stereotype of Stoicism emphasizes its attitude of resignation to events, since everything is fated and cannot be changed. The Stoic attitude is properly understood, however, not as blind resignation to fated events, but rather as a belief in human rationality as an integral part of the active principle in the universe.[25] Human beings are intimately involved in the operation of natural law, a law that is not separable from the material universe or from the human beings who inhabit it. Providence works within human nature, and the Stoics exude confidence that human nature is sufficient for achieving a moral life.

Evidence is lacking for an extensive debate among the early Stoics about the fine points of a theory of natural law or even of a very detailed definition of it. Cicero confirms that Zeno believed that natural law was divine: *Zeno . . . naturalem legem divinam esse censet.*[26] Human beings are endowed with reason (*logos*), the divine principle that shapes our impulses. For people to live according to nature means, then, to live according to reason. Since we are not gods but limited and fallible mortals, however, we must choose our actions. Choice implies freedom, including the freedom to err. The Stoic admonition is to choose according to reason, but that is a hortatory principle rather than a set of criteria.

The central concept of Stoic ethics is "naturalness."[27] This assumes a supreme confidence in the goodness or potential for goodness in human nature and follows from Socrates' belief that if human beings know the good, they will do it. "Nature," however, is an ambiguous term. It can mean that which is, already, all around us; or it can mean that which ought to be if all people accomplished their true end (*telos*) and lived a life fully in conformity with virtue.[28] Zeno's definition of nature as "a craftsmanlike fire, proceeding methodically to genesis" seems in its intent to be fully in accord with Aristotelian definitions.[29]

In short, the Stoics offer a general guideline about how to decide what to *do* (that is, to live according to reason), but they say nothing at all about what human beings are *due* (that is, what are their rights). The law of nature, the law common to all, the will of Zeus, or right reason are sufficient to guide good Stoics through life by helping them choose what to do and what not to do.[30] But even then, the Stoics argued, a perfect act depended not on the context of the action but on the virtue relating to how or why it was done, which in turn depended on the attitude or intention of the doer.[31] Virtue was determined not by its consequences in the world but by the degree to which actions followed from a disposition perfectly attuned to the rationality of nature.[32] The Stoic preoccupation was with intentions and with conformity with nature. There was no space for the play of human autonomy apart from the grand plan.

We strain to see in Stoicism a basis for a belief in individual rights. Persons were individuals in Stoic thought to the extent only of their time and place within the world soul. Margaret Reesor points out that both the world soul and the individual soul are series of patterns in time. "It is the function of the soul of the individual," she says, "to produce qualifications that are individual to him; it is the function of the world soul to produce the qualifications of individuals. It is inconceivable, therefore, that a man's individuality can be realized in any other society, with any other group of individuals, or in any other period than that in which he is actually living."[33]

Stoicism is a one-way street. Self-sufficient individuals act in accordance with nature, but nature owes them nothing back. Certainly nature has not endowed them with "unalienable rights."

How, then, did Stoicism advance the climate of potentiality for an eventual emergence of the idea of individual rights? The answer is threefold.

First, it shifted the definer of persons from the city, as in the case of Plato and Aristotle, to the larger world, or cosmos. To the question: "To whom or what do you belong?" the good Stoic would probably answer, "Not to Sparta or Athens, but to my rationality, which is the part of me most akin to the Law of Nature." No longer was the idea of citizenship limited to local communities.

Second, new emphasis was attached to the individual as a moral agent. Stoics, to be sure, labor as hard as Heracles at being virtuous without thinking of themselves as autonomous or independent agents, but they are moral agents nevertheless.

Finally, the Stoics elaborated and extended the idea of natural law, providing a framework to which many subsequent doctrines could be attached. B. F. Wright locates the earliest sources of American theories of natural law in Plato and Aristotle but concludes that it was the Stoics who produced a theory of natural law adapted to legal and political implications from which human laws and institutions could be seen as at least approximating the laws of nature. These Stoic ideas, as appropriated by Cicero and the Roman jurists, were the sources from which modern ideas of natural law are derived.[34]

ROMAN LAW AND NATURAL LAW

If Rome's mission was war, her vocation was law.[35] Law has been called the most original product of the Roman mind. While in most other areas of intellectual activity the Romans were subject to the Greeks, here they were masters. In their hands law became a scientific subject for the first time, with its own abstract principles derived from actual rules and practices. The Romans typically were not given to abstractions, but this capacity for abstract legal thinking turned out to be one of the most fertile of all, for it meant that they could easily combine old principles and rules to form new ideas and rules.[36] Barry Nicholas emphasizes this capacity for abstractions:

It was the strength of the Roman lawyers that they not only had the ability to construct and manipulate these abstractions on a scale and with a complexity previously unknown, but had also a clear sense of the needs of social and commercial life, an eye for the simplest method of achieving a desired practical result, and a readiness to reject the logic of their own constructions when it conflicted with the demands of convenience. If the law is "practical reason" it is not surprising that the Romans, with their genius for the practical, should have found in it a field of intellectual activity to which they were ideally suited.[37]

The Romans were so given to the ordering of relations in a legal sense that they even adopted a legal relationship with the gods. There was no need to love the gods, only to give them their due and to expect due consideration back. Roman prayers typically had the character of a legal contract: *do ut des,* "I give so that you will give."

The pragmatic Romans solved their legal problems in a practical fashion as they met them—*solvitur ambulando,* "it is solved by going." At first the Roman city-state had few dealings with foreign law, which in any case was not acknowledged by the Romans as even existing since it was not their own. In the early days there was no concept of international private law, and Rome recognized the rights of foreigners only insofar as she conferred one-way concessions or treaties upon them. In the beginning, therefore, the "law of nations"—*ius gentium*—was only a way of describing accepted practices extended to ambassadors. From the time of Cicero (106–43 B.C.), however, the term came to refer to the legal institutions common to various peoples. Under the *ius gentium* Roman jurists recognized a whole range of legal relations as valid between Roman citizens and foreigners or between foreigners and foreigners, depending on the decrease in national or municipal particularism. By the first quarter of the second century B.C. the term *ius gentium* was used to group together an array of rules governing these relationships that had been found so useful as to be put into law.[38]

This broader notion of the *ius gentium* was a Roman creation and had no validity except in a context defined by Rome. Gaius (second century A.D.) devised the distinction between the *ius civile*, each people's particular law not met elsewhere, and the *ius gentium*, the law revealed by natural reason and observed everywhere. This was the first time that the conception of universal reason appeared not only in the books of philosophers but also in the actual corpus of Roman jurisprudence.[39]

Rome took seriously her task of governing her newly conquered provinces. She was so confident of her own laws that the provinces were led to submit to them, too. This meant that gradually Roman law came to hold sway over a very large area and for a very long time, so that a significant portion of the human race has been affected by it ever since.[40]

The power of Roman law was greatly enhanced by its marriage with Stoic philosophy and especially with the doctrine of natural law. At first Rome had only the local laws of her own citizens, the *Quirites*. Slowly the law of nations, *ius gentium*, began to carry the weight of law among Rome's allies and enemies alike. A later term for the *ius gentium* was *ius commune*, which means almost "common sense." The evolution of the *ius gentium* was advanced by Cicero and predicated on Stoicism. Stoicism furnished the philosophical basis that, over a long period of time, transformed the *ius gentium* from an exception into a rational system flexible enough to embody a system of equity for all of Western society.[41]

Stoicism provided Roman law with a more cosmopolitan outlook appropriate to a world widened by the conquests of Alexander and transformed into an enduring empire by the Romans. The major thrust toward empire, sped by the wars with Carthage, occurred during the very period in the second century B.C. when Stoic philosophy was most influential at Rome. As Rome assumed a role of administering jurisdiction over the world it had conquered, it needed a broader conception of law to confirm and justify such a role. Stoic philosophy as adapted by the Romans and most especially by Cicero was perfectly suited for this function.[42] Without Stoicism, Rome could not have made her greatest contribution to Western culture.

Our major source for Roman law is the *Digest*, also called the *Pandects*, compiled at the behest of the emperor Justinian between A.D. 530 and 533. Justinian, eager to restore the greatness of the Roman Empire and conscious of the importance of law to that project, commissioned Tribonian and a group of sixteen legal scholars to read all the law books available and abridge them into one work. The result was a work one and a half times the size of the Bible. Justinian insisted, however, that all the constituent texts had to be abridged and edited to include nothing that was obsolete in his own time. This meant that most earlier Roman legal documents cannot be known in their original form except for the *Institutes of Gaius*, a textbook of the second century A.D., which was discovered in 1816 underneath a text of St. Jerome. A second commission in 534 revised an earlier collection of imperial constitutions dating from the reign of Hadrian. The third component of Justinian's project was the *Institutes*, a short educational handbook for students published also in 533.

All of these works together comprise the *Corpus iuris civilis*, which is often considered to have influenced the Western world more than any other document except the Bible. Edward Gibbon in the *Decline and Fall of the Roman Empire* gives tribute to Justinian for his astonishing achievement:

The vain titles of the victories of Justinian are crumbled into dust, but the name of the legislator is inscribed on a fair and everlasting monument. Under his reign, and by his care, the

civil jurisprudence was digested in the immortal works of the
Code, the *Pandects*, and the *Institutes*: the public reason of the
Romans has been silently or studiously transfused into the
domestic institutions of Europe, and the laws of Justinian still
command the respect or obedience of independent nations.
Wise or fortunate is the prince who connects his own reputation
with the honour and interest of a perpetual order of men.[43]

The opening of the *Digest* holds that laws are of three
different sorts. There is the law of the state, *ius civile*,
expressing the interests of a particular community. There
is the law of nations, *ius gentium*, "which men have
devised for their mutual intercourse." And finally there
is the law that expresses a higher and more permanent
standard, the law of nature, *ius naturale*, that corresponds
to "that which is always good and equitable (*bonum et
aequum*)."

While this threefold distinction may have been an inser-
tion of post-classical writers, it nevertheless expresses a
practical solution formulated by Roman jurists to the
problem of Rome's expansion from a municipal to a world
power. Seeing local, imperial, and natural law as related
creates a commonality for all legislation.[44] Stoic natural
law contributed the theoretical basis for this common
enterprise. As Quirinus Breen puts it:

The Roman jurist did not plan an empire, projected no blueprint
for a world state. His ideal of goodness through justice was
undergirded by a largeness of conception of certain guiding
principles of private law. I refer particularly to his regard for the
law of nature (e.g., every man is born free, even the slave) and
the law of nations (e.g., the integrity of the empire's many
peoples as to their nationhood, languages, customs, literatures,
heroes). In truth, the civilian was right who said the Roman
law (specifically the *Digest*) is "reasoned justice."[45]

The Roman appropriation of natural law did not result
from an intrinsic interest in transcendental speculation
about the nature of law. Instead, it served what A. P.
d'Entrèves calls "a quest for the intrinsic character of a

given situation."[46] For the Romans, it is probably fair to say that natural law provided a way of describing what seemed to them simply the normal facts of their concrete situation and experience. The *ius naturale* thus provided not a thoroughgoing system of legal rules but rather a means of interpretation. Together with the *ius gentium*, it helped decisively in the adaptation of positive laws, peculiar to a particular locale, into a legal system for an international or rather transnational civilization.[47] Robert N. Wilkin describes the process as follows:

When the ideal law of the Stoics came into contact with the positive law of the Romans, intelligence and enlightenment were brought to bear on traditional practice and mechanical formulas. . . . It established the law as a rational process, and recognized the exercise of the ethical will as a part of reason. It was not a substitute for the positive law, but served, and has served throughout the years, as a *critique* and norm of positive law. It operates not directly on positive enactments, but indirectly through the minds of men; but that which controls the minds of men will in the end master their institutions.[48]

The incorporation of Stoicism into Roman thought occurred primarily through the teachings of Panaetius and Polybius in the circle around Scipio Aemilianus in the second century B.C., enhanced later by the visit to Rome of Posidonius, under whom Cicero had studied Stoic philosophy at Rhodes. These teachers offered to some of Rome's leading minds a deeper insight into the relationship of human beings to nature; they adapted Stoic thought to the Roman mentality, especially in matters of ethics and politics; they taught notions of fairness by which to temper the positive laws of Roman jurisprudence; and finally they combined Stoic philosophy and Roman theology into what one observer calls a "philosophical state religion."[49] The natural law theory of Stoicism gave the Romans a basis for appealing to ancestral custom, the *mos maiorum*. Central to this process of adaptation was the Roman lawyer Cicero.

THE ROLE OF CICERO

Roman law is the armature around which the Western civic project is constructed. The most articulate architect of that structure was Marcus Tullius Cicero.

Cicero was philosophically eclectic, but he had a keen instinct for the utility of Stoic natural law for Roman purposes. In perhaps his most influential work, the *De officiis*, he clearly approves of the Stoic views he represents, as he does also in the *De legibus*. Through Cicero, Stoic ideas gained favor among Roman lawyers and later among such influential fathers of the Roman Church as Lactantius and Ambrose.[50]

In the *De republica* Cicero situates natural law theory within the Roman context:

True law is right reason in agreement with Nature; it is of universal application, unchanging and everlasting; it summons to duty by its commands, and averts from wrong-doing by its prohibitions. ... It is a sin to try to alter this law, nor is it allowable to attempt to repeal any part of it, and it is impossible to abolish it entirely. We cannot be freed from its obligations by senate or people, and we need not look outside ourselves for an expounder or interpreter of it. And there will not be different laws at Rome and at Athens, or different laws now and in the future, but one eternal and unchangeable law will be valid for all nations and for all times, and there will be one master and one ruler, that is, God, over us all, for he is the author of this law, its promulgator, and its enforcing judge.[51]

The Roman perspective is clearly evident here. After noting the eternity and universal applicability of natural law, Cicero emphasizes its ethical force. It summons one to duty and averts wrongdoing. Neither the Senate nor the Roman people can abrogate it, and it requires no interpreter. It is the same at Athens as it is at Rome, valid for all nations at all times. Finally, the god of the Stoics, whether Zeus or Divine Reason, is the author of this law and, as it were, the jury, judge, and probation officer as well. This divine "mind of the world," however, is not an incorporeal spirit but a set of material impulses based on Reason. It differs from the human will not in kind but in degree.[52]

For Cicero the word *natura*—either alone or in phrases such as *ius naturale, ius naturae, lex naturae*—refers sometimes to a divinely ordained universal order, sometimes to what D. H. Van Zyl calls "those half-legal, half-ethical rules which express the principles of human justice,"[53] because they have to do with how human beings live with one another in communities and how they pay respect to the gods.

In the *De legibus*, Cicero says that law is the highest reason inherent within nature, and that the same reason, when it is confirmed and established in the mind of men, is law.[54] Chaim Wirszubski argues that if Cicero actually believed that his proposed code embodied natural law, he was naive. "But even if naive," Wirszubski continues, "his assertion is in the highest degree significant, because it means that in Cicero's opinion the fundamental laws of Rome ought to be unalterable, that is to say, the fundamental laws, i.e. the constitution, ought to be above the ordinary legislative power."[55] Cicero observed from the political turmoil of his own and the preceding era that positive laws alone could not ensure the tranquillity of the state and the well-being of its citizens. By postulating a moral basis to law, he hoped to mantle law with immunity to the whims of the people and the vicissitudes of the times. He had argued in *Pro Cluentio* 146 that we are slaves of the law so that we may be free: *legum idcirco omnes servi sumus ut liberi esse possimus.* If we are to be slaves of law, then the law must be supremely good.

Cicero is rightly considered the father of natural law in terms of its impact on the West through Roman law. According to Paul MacKendrick, Cicero fixed in our political theory these seminal ideas: that the law is the standard of justice; that there is a necessary connection between power and responsibility; that law rises out of community traditions in an organic manner; that power resides in the people; and that there is an intimate connection between the rule of law and high moral character. In all these aspects Cicero affirms the priority of ethics. MacKendrick concludes that Cicero, like Pericles and Plato but unlike the modern pragmatists, regarded ethics as more important than economics, even if he did stress the duty of the *princeps* to protect private property.[56] In this way, too, Cicero's debt to Stoicism was profound.

RIGHTS AND ROMAN LAW

The achievement of Roman law, both as a practical system and as an abstract theory identified with natural law, brought an advance also in the idea of individual rights, but only in a preliminary way.

The development of the *ius gentium* expanded the idea of law beyond the immediate kinship or city, thereby loosening the power of the *corpus* or immediate body or corporation to determine the definition of individuals. Still, the *ius gentium* arose out of Roman positive law, and in that law we do not see a place for the individual as a repository of subjective rights. H. F. Jolowicz considers Henry Maine's thesis that the Roman system had no conception of rights at all[57] to be an exaggeration, but he concedes that among the Romans it had nothing like its modern importance.[58]

More precisely, what we do not see anywhere in the *Corpus iuris civilis* is an expression of the belief that natural law is superior to positive law. This means that if Antigone had been a Roman rather than a Greek when she claimed to be obeying the higher or unwritten laws,[59] she would have been incomprehensible. For Cicero and the Romans generally, positive Roman law was coequal with natural "higher" law, and thus natural law could not be invoked to overrule positive laws.

The Roman conception of law, then, is anything but revolutionary. It contains no vindication of the "rights of man" but is rather a reflection of existing laws. It was never meant to give sanction to any idea that was not already in existence. As d'Entrèves concludes: "We must indeed divest ourselves, in order to understand the Roman conception of natural law, not only of the modern conception of natural rights, but of the notion of the subordination of positive to natural law with which later ages have made us familiar."[60]

The most obvious test case for this is the issue of slavery, the one institution common to the Greeks and Romans in antiquity and one always reckoned within the *ius gentium*. Slavery was antithetical to natural law and to every Stoic notion of equality. In the *De legibus* Cicero urges a "single definition" for human beings: "However we may define man, a single definition will apply to all. . . . For those creatures who have received the gift of reason have also received right reason, and therefore they have also received the gift of Law, which is right reason applied to command and prohibition. And if they have received law, they have received Justice also."[61]

We soon see, however, that a single definition does *not* apply. Slavery is perfectly legal because it is the way things are. It is the one glaring discrepancy between natural law doctrine and the *ius gentium*.[62]

The division of "how things are in nature" (*physikon*) and "how they are in custom or law" goes back to Aristotle,[63] but Jolowicz sees the slavery problem as evidence of the fact that when the Romans said "natural law," they really meant "Roman law." For example, although all states had procedures for the manumission of slaves, rules about it differed greatly from state to state. Whenever a stipulation concerning manumission is stated, the particular Roman institution is meant, and the rules of other states on the subject do not matter at all. In practice this was the meaning of *ius gentium* for Roman lawyers. The rest was "philosophical ornament."[64]

For the Romans, a "natural person" was one who possessed legal rights and capacities. Apart from criminal law, Roman slaves were not persons because they were incapable of rights and duties and because they themselves were the objects of ownership and other proprietary rights. Their status was absolute; it did not depend on being owned by a master, and there could be an ownerless slave just as there could be an ownerless animal.

While slaves had no rights, there were other groups

completely or partially prevented from the full possession of or exercise of rights. These included women, young people, the mentally ill, and the prodigal.[65] Children acquired legal personality as soon as they were born, but in order to count as born they had to have lived for at least a moment outside of the womb. According to the *Digest*, an unborn child was not a human being.[66]

The Roman term *obligatio* referred to a personal right, but only as a constraint to cause a person to do something or leave something undone in the interest of someone else. Mostly this had to do with matters of pecuniary value and with patrimonies. As J. Declareuil sees it, these constraints—whether positive or negative—primarily reveal a jurisprudence that tended to reduce legal relations to an economic plane.[67] Thus rights in Roman law refers primarily to *res*, to "things." A thing can be a physical object or a debt one is owed, but both property and debts due have in common that they are assets of economic value. When Gaius and Justinian speak of the law of things, they are referring to the part of the law that governs the formation, exchange, and use of economic assets.[68]

Geoffrey Samuel locates the starting point of the idea of subjective rights in Roman laws of property. He stresses that the history of "right" is complex because it follows more than one philosophical line. One strand of the idea of "natural right" has to do with property and ownership, while the other concerns the more abstract moral basis for constitutional theory. This latter line places more emphasis on natural law, *ius*, justice, and *dominium* as universal ideals.[69]

In part this is an epistemological problem, because the word *ius* or *nomos* meant very different things, for example, to Aristotle, Aquinas, and Locke. For Aristotle, the law was a "thing" inevitably intertwined with the polis or state. For Aquinas, *ius* was objective juridical connection. For Locke, *ius* was subject to the positive rules of property law. "Thus to compare, even unhistorically," says Samuel, "the concept of a right, or its correlative, in the works of Locke and Aquinas would be to compare two quite distinct structures of legal epistemology."[70]

Another way to get at the problem, suggests Samuel, is to locate the difference between real rights and natural rights in private and public law, respectively. The problem with this strategy, however, is that the division between public and private law did not have much practical meaning until after the end of the medieval period.

Samuel thus posits two historical stages. The first stage of legal "rights" has to do almost entirely with physical property, which was what determined an individual's sovereignty within society. The only true "subjective right" in private law is located in Roman laws of property, that is, between persons and things. The second historical stage, the "inductive," was concerned with moving away from the relationship between subject and property and toward the relationship between subject and subject. The third or "deductive" historical stage in the process culminates in such claims as "I have a right to vote" or "I have a right to free speech."

The key to understanding modern subjective rights lies in its firm foundation in Roman "black letter" law, that is, in the positive legal details of property rules. From that beginning the evolution of rights ultimately reached the third stage, in which subjective rights transcend the limitations in the *Institutes* to become a means of understanding human society as a whole, what Samuel calls "a metalegal concept" capable of validating not only law but also morality and politics.[71]

The fundamental question to which we return, however, is whether at any period in the Roman scheme the individual had any absolute value simply by virtue of being a human being. The answer seems to be no. While in Greek philosophy the law of nature can be seen as the individual's best defense against the law, in Rome the emphasis was on the framing of law itself. That meant that Roman law necessarily would be concerned with the public good rather than the private good of individuals. Surely the public good was seen as protective also of the private good in a sort of "trickle down" effect, but the status of individuals is nevertheless subordinate to the law.[72]

Our great debt to the Romans is their belief in the rule of law. This belief embodies the persuasion that reason rather than force is sufficient for dimming human differences and for enabling us to live together without all being the same. In addition, Roman jurisprudence sought—under the influence of natural law—to approximate what was "always just and good," *semper aequum et bonum*.

While Roman law contains only the seeds of a theory of individual rights, there could be no such rights at all apart from a prior commitment to the rule of law. That is what the Romans confirmed for the world, dignified and ameliorated by the humane claims of Stoicism.

A belief that individuals are endowed by nature with certain unalienable rights still lay far in the future. In the meantime, the history of the idea of rights was to take a dramatic turn in the Middle Ages.

CHAPTER 2

Law, Individual, and Church in the Middle Ages

Scire Deum satis est, quo nulla scientia major.
It is enough to know God, than whom there is no
greater knowledge.

IF an ordinary person in Europe in the early
Middle Ages were asked, "To whom or what do you belong?" the answer would probably be "to the Church."
Personhood by virtue of membership in a group, conceived by the Greeks and elaborated by the Romans, was
now embraced by medieval Christianity.

In what might be called a "wholeness" theory of society, the social, personal, and religious components of a
Christian's life could not be separated. The Church's
claims of direction over the lives of its members were
both corporate and individual, both public and private.
The body of citizens, *corpus civium*, of the classical Roman world was now transformed into the body of Christ,
corpus Christi. Neither historical situation permitted a
notion of individuality apart from the group.

Both Greek philosophy and Roman law were pressed
into the service of the Church in the medieval period.

Although they required many transformations to accommodate Christianity, they represented a continuity with the classical past that never was entirely broken. The challenge of combining the classical tradition with Christianity was enormous:

> An immense task lay ahead of the medieval man. The present had to be secured, the past reconquered. The lesson of Roman law was that the greatest of all legal systems had been based purely on reason and utility; the lesson of Aristotle, that the State is the highest achievement of man and the necessary instrument of human perfection. How could a Christian community be taught the elementary duties of good life and fellowship? How could Roman law be accepted as the universal law of Christendom? How could Aristotle, a pagan philosopher, be adapted to the Christian view of life?[1]

The story of the evolution of rights in the Middle Ages may be approached from four perspectives: the role of Stoicism, the transformation of the theory of natural law, the union between the Church and Roman law, and the individual as subject in medieval society.

STOICISM IN THE MIDDLE AGES

Stoicism was the Greek philosophy most adaptable to Christianity, just as earlier it had been the philosophical system most congenial to Roman culture. Stoic influence permeated theology and law, the two primary projects of the Middle Ages. For Christian intellectuals, the Stoic inheritance provided patterns and insights to enrich their efforts to forge connections between their past, present, and future.[2] In medieval law, its greatest influence was the incorporation into Roman law of Stoic natural law theory.

By combining the previously antithetical notions of nature and law, *physis* and *nomos*, and then by merging that combination with a divinely ordered universe, the Stoics had posited a worldview easily open to Christianization. What had been a contradiction in fifth-century

Greece became a philosophical system in the Hellenistic period and a handmaid of the "law of nations" in the Roman Empire. Now, with natural law as godparent, Stoicism was ready for baptism.

The appeal of Stoicism in the Middle Ages lay in its promise of certainty, universal harmony, and a method of understanding the troubles of the world. If everything happens according to divine Providence, then we need only endure events and accept everything that happens with a spirit as unruffled as possible. Although this is not essentially a Christian doctrine, it came to sound like one, and people acted consistently as if they believed that it were.

Both Stoicism and medieval Christianity attempt to make a forbidding universe more friendly. Both emphasize morality, the ideal of human community, the importance of personal ethics, and a persistent yearning for harmony and unity.[3] Because of these affinities, Stoicism attracted more adherents than any other system except Christianity, including many who professed Christianity, and affected human institutions more than any other Greek philosophy.[4] It was the only philosophical system that directed its message toward all human beings without distinction, offering internal liberation whether one's external conditions were free or slave, Greek or barbarian, even male or female.[5]

Stoicism passed into the Middle Ages through the works of other writers in addition to Cicero. The Roman Stoic Seneca (c. 4 B.C.–A.D. 65) was held in especially high esteem. Augustine refers to Seneca frequently,[6] as do John of Salisbury, Alain de Lille, Roger Bacon, and Thomas Aquinas.

A case study in the early appropriation of Stoic thought is provided by Ambrose, the bishop of Milan (c. 340–397). Marcia L. Colish shows that Ambrose, unlike a number of the Church Fathers, did not feel the need to agonize over Tertullian's question, "What does Athens have to do with Jerusalem?"[7] He simply appropriated Stoic ideas for his own ends. For example, in the *De fuga saeculi* Ambrose holds that there is a natural law inscribed on the human heart and a written law inscribed on the tablets of the Ten Commandments. Human beings fulfill the natural law when they voluntarily obey God's commandments.[8] When all of his works are taken together and his use of Stoicism is taken in context, it is clear that Ambrose is not trying to prove the superiority of Christianity or even to bring Stoicism systemically into accord with the Gospel. In the field of ethics, which is his primary interest, Ambrose simply draws on Stoic ideas and formulae as ways of posing and arguing issues.[9]

The most difficult obstacle for Christianity in appropriating Stoicism was the materialistic basis of Stoic philosophy. The universe and everything in it, even divine Providence itself, was considered by the Stoics to be actual and material rather than abstract or ideal. Medieval Christian writers dealt with this materialism in various ways. Influenced by Cicero and Seneca, Lactantius interpreted biblical texts in the light of Stoic materialism almost unconsciously. By the fifth century A.D., however, Stoic materialism itself had softened, perhaps owing to the impact of Neoplatonism.[10]

Stoicism had to be reconciled with Christianity in another important respect. Where Christianity speaks of original sin, Stoicism holds that the moral life is not imposed on human beings from the outside but that we are born good and inclined toward goodness. Furthermore, everyone can grasp by intuition the basic principles of morality, even without special knowledge or training. Moral life is the same everywhere and for everyone. By instinct and hard work, rather than by perfect faith, all human beings can aspire to moral perfection.[11] This is aided by the Stoic notion of conscience. Seneca sounds not a little like Benjamin Franklin when he says that he examines himself every evening to review how well he had done that day.[12]

What persisted, however, was the aspect of Stoicism that contributed so profoundly to the natural law theory that would ultimately inform the Bill of Rights—namely, the conviction that nature is not irrational but coincides with universal reason. Further, this reason is synonymous with Divinity. Even when covered over with Grace and Faith, the Stoic origins of this idea persisted, never to be lost from sight altogether.[13]

NATURAL LAW AND THE CHURCH

Early in the twentieth century, Ernst Troeltsch proposed that natural law came as an alien element from the ancient world into the teachings of Christianity, providing a social and political program lacking in the Gospel.[14] Troeltsch's argument is persuasive. The teachings of Jesus have little to do with hierarchy, political power, or institutional organization. Rather, they urge that it is a good thing to give away one's cloak and that the earth is meant for the meek, the poor, and the peacemakers. The sociopolitical infrastructure for a dominant Christian culture in the Middle Ages was provided instead by two legacies from the classical past: Stoic natural law, which contributed the theory, and Roman law, which contributed the practice.

The two Church Fathers primarily responsible for appropriating the pagan idea of natural law for Christian purposes in the early medieval period were Ambrose and his great pupil, Augustine (354–430). Together they took the natural law tradition they inherited from Cicero and established it in a permanent place in the Church. Eventually the Church Fathers came to use *natural law* simply as a general term of approbation for whatever ideas they were forwarding at the time.[15]

In time, natural law became synonymous with church doctrine, offering something to everyone and at the same time providing ideas with the protective covering of immutable truth. A. P. d'Entrèves addresses both the formal continuity and the transformation of the doctrine by the Church Fathers:

As far as the "formal" continuity of the notion is concerned, there is no doubt that medieval natural law is the progeny of the Greeks and the Romans. To medieval eyes the idea of the law of nature appeared surrounded by the glamour of the Roman

legal inheritance. It had, however, received as it were the necessary christening by being accepted and embedded in the teaching of the Christian Fathers.[16]

The Christian version of natural law doctrine is stated
uncompromisingly in the *Decretum Gratiani*,[17] the oldest
collection of church law, compiled around 1140: "Mankind is ruled by two laws: Natural Law and Custom.
Natural Law is that which is contained in the Scriptures
and the Gospel." This formulation embodies an earlier
statement by Isidore of Seville (d. 636): "*Ius naturale* is
that which is contained in the law and the Gospel, by
which each is commanded to do to the other what he
would have done to himself and is forbidden to do to
another what he would not have done to himself. . . . All
laws are either divine or human. Divine laws are based
on nature, human laws on custom. The reason why these
are at variance is that different nations adopt different
laws."[18]

When Gratian equates natural law with the Scriptures
and the Gospel, he summarizes the entire program of
medieval moral and legal philosophy. This is because the
Christian version of natural law has two meanings: the
law of nature is contained in the Scriptures, but also the
Scriptures do not contradict the law of nature. This
achieves the conclusion, extraordinary for Christianity,
that reason and revelation are equivalent.[19]

Aristotle also made his way into the Middle Ages and
into the transformation of natural law, but his influence
was felt much later when translations of his work became
available in the twelfth century. Aristotle's thought is
more difficult than Stoicism and less congruent with
Christianity. "Aristotelianism," says Gerard Verbeke,
"had to face many difficulties and much opposition during
the first centuries of Christianity. Christians were openly
hostile to Aristotle. They took him to task for having
denied divine providence, for having rejected immortality
of the soul, and for having defended the eternity of the
world."[20]

The gargantuan labor of reconciling the Aristotelian

and Christian views of life was the lifework of the great
Dominican scholar Thomas Aquinas. Born near Naples
in about 1225, Aquinas entered the Dominican Order
against the wishes of his aristocratic family. After a time
in Paris he returned to Italy, where he became acquainted
with William of Moerbeke, the translator of Aristotle into
Latin. Aquinas's writings, a huge output totalling some
thirty-four volumes, were completed in the twenty-year
period between 1254 and his death in Naples at the age of
forty-nine in 1274.

The *Summa contra Gentiles*, an effort to give Christianity a rational basis, is directed to an audience that does
not take Christianity for granted but includes also pagans,
Jews, and Moslems. It argues for a natural understanding
of religion, addressing specifically Christian doctrines
only in the last third of the work. Aquinas could accommodate Greek philosophy to Christian theology because
he was a theologian who did not separate religious from
philosophical thought. There is, he says, a double ordering
of things, *humanitas* and *christianitas*. His theme,
"Grace does not do away with nature, but perfects it,"
blessed nature in a way that the apostle Paul could never
have countenanced. Nevertheless, if grace does not abolish nature, neither does nature abolish grace. Nature is to
grace as Vergil is to Dante's Beatrice: it can get you only
so far. Then grace is required.

Aquinas considered that although grace did not bring
the natural state into existence, it was necessary for the
proper functioning of the state. The natural laws of the
human state were therefore valid, but to be adequate for
a Christian society and in order to be perfect, those laws
required grace as mediated by the Church.

In the *Summa theologica*, Aquinas struggles with the
relationship of rational creatures to divine providence.
His analysis demonstrates his understanding that natural
law was a way of interpreting human nature and the relationships of human beings to God and the universe. Natural law is not intelligible apart from its link with the
eternal divine order. His assessment of natural law sounds
quintessentially Stoic:

But of all others, rational creatures are subject to divine Providence itself, in that they control their own actions and the actions of others. So they have a certain share in the divine reason itself, deriving therefrom a natural inclination to such actions and ends as are fitting. This participation in the Eternal law by rational creatures is also called the Natural law. . . . As though the light of natural reason, by which we discern good from evil, and which is the Natural law, were nothing else than the impression of the divine light in us. So it is clear that the Natural law is nothing else than the participation of the Eternal law in rational creatures.[21]

Elsewhere in the *Summa,* Aquinas addresses the relationship of natural law to human justice:

St. Augustine says: "There is no law unless it be just." So the validity of law depends upon its justice. But in human affairs a thing is said to be just when it accords aright with the rule of reason: and, as we have already seen, the first rule of reason is the Natural law. . . . And if a human law is at variance in any particular from Natural law, it is no longer legal, but rather a corruption of law.[22]

Aquinas appropriates another doctrine of Stoic natural law by insisting that human beings possess a natural inclination to know the truth about God. "In this respect," he writes, "there come under the Natural law all actions connected with such inclinations."[23] Sin has not invalidated the human inclination to know God, but faith is required since natural principles permit only the *possibility* of overcoming sin.

One of Aquinas's great strengths is the fluidity of his thought. He admits that the natural law can change by addition or supersession on grounds of utility. To admit of the possibility of a changing truth—a possibility Plato found repugnant—required great courage for Aquinas. D. J. O'Connor describes Aquinas's dilemma concerning the changeability of truth in this way:

Finally, it is worth noting that there seems to be a common origin for many of the difficulties that face St. Thomas in working out his theory. It is the conviction, shown most clearly in his theory of knowledge, that no knowledge is of any value unless it is certainly true and known to be so. But if there is one lesson to be learned from the history of philosophy, it is that if we regard knowledge as tentative, experimental, and corrigible, we shall gradually acquire some information about what the universe is like and about our place in it. But if we regard it as intuitive, certain and incorrigible, we shall not learn any facts about anything because we have set our standards too high.[24]

Aquinas influenced the evolution of the idea of natural law in part because he was a practical as well as a speculative thinker. As the person who coined the term *scientia politica*, "political science," he granted validity to the state and to human laws, thus paving the way for a place for the individual apart from superior authority. This was an important first step, although only a step, toward the transformation of individuals into full-fledged citizens.[25]

Aquinas was able to combine philosophy, theology, and politics because of his knowledge of Roman law. He was acutely aware, for example, of the difficulties posed by the notion of the *ius gentium*. Ulpian says that natural law, the *ius naturale*, is common to both man and animals, while the *ius gentium* applies only to human beings although it is the same everywhere. One ambiguity here is that "natural reason" is not common to animals and so can hardly be considered a basis for the *ius gentium*. Aquinas saw the *ius gentium* as so important that he dealt with this problem in two different treatises.

Aquinas's great achievement was to provide a rational basis for both ethics and politics, the very institutions that earlier Christians considered hopelessly mired in sin and subject only to the remedy of grace. His momentous discovery was that natural law provided a medium by which to incorporate Aristotelian/Stoic ethics and politics into a Christian view of life. Once again human beings could be conceived of as political animals, and life in community could be seen as a place for the harmonious integration of individual lives.[26]

That the Christian community can be based on natural law, human reason, and political institutions as well as on God's will is a great breakthrough in human thought. The state is the condition of our existence, Aquinas would say, and in some cases disobedience to it may be a duty. It is important to emphasize, however, that Aquinas's doctrine is not individualistic. While resistance to the state might sometimes be necessary, there is in his thought no call to revolution against the state.[27]

Thus, while Aquinas dignified the human capacity for reason and effected a new harmony between human and Christian values through his interpretation of natural law, his doctrine by no means constitutes a thoroughgoing rationalistic system. "The proud spirit of modern rationalism is lacking," observes d'Entrèves. "There is no assertion of man's self-sufficiency and inherent perfection. There is no vindication of abstract 'rights', nor of the autonomy of the individual as the ultimate source of all laws and of all standards."[28]

Aquinas accomplished for medieval theology and philosophy what Roman jurisprudence accomplished for medieval law: an accommodation to Christian principles that retained a faith in human reason as a basis for moral activity and civic justice. In both cases natural law provided the theory that justified the accommodation.

ROMAN LAW IN THE MIDDLE AGES

Governments in theory operate either from the top down or from the bottom up. The decisive issue in these contrasting theories, which Walter Ullmann calls the ascending and descending themes of government and law,[29] is the location of the power to create laws. In the ascending theory, the people are the source of law. Whatever governmental arrangements they make, they retain the original power and must give their consent to the governance. In this theme the people also retain a right of resistance. This state of affairs is at least partly evident in classical Athens, republican Rome, and the Germanic communities chronicled by Tacitus.

In the descending theme of government, the source of laws resides not in the people but in some otherworldly being or divinity considered the source of all power both public and private. Earthly rulers have a direct relationship with that source and preside as its surrogate. Officeholders are appointed by the rulers and serve at their pleasure. There is no consent, no representation, no accountability, no right of resistance. Implicit in the descending theme is a hierarchical arrangement in which officers have power in direct proportion to their proximity to, or distance from, the highest ruler.

The shift in Rome from republic to empire was a shift from an ascending—although narrowly oligarchical—to a descending theme of government. Now the emperor as *princeps* was principal ruler and sole authority. Further, in the wake of his adopted father, Julius Caesar's being declared a god, Augustus expanded from the Hellenistic East the notion of the divinized ruler, a novel concept profoundly incompatible with republican Roman values. It would prove, however, a concept easily transferable to the pope as God's appointed ruler and to other religious and political claims of the medieval Church.

The ascending and descending concepts of government determine two different ways by which a person relates to the state: as subject or as citizen. For most of the medieval period the descending concept held sway, and the view of persons as subjects was predominant. Only during the later Middle Ages did the subject begin to be replaced by the citizen.[30]

The descending concept also determines that society will be seen as an all-embracing corporation. The faithful Christian, once incorporated into the Church, was from that point forward thought to conduct life not as a "natural" human self with autonomous social functions, but as a "new self" formed by Christ and the Church. This meant that as members of the religious corporation, individuals were no longer agents but subjects in public affairs. In their social and political life they were now subject to the laws that were given them, not creators of laws they had made.[31]

The organic theory of society—articulated by Aristotle, made concrete in the system of Roman law, and appropriated at the beginning of the Christian era by the apostle Paul—provided a strong foundation for a Church Universal. What it did not permit was a theory of the autonomous rights of individuals.

When the empire became Christian in the age of Constantine in the fourth century, Roman ideas and practices permeated the new arrangement from the beginning: Hellenistic philosophy,[32] the idea of the divine ruler, governance from above instead of from below, and a strong belief in the body politic as determinative of one's status as a person.

Ullmann observes that the fusion of Roman law with Christianity, together with monotheism and the legalism permeating the Bible, paved the way for the acceptance of a monarchic political order. The late Roman emperors practiced a highly bureaucratized form of monarchy that made Constantine's conversion easy to accommodate within the prevailing political culture. All that was required to incorporate the Church into the Roman body politic was a simple decree.[33]

Constantine's decree granting the Church a legal corporate personality brought it into accord also with Roman public laws governing religious practices. For example, the law that regulated the priests of the sacred cults, the *ius in sacris*, also formed the constitutional basis of the emperor as the *pontifex maximus*.

Roman law provided the foundation for the new regime, however, in more than strictly religious matters. From the early period Christian organizations were imbued with Roman institutional practices, of which none was more important than the idea of law itself, the most Roman idea of all. The Hebrew Bible was filled with laws, but even independent of that, pagan Roman law permeated the growing body of Christian doctrine.[34]

Roman law entered effortlessly into Christian doctrine most of all because of the apostle Paul, whose letters created in Christian scripture a climate friendly to Roman law. Paul came to Christianity as a Roman citizen deeply imbued with the corporational nature of Roman law with its hierarchical notions of civic organization. Those notions deeply influence his teaching.

Whereas Romans in the classical period had been members of the Roman state or *corpus*, now baptism brought individuals into the body of Christ, the *corpus Christi*. This doctrine is explicit throughout the Pauline letters. In 1 Cor. 12.12–13, for example, Paul writes: "For Christ is like a single body with its many limbs and organs, which, many as they are, together make up one body."[35] At 1 Cor. 12.27 he returns to the topic: "Now you are Christ's body, and each of you a limb or organ of it." In Eph. 1.23 he writes: "He put everything in subjection beneath his feet, and appointed him as supreme head to the church, which is his body and as such holds within it the fullness of him who himself receives the entire fullness of God." Another reference to one body occurs at Rom. 12.5: "For just as in a single human body there are many limbs and organs, all with different functions, so all of us, united with Christ, form one body, serving individually as limbs and organs to one another."

The message is clear: If persons are parts of a body, they cannot function alone. They are not autonomous individuals.

The incorporation of persons into the Church had fundamental political as well as religious significance. It meant that a human being was no longer defined as a living creature who is politically active—Aristotle's "political animal," *politikon zoon*—but is rather a new creature, a *nova creatura*. After addressing an issue in the church in Galatia about whether Christians should continue Jewish rituals, Paul exclaims: "Circumcision is nothing, noncircumcision is nothing; the only thing that counts is new creation" (Gal. 6.15). In a letter to the Corinthians he adds: "When anyone is united to Christ, there is a new world; the old order has gone, and a new order has already begun" (2 Cor. 5.17).

Not only are the "new creatures" removed from their

former state of nature, but now they are also members of a corporation. As such, they are instructed to obey all superiors whether secular or ecclesiastical. Paul is adamant about this: "Every person must submit to the supreme authorities. There is no authority but by act of God, and existing authorities are instituted by him; consequently anyone who rebels against authority is resisting a divine institution" (Rom. 13.1–2). For Paul, the authorities are "God's agents" who are "working for your good" (Rom. 13.4).

The same admonitions thread through the non-Pauline epistles of the New Testament. 1 Pet. 2.13–14, for example, admonishes obedience to superiors: "Submit yourselves to every human institution for the sake of the Lord, whether to the sovereign as supreme, or to the governor as his deputy." Slaves likewise are instructed to submit unquestioningly to their masters: "Servants, accept the authority of your masters with all due submission, not only when they are kind and considerate, but even when they are perverse" (1 Pet. 2.18). The masters are also to be the objects of prayer: "First of all, then, I urge that petitions, prayers, intercessions, and thanksgivings be offered for all men; for sovereigns and all in high office, that we may lead a tranquil and quiet life in full observance of religion and high standards of morality" (1 Tim. 2.1–2).

Earthly rulers receive their powers as a divine concession. Only God has power, and that power is supreme. God may confer power on earthly rulers, but subjects have no rights in the public realm other than those royally conceded. Furthermore, if the rulers do not fulfill their obligations, there is no power on earth that can make them do the right thing. They answer only upward.[36]

It was this Pauline doctrine with its emphasis on law, order, and hierarchy, rather than the more affiliative message of the Gospels, that was passed on to medieval society. John Chrysostom, explaining Paul's doctrine in the early fifth century, emphasized this hierarchical nexus between human law and divine law: "It is the divine wisdom and not mere fortuity which has ordained that there should be rulership, that some should order and others should obey."[37] In short, one's status is determined by membership in the group, and one's political and religious duty is to obey one's superiors.

Paul, the Roman citizen, had learned his Roman law well.

Tertullian (150–230) was one of the first Christians to cast religious ideas into legal form. Also a Roman jurist, he describes the relationship between God and human beings in terms of legal rights and duties, setting up a pattern that could fit easily into Roman jurisprudence. He, too, stresses the idea of the *corpus*, establishing a precedent whereby Paul's theology could eventually be brought to the service of government ideology.[38]

At first there was a certain pessimism about the sinful nature of human creatures and human institutions, resulting in a notion that Christians must live as aliens on this earth while waiting to get to the divine city hereafter. This is especially apparent in *The City of God*, in which Augustine praises the ancient Romans for their greatness but concludes that their world was only "smoke that weighs nothing" when compared with the Heavenly City: "Our City is as different from theirs as heaven from earth, as everlasting life from passing pleasure, as solid glory from empty praise, as the company of angels from the companionship of mortals."[39]

This early pessimism lasted until at least the end of the thirteenth century, impeding the development of an adequate theory of the dignity of temporal power.[40] Eventually, however, the incorporation of Stoic natural law and Roman positive law into the Church provided triumphalist Christianity with a systematic claim to the social and political institutions it now controlled. In time Christianity ceased to be hostile to the world, becoming comfortably at home in a thoroughgoing Romano-Christian civilization.

The new order was informed by two Latin texts above all others. The first was Jerome's translation of the Bible, known as the Vulgate, which was the primary source of political as well as religious ideas in the Middle Ages. "The Latin Bible," says Walter Ullmann, "was suffused with notions, ideas, and quite specific linguistic expressions which had been taken from the Roman constitution and law. It was the language of the cultured and educated classes of the late fourth century. This infusion of Roman law and jurisprudence into the Bible succeeded all the more easily, as the Old Testament in particular was thoroughly permeated with legalism."[41]

The second text was the *Corpus iuris civilis*, which provided for the Middle Ages the civic infrastructure of Roman law. Roman law supported the prevailing belief in a single universal empire of all Christendom. The conception of the Christian empire included both the political and the cultural unity behind the Church, and Rome became the center of the empire in which Christ's vicars had established the Church as the center of the universal ideal. "This 'cultural idea of Rome,' " says Hans Julius Wolff, "even more than the political idea of Rome, created in medieval thinkers, imbued with reverence for established authority, the belief that the law of the Roman Empire, as stated in the imperial codification, was the revelation of legal truth and therefore above all the customs by which men actually lived."[42] Roman law thus assumed its central place in the Middle Ages for both political and cultural reasons.

In about the eleventh century—after a period of several centuries in which rules were simplified, Roman ways were merged with tribal customs, and complexities were increasingly omitted—legal studies in Europe shifted remarkably. During this period several changes occurred in European civilization: the power of the papacy was greatly enlarged under Pope Gregory VII (1020–1085); feudalism became concentrated into a complete system; the Norman states achieved efficient administration and political power; and the intellectual project of the medieval Scholastics was firmly in place under the leadership of Anselm (1033–1109), the archbishop of Canterbury. In the context of this new prosperity and stability, a revival of interest in jurisprudence grew up in Provence and in the north Italian areas of Lombardy, Ravenna, and Bologna.[43]

By far the most important of these schools was that

at Bologna in northern Italy. It owed its origins to the leadership of the Marchioness Matilda, who, as a staunch supporter of Pope Gregory VII, wanted to establish at Bologna a center of legal studies favorable to the pope that could counterbalance the Imperialistic school at Ravenna supporting the divine right of kings. Under Matilda's sponsorship, Irnerius studied law in Rome and then returned in about 1088 to Bologna to open his school and institute Roman law as the first academic discipline in Europe.[44] Thousands of students from all over Europe eventually came to study at Bologna, which became the nerve center for the dissemination of Roman law throughout the Continent and beyond. One student, Vacarius, went to England to teach at Canterbury and Oxford.

Meanwhile at Ravenna, Peter Crassus was exploiting the potential of Roman law for defending the divine power of kings. With his tract, *In Defence of King Henry*, he introduced Roman law into the center of political controversy, a place it would keep until after the Reformation. Crassus used the *Code* as well as the *Digest* to justify the king's legal powers within his domain.[45]

The revival of legal studies was consistent with the scholastic method, which emphasized organization, logic, and dialectical methods. Medieval lawyers had a great share in this resurrection of order over the fragmentation of knowledge that had occurred in the so-called Dark Ages, but their work had a different cast about it because it dealt with a major text and engaged in a practical task. Paul Vinogradoff explains:

While their fellows in the school of Divinity operated on Scripture and Canonic tradition, and the masters of arts struggled, by the help of distorted versions of Aristotle, with the rudiments of metaphysics, politics, and natural science, the lawyers exercised their dialectical acumen on a material really worthy of the name, namely, on the contents of the *Corpus Juris*. . . . For the doctors of the new study the books of Justinian were sacred books, the sources of authority from which all deductions must proceed. It is not to be wondered that they were not content with casual fragments, but made researches into its component elements, and considered it as a whole.[46]

The reception of the Roman legal system had a special appeal to ambitious emperors, princes, and even clerics because it placed the state above all interests, both public and private. Roman law did not admit the feudal intermixture of public and private purposes, and therefore supported with great efficiency a descending theory of government, whether secular or sacred. It also supported economic development with its elaboration of contracts and property rights. As common law grew, Roman jurisprudence became a powerful force in the courts as well as in the schools. In all these ways Roman law in the Middle Ages represents the power of ideas to organize social and political life.

THE INDIVIDUAL AS SUBJECT

Roman law undergirded the biblical basis of the Middle Ages, tending to focus not on the individual but on the corporate body as a whole. The idea of the rule of law within the Church was bolstered by the notion that law was the "soul of the body politic." Although the Bible did not set forth anything like a complete system, it did point toward monarchy, a descending form of government, the idea of the individual as subject, the necessity of obedience to the external rulers, and a great respect for designated offices within the body.[47]

In such a system, the only competent authority is the ruler or emperor—the *dominus mundi*, master of the world. The ruler represents God on earth, serving as God's vice-regent and vested with virtually unlimited powers derived from above. Those powers were personal, inalienable, and nontransferable.

Ullmann points out that there are differences as well as similarities between the monarchic system of the papacy and monarchy as practiced in the Roman Empire. Both represent the wholeness doctrine, however, and both see the individual as a subject rather than as a citizen with

autonomous rights. Although the doctrines might take
different forms within the two structures, the papacy borrowed on a large scale from Roman institutions.[48] For
example, the papacy borrowed from the Roman emperors
the letter known as a "rescript" or "decretal letter" to
exercise its binding authority. These letters constituted
church law, now vested with all the authority of Roman
law.[49]

Ordinary Christians had no share in making the policies
by which they were governed. Nor did they have jurisdictional rights over property. Since all property came from
God, and God is the source of the ruler's authority, the
ruler had the authority to dispose of the individual's property. In the twelfth century the civilian Martinus stated
this thesis explicitly, declaring that the expression "everything is understood to be in the prince's power" meant
that the ruler was the owner of all the property of his
subjects and could dispose of it at will. This was his power
of *dominium* by virtue of his being God's vice-regent on
earth.[50]

Nor had there developed at this point any idea of human
equality in the civic sphere. Pope Gregory the Great (c.
540–604) granted that by nature all people are equal, but
insisted at the same time that there is some sort of "occult
dispensation" by which some people because of their merits rank higher than others: "All men are by nature equal.
. . . Nature created all men equal, but by a varying order of
their merits, an occult dispensation ranked some behind
others."[51] Even in the later Middle Ages the doctrine that
members of the society by virtue of their membership had
equal standing in the public realm was unknown.[52]

There *was* a theory of inalienable rights in the Middle
Ages, but it belonged to corporations, not to individuals.
During the thirteenth century Roman and canon lawyers
developed the idea that kingdoms had to have certain
guaranteed rights if they were to survive. At the same
time, they began to think of the king not as a *dominus* in
an absolute sense, but as a guardian of the responsibilities
entrusted to him.[53]

Medieval theorists thus attached the idea of inalienable rights to the common public good rather than to individuals.

In the later Middle Ages legal specialists also attempted to develop a theory of privileges for women, children, and clerics through a system of renunciations. *Renuntio* means the surrender of one's legal privileges in return for special protection. Drawing on the organic theory of society, legal scholars developed the doctrine that the protection of women and children as well as of the Church was required because women, children, and Church were prey to their more sophisticated environment. Later, emperors and kings were added to the protection list since they too fulfill a unique role. In every case, the criterion for a legal renunciation was in one vital respect the same: inalienable rights were those that touched the public interest.[54]

In summary, the individual had not yet emerged in the medieval world. This is due to a host of factors, but chief among them is the primacy of Roman law with its emphasis on the group rather than on the individual in both Church and society. Paradoxically, the influence of Roman law eventually would prepare the way for the secularization of government and the new place of the individual within it. By the end of the twelfth century, Western Europe was in the grip of Roman principles of government supplied by Roman law, having undergone what one observer calls a "bloodless revolution" such as Europe had not known before.[55] Roman law would become both a source of inspiration and a means of accommodation to change—but not yet.

Natural law, too, contained the seeds of the potentially revolutionary idea that the "laws of nature and of Nature's God" might someday be taken to mean that individuals as well as corporations are endowed with rights. The legal renaissance of eleventh-century Italy raised the possibility that there might be a superior code capable of abrogating human laws. This could not happen as long as the Church Universal remained all-powerful, but when the breakdown occurred in the Renaissance and Reformation, the way was clear for the flowering of these seeds of thought.[56]

The pervasive presence of natural law and Roman law in medieval Christian civilization thus helped enhance the possibilities for human freedom because they kept alive the possibility of conflicting loyalties that eventually would clear a space for the individual in society.

In the meantime, a theory of individual rights emerged from contemporary events in feudal medieval England, where Roman law was giving way to common law and creating yet another set of conditions conducive to human liberty.

CHAPTER 3

English Beginnings: Common Law and Magna Carta

Magna Carta is such a Fellow, he will have no Sovereign.

SIR EDWARD COKE

THE Romans considered Britain to be so far removed from the center of civilization that the poet Catullus (c. 84–54 B.C.) emphasized the separation of the "faraway Britons" by placing the adjective and noun, *ultimos . . . Britannos,* in two different lines of one of his poems.[1] This geographical remove helps account for the very different historical circumstances that shaped the rise of English common law.

English feudalism, evolving at a distance from the Roman jurisprudence that dominated the Continent, brought forth the gradual development of practical legal institutions that ultimately enhanced the role and status of the individual. From as early as the twelfth century in feudal England, common law shielded individual liberty against the aspirations of monarchs because it involved the element of consent.

FEUDALISM AND THE RISE OF COMMON LAW

In many ways medieval England exhibits in fact if not in theory an ascending form of governance. If the people were supposed to be "subjects," they may frequently not have known it since they were so busy with the daily realities of conducting public business, participating in guilds in which individuals had full membership and elected their own officers, and practicing self-governance in the villages. Customary laws, which as the term implies were the product of customary usage, permeated the affairs of the island, and the rulers tended to give at least tacit approval to these lay laws by having "all the laws in their breasts." The practical deployment of individual capabilities among persons in the lower strata of society thus provided a bridge between the medieval and humanistic theses.[2]

Feudalism was contractual in nature, a matter of oaths and loyalties exercised in both directions between lords and vassals. The emphasis was on mutual obligations, and the vassal had a means of resisting a lord who behaved as a tyrant. This was called the *diffidatio*, a withdrawal of *fides* or loyalty from the lord. This practice was personal, however, not institutional. The intense personalism of these arrangements contradicted the descending form of government and in some ways diametrically opposed it.[3] As theocratic kings the medieval lords had absolute power. As feudal lords, however, they were one among others.[4] Within this bargaining context, laws were arrived at by counsel and consent, often by cooperation and teamwork framed by the personal relationships between the king as feudal lord and his chief tenants.[5]

English common law is therefore "common" in more than one sense. It helped produce a common culture within feudal society, but it was also common as opposed to fancy. Because it was earthbound and daily instead of speculative and abstract, it tended to pay greater respect to the rights of individuals. These conditions made possible the resurrection of Aristotle's "natural man" and the emergence of individuals as citizens.

English contributions of learned tracts to political theory were few in comparison with the French and Italian. One reason for this was the relative insignificance in England of Roman law, which served as the focus and incentive for a great deal of legal theorizing. The tension between government and the governed across the Channel also took different and less intense forms in England, at least after the time of King John and Magna Carta in the thirteenth century.[6]

Natural law doctrine was later evoked in England to provide justification for practices historically established within feudalism. This could occur only because the underlying conditions were already in place. "No natural law theory," insists Ullmann, "no considerations of doctrinal character, could have exercised influence if the historic presuppositions had not been favorable."[7] The differing historical conditions help explain why individual rights evolved as they did in England in contrast to the Continent. The outcomes of the later French and Russian revolutions would be very different because they grew out of ideological abstractions rather than a long history of practical accommodations concerning the limits of power.

ROMAN LAW IN ENGLAND

In the early twelfth century, King Henry II (reigning 1154–1189) established royal courts to consolidate his power, thus beginning the unification of national law. Henry was the first of a series of kings under whom constitutional governance in England began to take shape. Upon accession to the throne he crushed a group of rebellious barons, but almost immediately his authority was challenged again, this time by the Church at Rome represented by Thomas à Becket. This challenge resulted from Henry's determination to limit the privileged position of the clergy. After arranging for Becket's murder, Henry continued to strengthen his secular control by setting up a rudimentary civil service.[8]

This process was aided by the fact that judicial decisions began to be recorded, creating an accruing body of law.

Lawyers in the king's courts came to depend not only on the scribbled notes of their colleagues but also on two learned law books, one written by Glanvil during the reign of Henry II and another by Bracton in the reign of Henry III in the thirteenth century. The result of these changes was that Anglo-Saxon common law, rather than the revised Roman law, became the supreme law of the land.

This does not mean, however, that there was an absence of Roman legal ideology. Hans Julius Wolff points out that Roman concepts were by no means completely barred and that Bracton dealt with some of them without even considering that they were something foreign. The Roman importations, however, did not interfere with the development of English law along the lines that had been established by the courts from the time of Henry II.[9]

Roman law with its attendant principles of natural law had been brought into England through the Church, whose clerics were the first justiciars of English law. An Italian named Vacarius taught Roman civil law and canon law at Oxford in the middle of the twelfth century and was enormously popular. Robert N. Wilkin holds the minority view that Roman law had a greater impact on the law of Britain than on that of the Continent:

It [Roman law] was so completely accepted in England that Englishmen thought it their own. It never was foreign after the twelfth or early part of the thirteenth century. It had an extensive influence on Bracton and through him on Coke. While we think of Coke as particularly a champion of the common law, his basic principles were the same as those of the Roman law and natural law. Through their acceptance into the common law of England natural-law principles became a part of the constitutional history of England.[10]

Others take a more measured view of the impact of Roman civil law on English common law. Paul Vinogradoff holds that while it exercised a very great influence during the critical period in the twelfth and thirteenth centuries, when the foundations of the common law were being laid, civil law did not become a constituent element of English common law acknowledged and enforced by the courts.[11] Whatever the degree of impact, the situation was that the legal advisers to the Crown ordinarily combined a knowledge of Roman legal theory with practical experience of English realities.[12]

Hans Julius Wolff agrees that England was the major exception to Roman law as the law truly "common to all" but suggests that even there Roman law could supply the rules needed to fill the gaps of national law. He traces the scholarly interest in Roman law back to Lanfranc, the chancellor of William the Conqueror and archbishop of Canterbury, who had studied with the pre-Glossator legists in Italy at Pavia.[13]

The study of Roman civil law in England progressed so far that the Church came to feel threatened by what it saw as the spread of secular learning. Two papal bulls, one by Honorius III in 1219 and another by Innocent IV in 1254, were directed against the teaching of Roman law in Paris and in "neighboring countries," including England. In 1234 Henry III forbade the teaching of civil law in London. In spite of these prohibitions, however, the teaching of Roman civil law was never entirely discontinued in the major centers of learning in England.

One of the most important English contributions to Roman law was Bracton's *Laws and Customs of England*, especially his discussions of *ius civile* and *ius gentium*. Even here, however, the influence of Roman law is found not in quotations from the *Digest* or the *Code*, but rather in maxims, many of which had come into England through the medium of canon law. The real measure of the extent of that influence lies in the development of juridical ideas, and here the Roman influence on English doctrine is considerable.[14] The old English Books with their grants of private property exempted from folkright are also Roman imports brought in through the Church in conjunction with the kings. The impact of these importations was to alter the earlier tribal custom of land tenure in England by substituting forms of Roman property law.[15]

MAGNA CARTA

A major advance in constitutional development in England came in the early thirteenth century with the signing of Magna Carta. With this event, what formerly had been private law and custom deriving from personal relations became written and public. As mere subjects with no power, King John's barons could not restrain God's appointed monarch. The barons, however, were not only subjects; they were also barons, and in that role they shared comparable power with the king, who was also a baron. It was as barons rather than subjects that they forced King John to make his constitutional surrender in 1215 at Runnymede.

The situation leading to Magna Carta was one of détente, with different powers balancing each other out. The barons were in a position to destroy King John altogether. The king, while tactically at the disadvantage, knew that all of his castles were garrisoned and ready to fight. Knowing that their balance was temporary, the barons were careful not to overplay their hand. Ultimately they received John's assent to all but one of their forty-nine demands. On June 15 John sealed the articles. For three days they were worked over, apparently with Stephen of Canterbury leading the task, and on Friday, June 19, both parties came together, read the agreement, and sealed the final copies.

Magna Carta is venerated by some as "the greatest constitutional document of all times—the foundation of freedom of the individual against the arbitrary authority of the despot."[16] By its own terms, however, it claimed to be a reassertion of ancient customs and a restoration of earlier liberties. Chapter 39, called by Sir Edward Coke "the golden passage" of English law, is the crucial chapter of Magna Carta for the history of due process and the protection of personal freedom. This provision was not original. Rather, it restated an axiom that had received its first clear formulation in the edict of the German Emperor Conrad II in 1037, found in the *Liber feudorum*, that no soldier could be deprived of his fief except by judgment of his peers: "No freeman shall be captured and imprisoned, or disseized, or outlawed, or exiled, or in any way harmed, except by a lawful tribunal of his peers and by the law of the land."[17] Judgment by peers had been laid down in a number of documents throughout Europe; in England it appeared in the Laws of Henry I in the form, "Each man is to be judged by his peers in the same neighborhood."[18]

Chapter 39 reads as follows:

No *freeman shall be taken or imprisoned or disseized* of any freehold, or liberties, or free customs, or outlawed, or banished, *or in any other way destroyed, nor will we* go upon him, nor send upon him, *except by* the legal judgment of his peers or by *the law of the land.* To no one will we sell, to no one will we deny or delay right or justice.

Its close relationship to the Fifth Amendment of the U.S. Constitution may be noted by the parallel concepts found in italics:

No person shall be held to answer for a capital, or otherwise infamous crime, unless on a presentment or indictment by a grand jury, ... *nor shall any person* ... *be deprived of life, liberty, or property, without due process of law.*

Chapter 39, which became Chapter 29 in the definitive form of Magna Carta, outlived all the other details of the document. Although it was stated as a universal principle at the time and eventually would become one, in 1215 it applied only to all freemen—that is, freeholders entitled to a franchise with tenancy. At the time, this may have amounted to only about 10 percent of the population. Not until four hundred years later would the English Revolution put an end to the feudal tenures Magna Carta was designed to sustain.[19]

There was no thought that these rights were ever divinely granted by any divine law or even natural law, not because they were conceded by any higher authority, but because they had gradually come into being and then emerged into the public sphere. "In brief," concludes

Ullmann, "the individual's safety, freedom, and property were declared inviolate, were removed from arbitrary interference—in a thoroughly feudal document."[20]

This article has been seen as the origin of the rule of law and of the principle of due process of law.[21] Nevertheless, these processes were part of the feudal compact rather than the emanation of new theories sprung full-blown from the brain of Zeus or any man. As J. C. Holt puts it, "The liberties of the twelfth and thirteenth centuries were no infection spreading from one country to another; they were part of the very atmosphere."[22] The grievance of the barons was that King John had set aside the feudal compact. What they had wanted to see established was not the king's law but the "law of the land," that collection of written and unwritten rules that had been common to the barons and to the king as a baron.

After Runnymede the understanding was established that the governor as well as the governed is subject to the rule of law. This principle obtained when Charles I acceded to the Petition of Rights, when William III and Mary II accepted the Declaration of Rights in 1689, and when George III was served with the American Declaration of Independence. Edward Coke (1552–1634) may have devised an abstract principle out of the pragmatic arrangements settled at Runnymede—the matter of Coke's understanding is much debated[23]—but the proposition that the personal liberty of subjects is the highest function of law became one of enduring worth.[24] Even though only four of the original thirty-seven clauses remain in force,[25] the ideals of Magna Carta have inspired and protected individual liberties for nearly eight centuries.

MAGNA CARTA AND NATURAL LAW

In the mid-seventeenth century, customary or common law came to be compared invidiously with the wider claims of abstract natural rights. An early proponent of natural rights was Henry Parker, whose writings had an important influence on Hobbes. Parker, in supporting Parliament against the power of the throne, rejected dependence on common law as a source of great harm. Equating Parliament with the state, he identified the fundamental laws that governed both not with custom or statute but with the law of nature: "Fundamental law is such a one as is coucht radically in Nature itself (and so becomes the very pin of law and society) and is written and enacted irrepealably in her *Magna charta*, which we are not beholden to any sublunary power for, but belongs to us as we are living and sociable creatures."[26]

This challenge on the basis of natural law would grow. By the time of the American Revolution, the authority of Parliament was being challenged by radicals at home and by American colonists abroad. The issue was the sovereignty of Parliament, concerning which the colonists and their English radical sympathizers such as William Pitt, first earl of Chatham, and Charles Pratt, first earl of Camden, held that the actions of Parliament were limited by fundamental, natural law. Chatham, for example, considered Magna Carta "the Bible of the English Constitution," a "political bible" that could not be used to support government action against the colonists.[27] Camden attacked the Declaratory Bill of 1766 as "absolutely illegal—contrary to the fundamental laws of nature, contrary to the fundamental laws of this constitution."[28]

Events in France and America influenced the political climate in England in the later eighteenth century, bringing a concomitant challenge to the common law tradition of Magna Carta. In stressing unlimited and inalienable rights, leading thinkers rejected mere appeal to precedent. James Mackintosh observed: "It is not because we *have* been free, but because we have a right to be free, that we ought to demand freedom."[29] Thomas Paine took the issue even further, rejecting all historical assumptions in favor of natural ones. Paine saw Magna Carta not as the fountainhead of liberty but as a document partially securing inherent civil liberties. Carrying the thought of Hobbes and Locke one step further, Paine replaced common law and precedent with ideas of abstract law and natural rights. Paine's ideas, however, did not fare well in an England marked by conservative reaction against the

French revolution.[30] More popular was Edmund Burke's insistence on the continuity of English laws and institutions, strongly rooted in antiquity even while undergoing change in response to circumstances.[31]

Magna Carta does not represent in any sense a democratic revolution. The constituted tribunals were tribunals of one's peers, that is, others of like status. It was unthinkable that one would be judged by anyone of lower status. The great breakthrough, however, was that individual rights were confirmed by a written document rather than imagined as a theory or conceded as a gift by one individual to another.

The impact of feudalism and English common law on human liberty was expressed succinctly in a special medal struck for Edward III's coronation in 1327, signalling a return of the ascending theme of government. The motto on the medal reads *Voluntas populi dat jura*, "The will of the people gives the laws."

EARLY ENGLISH THEORIES OF RIGHTS

An important transitional figure in the late medieval period in England is William of Ockham (or Occam) (c. 1290–1349). Ockham saw the natural moral law as the positive law of divine will. He broke with Aquinas by positing that everything God does is done because God wills it, not because it is somehow suitable to the nature of human beings. Thus Ockham saw no universals, only individual particulars. By asserting that universals are only names (*nomina*) for similarities among existing things—rather than, as Aquinas insisted, their real essences—Ockham with his nominalism paved the way for a more radical individualism.[32] In many universities he came to represent the modern way, *via moderna*, as opposed to the *via antiqua* of Aquinas. Michel Villey holds that Ockham provides in his *Opus nonaginta dierum* the first systematic account of subjective rights.[33]

Ockham advanced individualism also by his emphasis on natural law in his political writings.[34] As one provision of natural law, he states that rulers should be elected by consent—which may be the first time in political thought that governmental legitimacy was determined by consent based on natural law.[35]

Given the subsequent role of private property in arguments about rights, it is significant that the context of Ockham's political writings was the controversy between the papacy and the Franciscans over apostolic poverty. The Franciscans argued that they should not own property but only exercise the use of it for their immediate needs. Ockham's *Opus nonaginta dierum* was written in direct refutation of a papal bull issued in 1329 by Pope John XXII entitled *Quia vir reprobus*. In that document the pope attacked the Franciscan position by arguing that God possesses lordship (*dominium*) over the earth just as individuals do over their possessions. Thus, property is natural to human beings and is sustained by divine law. One scholar takes the view that it was the reaction to Ockham, rather than Ockham's own work, that led to a radical natural rights theory. If God has property in the world, such a view holds, then human beings can, too, and in this one way resemble their maker. This basic fact about human beings can thus lead fairly directly to an individualistic political theory not far removed from the classic theories of rights of the seventeenth century.[36]

Ockham's younger contemporary, John Wyclif (1320–1384), has been credited with advancing the theme of the individual as a fully fledged, autonomous, independent member of society who had inherent, inborn rights. What made Wyclif especially important was his resistance to the corporational or collectivist point of view and his appreciation of subjective judgments, the same values that led him to translate the Bible into the vernacular. For Wyclif, the validity of law and public actions depended on the "moral worth" of the body or person creating the law.[37]

The evolution of individual liberty in feudal England, together with events originating in the late Middle Ages on the Continent, would combine to create entirely new ways of thinking about human autonomy and individual rights.

CHAPTER 4

Enlightenment Humanism and the "New Thought"

> *The State of Nature has a Law of Nature to gov-*
> *ern it, which obliges every one; and Reason,*
> *which is that Law, teaches all mankind who will*
> *but consult it, that being all equal and indepen-*
> *dent, no one ought to harm another in his Life,*
> *Liberty, or Possessions.*
>
> JOHN LOCKE

THE emergence of the individual in political thought is one of the supreme achievements of the human mind. The gestation of the idea was long, stretching from the late Middle Ages through the Renaissance and Reformation to the eighteenth century. In classical Athens and Rome the status of human beings was defined by membership in the city or state. In the medieval period it was conditioned by membership in the *corpus Christi.*

Now the individual emerges as independent citizen in the social sphere, and now for the first time a belief in individual rights grows out of natural law theory. This chapter of the story of rights begins with certain cultural innovations during the late medieval period; continues with the humanistic scholars of the early Italian Renaissance; shifts to northern Europe with the thought of Grotius and Pufendorf; acknowledges the roles of Hobbes, Rousseau, and Montesquieu; and concludes with the seminal thought of John Locke. While such a survey passes over many key figures and moments, it traces in outline the emergence of individual rights in political thought, without which there would have been no United States Bill of Rights.

THE MEDIEVAL LEGACY

From the late twelfth century on, a combination of factors converged to widen the arena for individuals within the political realm and to enhance humanism in all areas of life. These cultural and intellectual innovations, some of them in unexpected ways, helped bring major breakthroughs in political thought.[1]

In the visual arts there was an increased naturalism, in which idealized stereotypes gave way to the portrayal of more individualistic traits. Architecture, sculpture, and painting were increasingly entrusted to laypeople.

Important works were now written in or translated into the vernacular, making all kinds of knowledge more widely accessible. With the spread of written work available in the vernacular as well as Latin, knowledge of many subjects was no longer limited to a small circle of educated clergy.

The writing of history changed, with a new emphasis on the role of individual human beings in the making of history. Otto of Freising, for example, claimed that history should be pleasant to read: "We have not set out to write tragedy, but a pleasurable history."[2] Grim themes of *memento mori* (remember to die) gave way to *memento vivere* (remember to live) as optimism and a zest for living replaced resignation and escapism.

Interest in the natural sciences grew, bringing with it an enhanced enthusiasm for discoveries about the natural world in which we live. Roger Bacon (c. 1219–1294), for example, experimented with convex lenses and rediscovered the crossing of the optic nerve.

"Political Platonism," with its emphasis on the perfection of a closed ethical/political system, was replaced by Aristotelianism, which saw both politics and ethics as imprecise endeavors that allow for many variations and different ways of life. Aristotle was more interested in empirically observing how people really behave. While Aristotle's central thesis about organic society would give way to a citizen-centered model, his intellectual methodology proved more amenable to humanistic thought than Plato's.

This breakdown of Platonic wholeness opened the way for renewed appreciation of Aristotle's views on natural law and the concept of citizen as constituent of the state. Aristotle had shown that person and citizen were two different categories, so that the good citizen need not be a good person and vice versa.[3] Ideally the two would be the same, but this wedge between ethics and politics opened the way for a wider arena of political action and a larger role for the individual on the stage.

Classical Greek and Latin authors were read with a new openness of mind. Rather than being scrutinized for conformity with Christian doctrine, they were interesting now for how they could enhance understanding of human life.

In a seemingly small but consequential advance, eyeglasses were invented, making it possible for more people to read the works that were increasingly available. The first documented manufacture of spectacles was that of Bernard Gordon in 1305 at the University of Montpellier.[4]

Finally, the continuity of Roman law with its concepts of the citizen and the state provided what Walter Ullmann calls "preparatory familiarity" for a new understanding of individuals as citizens in their own right.[5]

DANTE AND THE ITALIAN RENAISSANCE

The poet Dante (1265–1321) contributed significantly to the new ways of thinking with his inclusive view of the human community, *humana civilitas*. For Dante, this concept embraced not only Christians but Muslims, Jews, and pagans as well. While Dante subscribed to Aquinas's "double ordering" of things human and divine, he also evinced a great belief in human freedom. Grounded in this belief, Dante articulated in his *De monarchia* a new relationship between governors and governed: "Citizens are not there for the sake of governors, nor the nation for the sake of the king, but conversely the governors for the sake of the citizens, the king for the sake of the nation."[6]

Dante appears to have been the first to speak of human liberty as inherent in human nature and not granted by any exterior authority except God. Now citizens were seen to have choices about how they live with one another and how they organize human society. For Dante, liberty was the guarantee that human beings would be happy on this earth since freedom means that human beings exist for their own sake, not for the sake of something or someone else.[7]

Dante's *De monarchia* also contributes to other new forms of political thought. A faithful follower of Aquinas, Dante advocated *civilitas* as an antidote to political fragmentation and urged a world state composed of free states. For Dante, freedom was the "greatest gift conferred by God on man," and only free citizens had the possibility of developing all their capacities.

Following Dante, Lucas of Penna (c. 1320–1390) also combined Platonic, Stoic, Aristotelian, and Ciceronian ideas with the Christian faith to come up with a new and more inclusive amalgam. Lucas saw human beings as part of universal nature as well as creatures of God. Therefore people are endowed by God with inborn and indestructible rights, regardless of human legislation.[8] True happiness is a function of the freedom into which human beings are born, *ad libertatem nati sumus*, and which they can exercise against even legitimately instituted laws if the demands of officials are unjust. Lucas believed strongly that human happiness depended, to a very marked degree, on the adequate payment of wages, basing his belief on Lev. 19.13: "You shall not keep back a hired man's wages till next morning." Penna believed that rights, while only contributory to happiness, nevertheless could be exercised against even legitimately instituted laws.[9]

The thought of Pietro Pomponazzi of Padua (1462–1524) provides another striking example of the shift in the status of the individual in the Renaissance. Pomponazzi has been called the last of the Scholastics, but he is just as aptly considered the first representative of the Enlightenment.[10] In his treatise *On Fate, Predestination, and Free Will*, Pomponazzi never attacks the faith held by the Church of the Middle Ages, but he does heighten the distinction between faith and reason, leaning heavily to the side of reason. While not challenging the theory of a transcendent world, he makes clear that he does not need a theory of transcendence on which to base his ethics. In his worldview the human sciences now have a basis independent of theology.

Pomponazzi's thoughts on individualism in *On the Immortality of the Soul* differ diametrically from those in an essay of the same name by his slightly earlier contemporary, Marsilio Ficino of Florence (1433–1499). Both philosophers strive to define the individual, but Ficino does this by tying the freedom of human beings to the supernatural transcendence of their souls, while Pomponazzi believes that the justification of individuality resides not outside of but within nature. For Pomponazzi, the soul is a direct continuation of the body. In this emphasis on nature he is following Aristotle the biologist rather than Aristotle the metaphysician.[11]

Even though his thought had to be revised in many important respects, the rediscovery of Aristotle helped foment the intellectual revolution in the thirteenth century. For Aristotle the state was a natural unit that had grown entirely according to the laws of nature, independent of theology or divine intervention. This led to an abandonment of the "wholeness" point of view because it addressed not the Christian as the "whole person subject to the Ruler" but the state as a collection of persons. With the reintroduction of the concept of the state, the concept of the citizen also emerged. Both notions would prove troublesome to medieval Christian society and government.[12]

What has reappeared is the "natural man," whom Paul had pronounced washed away by baptism. Being incorporated into the Church had meant loss of autonomy from cradle to grave. Now the unipolarity of the individual as Christian gives way to the bipolarity of the individual as a natural person and as a Christian. The wholeness theory began to give way to departmentalization: persons as citizens, as moral agents, as religious practitioners. The individual as many-faceted citizen begins to replace the individual as subject to higher authority. Now citizens begin to take responsibility for shaping their communities and creating their laws—and now the ascending theme of government reappears after a long eclipse.[13]

Even though most thinkers of the Renaissance still had to confront Aquinas's "double ordering" of things human and things divine,[14] social life by the fifteenth century could once again be considered a creation of human beings as it had been in ancient Athens and republican Rome. Now, however, individuals occupy a greatly enhanced role as decisive constituents of their communities.

The stage was now set for the "new thought" of the Enlightenment and for a thoroughgoing theory of natural rights inhering within the individual. Two common threads, rationalism and the rule of law, run through the ancient, medieval, and Enlightenment eras of natural law theory. The rationalist character of natural law theory—and the belief that human reason is sufficient to discern it—goes back to Aristotle and Stoic philosophy. The connection of natural law with human law—and thus a belief in the rule of law itself—goes back to Rome and the "law of nations."

Three new features become prominently associated with natural law theory by the eighteenth century: the removal of the divinity from a central role in the doctrine; the emphasis on the freedom and agency of the individual in the public realm, as distinguished from the inner spiritual freedom promised by Stoic doctrine; and the assumption that the natural rights of individuals can justify the overthrow of governments. In short, natural law becomes radicalized.

GROTIUS AND PUFENDORF

Historians disagree on the role of Hugo Grotius of Holland (1583–1645) in the first transition, the removal of divinity from a central role in the doctrine of natural law, but by many he is considered a decisive source for the new thought.[15] Natural law theory underlies Grotius's *Laws of War and Peace* (1625), continuing intact the theory appropriated by Christendom even after medieval Christendom had been shattered by the Reformation, of which Grotius was a product. But Grotius holds in a famous dictum that natural law would be valid even if God did not exist: *etiamsi daremus non esse Deum*.

Although he believed in God and in a divine origin of natural laws, Grotius sees natural laws as absolutely valid, like the laws of mathematics, in such a way that even God could not change them. In the *Laws of War and Peace* he writes: "Measureless as is the power of God, nevertheless it can be said that there are certain things over which that power does not extend. . . . Just as even God cannot cause that two times two should not make four, so He cannot cause that which is intrinsically evil be not evil."[16] Grotius defines natural law in terms of the dictates of reason: "The law of nature [*ius naturale*] is a dictate of right reason which points out that an act, according as it is or is not in conformity with rational and social nature, has in it a quality of moral baseness or moral necessity; and that, in consequence, such an act is either forgiven or enjoined by the author of nature, God."[17]

The main contribution of Grotius was his systematizing of international law on the foundation of natural law. In separating natural law from theological ends, he did not necessarily act independently of theological influences. Nevertheless, he attached the old notion of natural law validated by the exercise of reason to the creation of an international legal system—and did so at a time of conflict between Catholics and Protestants, which gave the secularization new significance.[18] H. A. Rommen sees Grotius as a transitional figure between two great eras. While maintaining many ties from an earlier age, he ushered the theory of natural law into the modern period with the distinguishing characteristics of rationalism, sociality, and particular political aims.[19]

It may have been Grotius who set in motion the sharp division between faith and reason that would result in a natural law theory free of theology, culminating in the Declaration of Independence and the French Declaration of the Rights of Man and of the Citizen.[20] God may still have a place in natural law language, but it is largely a rhetorical place.

Ancient Epicurean philosophy upheld the existence of gods but located them in the remote spaces of the universe, where they lacked any interest in human affairs. There is something almost Epicurean about the remoteness now attributed to divinity in natural law theory. Sometimes known as Deism, this system of thought grants divine existence but not divine involvement in human matters. Nature's laws are discernible by human reason and do not require a God or gods to confirm their validity.

But there is a problem here. If, like two plus two equals four, natural laws are eternal and never change, then how do they relate to history, which is always changing? This fundamental issue was addressed by Renaissance thinkers in several ways. For his part, Grotius stood firm. He saw his legal theories as clear, coherent, and self-evident. To achieve such clarity, one must deal only in abstractions. Ragged facts must be stripped away. Grotius announces proudly that he has eschewed all facts: "With all truthfulness I aver that, just as the mathematicians treat their figures as abstracted from bodies, so in treating law I have withdrawn my mind from every particular fact."[21]

Following closely on Grotius was Samuel Pufendorf (1632–1694). Pufendorf was a German Protestant who worked in the courts of northern Europe, first Sweden and later Prussia. In 1658, at the age of twenty-six, he wrote the *Elementa jurisprudentiae universalis*, in which he praises Grotius and treats even Hobbes with respect. By the time he wrote *De iure naturae et gentium* in 1672 he had changed his views and came to a vigorous attack on Hobbes and the more radical theories of natural rights. He distinguished between "positive" and "negative" communities, holding that for a transition to be made from a negative natural state, where nobody owned anything, to a state of exclusive private property, express social arrangements had to be agreed upon. It was these general agreements for social utility that conferred rights. Rights, being derived from socially constructed agreements, could therefore not in turn be invoked against the agreements. They could be used, however—and often were—to support authoritarian regimes.[22]

This was a critical turning point, a break in the tradition. From the point of Pufendorf on, it became fashionable to poke fun at the Scholastics and the marriage arranged by Aquinas between Aristotle and the Church. From this time henceforward, an anti-Aristotelian nominalism became, expressly or tacitly, the basis of philosophy.[23]

For Aristotle, "nature" referred not to a continuous process of change but rather to the "end" or terminus toward which something aims. This end was identical with the essence of the thing progressing toward it, and the "good" it had "according to nature." Put another way, the essence of an oak tree is in the acorn, and the good end of the acorn is to become the oak tree it is meant to be.

The question, if it be a question, is whether human individuals and human institutions are oak trees. If an acorn at a tender age falls in with parasitic mistletoes or a mob of thorn trees, it will blithely continue on its good way to becoming an oak tree. A twelve-year-old child in analogous company might not be so unaffected.

Further, Aristotle, as we have seen, defines individuals as human by virtue of their membership in the polis or state. Politics, not nature, is the determining factor. Enlightenment thought in the tradition of Locke locates the essential worth of individuals not in their citizenship nor even in their creation by a Divinity but rather in their nature.

A third Aristotelian hallmark is the schism between *praxis* and *poesis*, that is, between exercise of reason and mere production. For Aristotle, production or *poesis* falls completely outside the realms of morals and politics, which alone define a truly human life. For Hobbes as well as Locke and the other liberals, activity in conquest, industry, and production came to be seen as creative and meaningful.

The aristocratic polis of men at leisure thus gives way to men of action. Similarly, the polis, corporate state, and *corpus Christi* give way to the social contract.

THE SOCIAL CONTRACT

The emphasis on the individual in natural law thought is signalled by the appearance of the social contract as the basis of civil society. The term "contract" contains the clue to the new arrangement. It implies the equality of the individuals involved because contracts are bilateral agreements made by two parties, each possessing independent status. Most observers consider the social contract as an entirely modern product,[24] although early origins have been discerned among the Greek Sophists, especially Protagoras.[25]

Once individuals are considered autonomous human beings endowed with inherent natural rights, they are no longer "subjects" or mere "members" of a higher power. On the formal level, the contract implies the choice of entering into mutual obligations that exist by virtue of natural law. On the substantive level, it implies the bartering of the natural rights of individuals in exchange for achieving political and social organization. "The idea of contract," says A. P. d'Entrèves, "was the only possible means of setting the natural rights of the individual within the framework of the State."[26]

The third new component of natural law theory is the notion of natural rights flowing from it, a notion that can justify revolution if those rights are abrogated. In the medieval period one could disobey the ruling powers *if* the rulers were not acting in accord with the natural law. Peter Stein considers the importance of some of the early "glossators" or commentators on Roman law in this regard. Placentinus, for example, in commenting on a fragment declaring that anyone who disobeys the order of a magistrate is guilty of fraud, demonstrates a liberal outlook when he adds the qualification, "unless he is obeying the Gospel or natural law."[27] After the Reformation, Protestants tended to base their resistance to kings on history or scripture rather than on natural law. In neither case, however, was natural rights theory sufficient to support a right to political revolution.

The theory of the social contract is therefore related to natural law, now invoked to support the claim that human beings are individuals capable of making their own judgments and acting in their own behalf. The component ideas of this thesis were not new, namely, that individuals are born free and equal at least spiritually and that there was some sort of original state of nature. What was required was a "shift of accent" in order to arrive at the notion of society as an arrangement created by its members through the exercise of their own will.[28] That shift of accent is the emphasis on the individual.

Natural law, like Proteus, assumes different forms in different hands. By various theorists natural law has been identified with the divine, the rational, the distinctively human, the normally operating, the frequently recurring, the primitive, the elements not subject to human artifice or control, the self-evident, the nonhistorical.[29] While there is no one founder of liberal theory, there is a liberal theory tradition that would be far different without the influence of any one of the following: Hobbes, Locke, Montesquieu, Smith, Hume, Burke, and Mill.

The sum of their endeavors was to transform natural law from a basic order in the universe, determined by God's sovereign will, into a guarantee of individual rights and a basis for political equality. "The rational individual," observes Paul Sigmund, "rather than the ordered universe, was now the starting point. The old hierarchies had disappeared. The earlier assumption that in all but the most obviously unjust societies the existing order represented God's will and reflected the order of the universe was now challenged by a new awareness of the possibilities of a restructuring of society by autonomous, rational, and equal individuals."[30]

For some this is a great decline from the time of the older idea of natural law, which served as an ethical system with material content. As H. A. Rommen sees it, for example, the earlier function of natural law was to serve as a moral basis for positive law and to represent the ideal, eternal ends toward which the historical state should strive.[31] We shall presently see, however, that at least in the Lockean tradition the moral element is not disjoined from the practical workings of the natural law.

HOBBES, ROUSSEAU, MONTESQUIEU

Before turning to John Locke as the central protagonist of this portion of the story, reference must be made to three other giants of his era: Thomas Hobbes (1588–1679), Jean Jacques Rousseau (1712–1778), and Montesquieu (1689–1755). In spite of the great differences among the three of them, and of all of them from Locke, they shared the conviction that a medieval or Aristotelian world view could no longer provide an adequate basis for political society. Modern science, empiricism, and powerful new intellectual currents all put society in need of new political foundations.[32]

These thinkers, influenced by the new ways of looking at nature, looked anew at social institutions. Knowledge itself came to be understood in new ways, not now as disinterested speculation and an end in itself, the highest form of Platonic or Aristotelian good, but as a tool or means for achieving human well-being. Similarly, these men came to understand that societal institutions had no fixed end or state apart from the human beings who comprised them.[33]

Hobbes, Locke, and Rousseau all shared a notion of the

"pre-social" human being, which assumes that individuals exist prior to the social institutions they invent. Thus the task of political philosophy is to describe the nature of that individuality and then to proceed to an analysis of what the rights and obligations of those individuals would be in their state as citizens. Andrzej Rapaczynski summarizes the place of these three thinkers in the tradition of political thought:

A theory of natural law and natural right . . . had a very long standing in political philosophy. But what distinguished the appeal to natural law in Hobbes, Locke, and Rousseau from the older political theories was their view that nature does not operate with the help of moral or quasi-moral norms: it does not prescribe, allow, or condemn, but forces, inclines, or incapacitates. The question that they, therefore, thought had to be answered before any natural law was used to legitimize a political system was whether the operation of the mechanical laws of nature provided a sufficient ground for inferring a system of normative principles.[34]

Hobbes was not a liberal but rather an important critic of liberalism who would later exercise enormous influence on Kant and Marx. A positivist and absolutist, he denied any element of teleology or ultimate direction in politics and transformed normative politics into a purely descriptive political science. In *Leviathan* (1651), Hobbes denied that human beings are by nature social beings but are instead moved only by selfishness and a desire for power. In the natural state, human society was in a condition of "a war of all against all." The solution was for individuals to give up or "alienate" their autonomy and their judgment to absolute rulers.

Locke would agree with Hobbes that primitive human liberties have to be alienated for political society to be created, but he would add that individuals need not give up their freedom of conscience in the process. For Locke, freedom of conscience is possible even while we obey the magistrates in all our actions, whereas Hobbes eliminates freedom of conscience as well as of action.[35]

Rousseau was a severe critic of natural law and the order of civil society proposed by liberals such as Locke. His polemic against the natural rights tradition stems from the radical break he posited between nature and society. For Rousseau, history replaces the natural order as the foundation of human rights. In his *Social Contract* (1762), Rousseau holds that men by nature are free and equal. The only way to reconcile with civil society their freedom and equality in the natural state is for human beings unanimously to surrender to the general will under collective, impartial laws. These laws, however, are particular to each nation and do not apply to humankind in general.

Rousseau sees productivity, a central Lockean thesis, as degrading to human lives, thus leaving very little room for Locke's ennobling and enriching interaction between nature and society. Finally, and perhaps most importantly, Rousseau considers individual autonomy in a rigidly formalistic way, as contrasted with Locke's more fluid and nonformalistic version. It was this insistence on freedom of the will from any determination that led to potentially totalitarian implications for Rousseau's followers such as Marx and Hegel.[36]

Montesquieu believed that laws underlay everything human, divine, and natural, and that through empirical investigation these laws could be discerned. The influence of his *Spirit of the Laws* (1748) was especially felt in the framers' determination to establish a mixed constitution and separation of powers as safeguards of human freedom. He was an Aristotelian in his commitment to moderation in politics, which contributed to his elaboration of a system of checks and balances far more intricate than the one proposed by Locke.[37]

If our focus were on the history of the political thought underlying the body of the U.S. Constitution promulgated in 1787, Montesquieu would occupy a post of central importance. But for the genealogy of the natural rights theory leading to the Bill of Rights, we turn instead to John Locke.

THE ACHIEVEMENT OF JOHN LOCKE

If Charles Dickens had written a novel along the lines of the present inquiry, his uncanny gift for diagnostic names could not have improved on that of the individual who enters the story next. Like a lock in a canal, which raises the water from one elevation to another, John Locke (1632–1704) elevated the status of individual rights for subsequent Western political theory. Thomas Erskine, in his speech in defense of Thomas Hardy in his trial for high treason, referred to Locke as "the man, next to Sir Isaac Newton of the greatest strength of understanding which the English, perhaps, ever had."[38]

By temperament as well as experience and intellect, Locke was ideally suited for appropriation by American thinkers of the eighteenth century. His classical education, active engagement in politics, and intellectual brilliance formed him in ways readily adaptable to American thought. Locke's father, a liberal Puritan and attorney who had fought on the side of Parliament in the first rebellion against Charles I, inculcated in his son the values of simplicity, temperance, and tolerance. Locke studied classics, Hebrew, and Arabic, first at Westminster School, then at Oxford, where he developed an aversion to Scholastic philosophy while being exposed to many new forms of thinking, including empirical science and medicine.

After a period of lecturing in Latin, Greek, and moral philosophy, Locke became increasingly involved with the intellectual and political movements of his time. As an assistant to Lord Ashley, earl of Shaftesbury, he helped frame a constitution for the colony of Carolina. His service as secretary to the Council of Trade and Plantations was further evidence of his ability and ease in the world of practical politics. Prolonged visits to Paris and Holland introduced him to some of the leading thinkers of his period.

His close association with Shaftesbury, who was tried for treason after leading the parliamentary opposition to the Stuarts, forced Locke to flee to Holland, where he wrote his first published works. He supported the successful revolution, which put William of Orange on the throne, then returned to England in 1689 escorting the future Queen Mary. From that time until shortly before his death, Locke served in various official and unofficial political capacities while writing voluminously on philosophy, religious toleration, education, and politics.

LOCKE'S OPPOSITION TO INNATE IDEAS

Central to Locke's political thought was his philosophical opposition to the theory of innate ideas. Unlike Plato, he firmly believed that we derive our ideas from experience; no realm of ideas exists apart from the experience of human beings. Similarly, no general principles exist to which everyone gives assent. Locke did hold that there are eternal principles of morality, which human beings may come to through reason, experience, and reflection, but even these are not innate. There is no one truth of things, he would say; life is not neat. Locke's conviction on this point was so steadfast that he was willing to live with any theoretical inconsistencies that might follow on it for the sake of the common sense it permitted.[39]

Locke broke through much of the prevailing thought about the human condition by holding that we are all "short-sighted." He came to understand that the only reliable thing that can be said about human knowledge is that it is, and can be, only partial. This simple truth has enormous consequences, because it means that any form of authoritarianism, whether intellectual or political, is based on the false premise that one person or system has all the answers.

Locke's attack on the doctrine of innate ideas could seem to compromise his belief in natural law. He deals with this dilemma by holding that while moral ideas are not innate, they may be arrived at by rational individuals. In the passage in which he attacks innate ideas, he explicitly upholds his belief in natural law: "There is a great deal of difference between an innate law and a law of nature; between something imprinted on our minds in the very original and something that we, being ignorant of, may attain to the knowledge of, by the use and due application of our natural facilities."[40]

For Locke, the problem of innate ideas is closely related to the problem of political authoritarianism. If ideas are innate, they lie outside the empirical realm and thus beyond the scrutiny of reason. In religious and intellectual matters as well as political, this encourages unquestioning assent to any ideas that are claimed to be fixed and unchanging—and to those who profess them.

TWO TREATISES OF GOVERNMENT

Locke published his *Two Treatises of Government* anonymously in 1690, acknowledging his authorship through a codicil to his will only after his death. Called by one observer "the most influential work on natural law ever written,"[41] *Two Treatises* was no disembodied speculation from the study but was born of the pressing politics of the day. In his preface he acknowledged that his purpose was to help establish the title of King William, "Our Great Restorer," to the throne.

The pressing issue which *Two Treatises* is meant to address is arbitrary and absolutist government. Here Locke launches a powerful attack against the most popular justification for royalist absolutism of his time, the political tracts of Sir Robert Filmer (1588–1652). Locke offers instead a radical constitutionalist theory of popular sovereignty and an individualist theory of resistance. Against the prevailing Whig convention of appealing to history, Locke formulates his arguments in the language of natural law and rights. "This move is completely understandable," observes James Tully, "in light of Locke's reconstruction of the epistemological superiority of natural law theory and his complementary dismissal of any theoretical appeal to history. . . . If Locke's project was to appear at all plausible to his immediate audience, he had to show that property, and equality, could be explained in a way consistent with natural law."[42]

Quentin Skinner notes the significance of the fact that Locke nowhere in his *Two Treatises* appeals to the prescriptive force of the ancient English constitution. By his silence, Skinner surmises, Locke is tacitly rejecting one of the most persuasive forms of political reasoning available to him, the appeal to history.[43]

Instead, Locke emphasizes the link between natural law and natural rights that lay in the belief in human reason, now freed from Aquinas's attribution of reason to God and attached instead to the rule of law. This version of natural rights holds that human beings are born endowed with such rights, not granted them by any superior authority.

For Locke, the function of natural law and of the state is to establish as inalienable the rights of the individual. In this state of nature, individuals are bound to be peaceful and take care of each other. Given the human predisposition to look out first for oneself and to violate the rights of others, however, it is necessary to set up civil government. Within the framework of mutual agreement or "social contract," human beings set up a single political body. This is not a contract between ruler and ruled but among free individuals. All participants must assent to this body politic, either tacitly or explicitly; by remaining in it as an adult, assent is implied. Even though individuals thus transfer to government the right to make and enforce laws and to decide on war and peace, they still retain their own powers of judgment. If they see tyranny developing over a long course of time, it is their right—although one never exercised lightly—to rebel against the tyrant and establish a new government. This "dramatically populist claim"[44] of a right to resistance resides in the whole body of the people.

Locke alters the tradition of natural law theory by according a central position to the state of nature and the social contract. He does not view nature as does Hobbes, as the war of all against all. Rather, it is a state of "peace, good-will, mutual assistance, and preservation" and also of equality in political authority, made up of "creatures of the same species and rank, promiscuously born to all the same advantages of nature and the use of the same faculties . . . without subordination or subjection."[45] For Locke, natural equality was the basis of the doctrine of consent to government.

Locke's accomplishment was that he moved from worshiping natural law as a static abstraction to affirming it as the moral infrastructure of tolerance and freedom, providing what we might call a pre-ethical proposition. That is, natural law now underlies rather than determines human freedom and worth.

Unlike Grotius or Pufendorf, Locke held a view of the social contract that did not permit persons to enslave themselves or to submit to absolute government. For Locke, the natural freedom of human beings was not merely a descriptive fact of the state of nature, as in Hobbes's theory, but was a moral *right*: "Every man is born with . . . a right of freedom to his person which no other man has a power over."[46]

Among the social contractarians, Locke is thus the only unqualified liberal.[47] The essence of his liberalism is not his belief in the social contract but rather his conception of individuals and the limitation on the state's function and power, which may or may not derive from the social contract. In this concept, the dignity of persons is ultimately independent of their interaction with other people; that is, it does not depend absolutely on their position in the community, as it did, say, with Aristotle. With Locke, one could leave society, at least theoretically, and still maintain one's dignity. With Aristotle, this is impossible.[48] Locke thus incorporates human beings into nature, closing the mind-body distinction that is at least as old as Plato.

LOCKE ON PROPERTY

Locke devised a remarkably workable political theory in part because of his practical solution to the dilemma of private property. By incorporating a doctrine of private ownership into natural rights theory, he achieved a prag-matic synthesis that avoided the extremes of both com-munitarianism and greed.[49] Locke's thesis is controver-sial, because anything having to do with property is always controversial. Its great strength, however, is that it seems to take the actual human situation into account.

Natural law theory from Aristotle to Rousseau and even the positivists holds that we come into existence with certain inherent rights, first of all, to life and property. The integrity of one's own being and security depends on the ability to secure one's life and well-being. That safeguarding of the person stems from the first natural right of all, the right of one's own individual life, which lies at the basis of the legal order. From this perspective, property is the direct outcome of ego and therefore not an arbitrary fabrication but a natural extension of personal-ity. H. A. Rommen states the thesis in bold form: "In the long run man cannot exist, cannot make good his right to marriage or to a family or to security of life, and cannot maintain his sphere of individual right to a life of his own, unless he is entitled to ownership through the acquisition of goods. The right to private property follows from the physical, ontological make-up of the individual person, from the body-spirit nature of man."[50]

Locke differs from earlier theorists, most of whom had been ambivalent about private property, in asserting that it is an integral part of human nature and a fundamental characteristic of human activity.[51] God's intention, Locke would hold, is that we work in and with nature to make it our own. It is our nature to work and to enjoy the fruits of our labors; indeed, our work makes us who we are.[52]

In his views on property, Locke once again revises his heritage from Aristotle.[53] For Locke, the state is not what defines one's very humanity, as Aristotle believed, but rather a pragmatic arrangement for protecting the private pursuits of individuals and to help avoid conflict. Its chief end, he says in Section 124 of the *Second Treatise*, is the preservation of property. True, Aristotle supports private property, arguing in the *Politics* that it helps reduce quar-rels, as each takes care of what is his own, and increases pleasure through the pleasure of giving things away: "We may add that a very great pleasure is to be found in doing a kindness and giving some help to friends, or guests, or comrades: and such kindness and help become possible only when property is privately owned" (1263b9). Earlier he asserts that moral goodness rather than legal compulsion—as in Plato's scheme—will ensure that individual property is made to serve the needs of all (1263b6).

Locke's break with the ancients has to do instead with the separation in classical Greek political theory between action and production. Production is now part of the good life. It is a liberating and morally significant activity.

Locke is thus an unabashed philosopher for mastery over the natural world. In this sense he insists on privatization over against Aristotle's politicization of human life. Human beings are shaped, he would argue, in the process of their encounter with nature; their labor is not something degrading or alien. Rapaczynski concludes that Locke thus closes the classical Greek schism between *praxis* or intellectual activity and *poesis* or productive labor: "The modernity of Locke's philosophy thus lies not in the elimination of the Aristotelian domain of action and its replacement with a purely positivist or utilitarian theory of human interests, but rather in an attempt to fuse the discourse of interests with the discourse of moral action and to synthesize *praxis* and *poesis* in a unified theory of human activity."[54]

Locke's theory of property serves two purposes. First, the precarious insecurity of human beings is relieved not, as Hobbes thought, by a political compact but by taming or appropriating nature to serve human ends. Second, appropriation transforms human dependence on nature into a form of self-sufficiency, thus conferring moral status upon human actions.

Not to acknowledge the moral and religious basis of Locke's views on work and ownership is to engage in anachronistic thinking. A new element had been introduced into the world since the era of classical Greece and Rome, namely, the emergence of the Church with its emphasis on charity. It is not surprising that a theory

about rights as claims should have evolved from an institution that allowed claims made by the needy or deserving.[55] Further, as Tully insists, enjoyment of the fruits of
one's labors is not the sin of acquisitiveness but the ability
to fulfill the Christian duty of liberality and charity.[56]
Charity, says Locke, is the first thing we should teach our
children:

"As to having and possessing of Things, teach them [children]
to part with what they have easily and freely to their Friends.
. . . Covetousness, and the Desire of having in our Possession,
and under our Dominion, more than we have need of, being the
Root of all Evil, should be early and carefully weeded out,
and the contrary Quality of a Readiness to impart to others,
implanted. . . . [The way to understand property as well as justice and honesty] is to lay the Foundations of it early in Liberality, and an Easiness to part with to others whatever they have
or like themselves.[57]

Locke's critics have accused him of many transgres-
sions: underestimation of the social dimension of human
life,[58] overconfidence in the individualistic assumption
that the common good is not real[59] or that the public
realm exists only to further the development of individual
persons,[60] flirting with absolutism and constituting only
a "freakish and fitful" aberration,[61] and serving as the
point man for acquisitive capitalism.[62] Nevertheless,
Locke's appropriation of natural law as a basis for individual rights, his combination of tolerance for partial knowledge with faith in divine will, his skepticism toward authority, and his political common sense all joined to
ensure his leading role in the story of human rights.

LOCKE AND GOD

Locke is sometimes painted with a broad brush as so
thorough a rationalist of the secular Enlightenment that
the religious basis of his thought is eclipsed. John Dunn
emphasizes the degree to which Locke's thoughts depend
on religious premises, noting that a high proportion of

Locke's arguments depend on his theological commit-
ments.[63] The cogency of many of Locke's arguments, says
Dunn, depends on a defensible theology, and we have no
reason not to think that Locke himself would concur with
this judgment.[64] Some would place Locke in the tradition
of more explicitly theological writers. Skinner observes
that Locke reiterates some of the most basic tenets of the
Jesuit and Dominican thinkers, including the central role
of natural law, the extrapolation of political theory from
an original state of nature, and the belief that natural law
must be treated as the will of God.[65]

Locke thus represents a new chapter in the history of
natural law, which had risen originally out of the combination of Stoic theory with Christianity. This combination held sway in the theology, jurisprudence, politics,
and history of the Middle Ages for a thousand years. Ernst
Troeltsch points out that even when this system gave way
to a more radical doctrine of natural human rights, a
doctrine that almost always is found on the radical and
progressive side, it still evolved from the mostly conservative natural law of the Church: "Secular and progressive
as it may be, this new Natural Law still continues, none
the less, to find its basis in God's ordinance. It is closely
connected with rationalistic theology: it can even be the
ally of Calvinism, in the extreme forms of that doctrine.
With all its zest for progress, the theory still remains
moderate: it retains a conservative and bourgeois character."[66]

James Gordon Clapp summarizes the reach and depth
of Locke's influence as follows:

Locke's influence was wide and deep. In political, religious,
educational, and philosophical thought he inspired the leading
minds in England, France, America, and to some extent, Ger-
many. He disposed of the exaggerated rationalism of Descartes
and Spinoza; he laid the groundwork for a new empiricism and
advanced the claims for experimentalism. . . . In America, his
influence on Jonathan Edwards, Hamilton, and Jefferson was
decisive. Locke's zeal for truth as he saw it was stronger than
his passion for dialectical and logical niceness, and this may

account for the fact that his works prepared the ground for action as well as thought.[67]

The contrast between the attitudes of Locke and Hobbes toward law proved to be decisive for what followed. Hobbes, in spite of his pessimism, constructed his entire system around the assumption that human rationality is capable of finding out the natural laws. Otherwise Leviathan cannot be created. Locke also is pessimistic, but his pessimism manifests a deep antirationalism. Abrams points out that for Locke, reason is inextricably bound with interest and prejudice. Law, on the other hand, is independent of human irrationality; it expresses the incontrovertible will and more dependable rationality of God. Locke's ultimate invocation is therefore not to a rationalized instinct for self-preservation but to the will of God's order.[68]

THE ENGLISH BILL OF RIGHTS

Contemporary with Locke was the English Bill of Rights, which resulted from the combination of feudal compacts, Magna Carta, natural law, and Roman law. Early in 1689, a convention gathered to replace the discredited James II with William of Orange. It drew up a Declaration of Rights, which was promulgated eight months later in statutory form as the Bill of Rights.[69] William and Mary agreed to accept the Bill of Rights in what is known as the Glorious Revolution.

The English Bill of Rights did not contain new laws but was instead aimed at preventing the arbitrary practices of James II and the other Stuart monarchs. It included clauses that forbade the monarch to keep a standing army in peacetime without consent of Parliament; provided free elections of members of Parliament and absolute freedom of speech in parliamentary debates; required parliamentary approval before the monarch could suspend laws of the land or levy taxes; stipulated the proper empanelment of jurors in criminal trials; brought an end to excessive bail, fines, and cruel and unusual punishments;

and required frequent meetings of Parliament. At the conclusion of its thirteen clauses, it states: "And they do claim, demand, and insist upon all and singular the premises, as their undoubted rights and liberties."[70]

A revolution would be required in the American colonies before a new Constitution with a Bill of Rights could be written for America. What happened to turn an abstract theory of natural law into inspiration for a revolution? How did a notion stripped of "every particular fact" when promulgated by someone like Grotius turn into a road map for forays into the untidy turns of revolution and power politics? In addition to Locke's midwifery and such precedents as Magna Carta and the English Bill of Rights, the answer lies to a surprising degree in the meaning of certain words and in the assimilation of Roman law to natural law and the new ways of thinking.

CONTRIBUTIONS OF ROMAN LAW TO THE NEW THOUGHT

The Roman law element in natural law placed individual liberties strictly within the human enterprise. This was because that was where the locus of Roman law always lay. Michel Villey has shown that the Romans and the early Roman law glossators never possessed any subjective concept of right. For them *ius* always meant something *objective*, that is, what is right in a particular situation. *Ius* seemed to mean something objectively right and discoverable by law, often in issues having to do with land or other private, bilateral relationships.[71]

The Latin term for "law" (*ius*), as in "law of nations" (*ius gentium*) and "natural law" (*ius naturale*), had two meanings. It could refer both to objective *rules* of action and subjective *rights* to act. Lawyers trained in Roman jurisprudence learned to distinguish between these two references but did not see them as antithetical. Thomas Hobbes contrasted the two meanings, exploiting the difference between the terms *ius* and *lex*, rights and law, by insisting that they ought to be distinguished "because RIGHT consisteth in liberty to do, or to forbeare; Whereas, LAW determineth, and bindest to one of them:

so that Law, and Right, differ as much, as Obligation, and Liberty."[72]

More than the interpretation of words, however, was at stake. The sociopolitical culture of the medieval period was also changing. The descending theory of government that dominated the early Middle Ages flowed from an abstraction, the theory of the divine right of rulers. It was a seamless theory, unflawed except in one detail: it did not take into account the ragged edges of real experience. Abstractions are deadly because they discount the complexities of things. Any idea dehumanizes if it is the only idea one has. In the closed systems of classical antiquity, even those with an ascending theme of government, only the citizens, a minority of the entire population, had full status as persons. In the scheme of the Middle Ages, the ruler and the Church had the "one idea" of divinely ordained power, with individuals considered mere subjects within their spheres.

With a return of the Aristotelian idea of the state as a collection of persons, grown up in accordance with the laws of nature without theological intervention, comes the return of the citizen. These citizens, however, are no longer individuals who are subjects to higher authority but individuals who act on their own authority. The concepts of state and citizen are dangerous to the corporational structure of medieval Christian society and government because they imply the autonomy of persons. Once those concepts are in place, the unipolarity of Christian culture gives way to bipolarity as individuals become both Christians *and* citizens.

Hans Julius Wolff discusses the ways in which Roman law provided the emerging natural rights theory with a political, legal, and civic basis. Out of its long history, natural law theory now joined with positive law for the benefit of the citizen rather than of the corporation:

The Protestant rationalists, in their quest for the true natural foundations of human life, as conforming to and perceivable by reason, again raised the postulate of an absolute law, and thus found themselves in line with a long tradition. Refusing to accept theological explanations, however, they sought their backing in ancient statements rather than in those of medieval philosophers.[73]

Roman law made it possible for the new rationalists, in spite of their reservations about the *Corpus iuris civilis*, to connect their theories to the foundation of the Roman jurists. A reconnection with the classical past commended this union, since Roman law evolved in the first place to meet the needs of an urban, upper-class, individualistic society—the same sort of society envisaged by the scholars of the new era of rationalism.[74]

For most of the natural law writers of the seventeenth and eighteenth centuries, natural law had come to mean natural rights. On the eve of the American Revolution, the German philosopher and mathematician Christian Wolff (1679–1754) was explicit about this: "Whenever we speak of natural law (*ius naturae*), we never intend the law of nature, but rather the right which belongs to man on the strength of that law, that is naturally."[75]

In his dictum Wolff emphasizes the rights argument, but it is significant also that he sees these rights as adhering to human beings "on the strength of that law." In other words, if there were no natural law, there would be no natural rights. Fundamental to natural rights theory is the prior theory of natural law and its Roman manifestation, a belief in the rule of law itself.

This was the contribution to individual liberty of Roman law as shaped by the humanism of the sixteenth century and the natural rights theories of the seventeenth and eighteenth centuries.[76] The way was now ready for Thomas Jefferson, James Madison, and the U.S. Bill of Rights.

CHAPTER 5

The Bill of Rights

They that can give up essential liberty to obtain a little temporary safety deserve neither liberty nor safety.

BENJAMIN FRANKLIN

THE presence of a Bill of Rights in the U.S. Constitution, like the history of natural law and civic liberties, reflects a long story marked by intention, accident, and compromise.

Constitutional scholars generally hold one of two positions about the origins of the Bill of Rights. One is that the document is mostly derivative of English constitutional practice, the other, that it is mostly an American invention. Bernard Schwartz, paraphrasing Oliver Wendell Holmes, considers the American Bill of Rights a magic mirror "wherein we see reflected not only our own lives, but the whole pageant of Anglo-American constitutional development and all that those struggles have meant in the history of freedom."[1]

As we have seen, however, the Bill of Rights grows out of a history much older than the constitutional struggles of either England or America. The purpose of the present chapter is to describe the process by which the first ten amendments became part of the U.S. Constitution, then briefly to place them within their larger historical context.

FRAMING AND PASSAGE OF THE FIRST TEN AMENDMENTS

The Bill of Rights was deeply influenced by events in Virginia fifteen years prior to its ratification. While Thomas Jefferson was meeting with the Continental Congress in Philadelphia in May of 1776, thirty-six of his fellow Virginians, including James Madison, George Mason, Edmund Randolph, and Patrick Henry, were in Williamsburg from May 6 through July 5, writing a Declaration of Rights and a constitution for the new Commonwealth of Virginia. Jefferson told a friend at the time that the work they were doing was "of the most interesting nature, and such as every individual would wish to have his voice in. In truth it is the whole object of the present controversy; for should a bad government be instituted for us in future it had been as well to accept at first the bad one offered to us from beyond the water without the risk and expence of contest."[2]

George Mason drafted both the Declaration of Rights and the first constitution for Virginia. The Virginia Declaration omits any references to English law or to the colonial charters. Instead, it claims the law of nature as the source of individual rights in language similar to Jefferson's in the Declaration of Independence. Furthermore, Article 5 states the doctrine of separation of powers as a rule of positive law, the first time that such a statement had been made in any constitutional document.[3]

James Madison proposed a religious liberty clause boldly asserting that all men possess a natural right to believe and worship, *or not to believe* [emphasis added], as they wish. After Patrick Henry killed that amendment, Madison rewrote it to avoid offending conservative Anglicans, stating simply that all people had a natural right to "the free exercise of religion." The Virginia Declaration of Rights was passed on June 12, 1776.

Benjamin Franklin had the Virginia Declaration at hand when he wrote a bill of rights for the Pennsylvania Constitution of 1776. John Adams used it as he wrote a similar bill for the Massachusetts Constitution of 1780, and a translation of the Virginia document into French formed the basis of the French Declaration of the Rights of Man and of the Citizen in 1789.

The Constitution of 1787, its supporters argued, was a great improvement over the Articles of Confederation because it strengthened the central government with powers to regulate foreign and interstate commerce, levy taxes, raise armies, and coin money, as well as with a strong chief executive and a court system not accountable to Congress or the states. These very strengths, however, also raised the specter of invasion by the federal government of liberties many of the states had already forbidden their governments to infringe. For many, the concern was not so much a strong national government per se as the potential abuse of powers it represented.[4]

For a while the absence of a Bill of Rights in the proposed federal Constitution threatened its ratification. Antifederalists promoted the idea that this was not a mere oversight but a conscious Federalist deception, and it was not long before most Federalists themselves came to admit what Robert Rutland calls their "Achilles heel" and "tactical error" in omitting a Bill of Rights from the Constitution.[5] One explanation for this omission is that in the Federal Convention of 1787, the framers faced the very practical problem of how to create a workable form of government, whereas in the Second Continental Congress of 1776, they had faced the philosophical problem of how to justify a revolution.[6]

George Mason, who served as one of Virginia's delegates to the Constitutional Convention in Philadelphia, refused to sign the document and campaigned in Virginia against its adoption. In a critique written before he left Philadelphia, he wrote: "There is no Declaration of Rights. . . . The Declarations of Rights in the separate States are no

security. Nor are the people secured even in the enjoyment of the benefit of the common law. . . . There is no
declaration of any kind, for preserving the liberty of the
press, or the trial by jury in civil causes; nor against the
danger of standing armies in time of peace."[7] Rutland
points out that Mason did not mention a bill of rights
until the Convention was nearing its conclusion, but even
before he left Philadelphia he had come to see this omission as a fatal error.[8]

Jefferson, reading in France a copy of the proposed Constitution sent to him by James Madison, admired the
elaborate system of checks and balances embedded in the
document but worried about "the omission of a bill of
rights providing clearly and without the aid of sophisms
for freedom of religion, freedom of the press, protection
against standing armies, restriction against monopolies,
the eternal and unremitting force of the habeas corpus
laws, and trials by jury in all matters of fact." Jefferson
wrote further to Madison: "Let me add that a bill of rights
is what the people are entitled to against every government on earth . . . and what no just government should
refuse, or rest on inference."[9] Jefferson even proposed to
a friend that nine states ratify the Constitution but that
the four remaining hold out until a bill of rights had been
added.

Another delegate, Edmund Randolph, who was governor of Virginia at the time and had even introduced the
Virginia Plan, which formed the first draft of the document, also refused to sign the Constitution and hoped to
summon a second constitutional convention to remove
its liabilities. This was alarming to George Washington
and especially to James Madison, who feared for the future
of the Constitution he had so assiduously championed. In
a narrow vote the Virginia Convention finally voted for
ratification, but its support was closely tied to proposals
for amendments to the new Constitution.

Soon after the First Congress convened under the new
Constitution, Madison announced that he would propose
amendments to the Constitution. In his notes for a speech
on June 8, 1789, he indicates that some of the amend-

ments have to do with "private rights" and as such relate "to what may be called a bill of rights." He considers the primary purpose of the amendments to guard "against the legislative, for it is the most powerful and most likely to be abused," as well as to guard against abuses by the executive and "the body of the people, operating by the majority against the minority." Madison sees the greatest danger to a republic to be the "prerogative of the majority" and hopes the amendments "may be one means to control the majority from those acts to which they might otherwise be inclined."[10]

From the various amendments proposed by seven of the state ratifying conventions, Madison ignored those that would have changed the substance of the Constitution and formulated a list of seventeen, basing his choices upon the Virginia Declaration of Rights. The House of Representatives approved seventeen of Madison's amendments, the Senate consolidated them into twelve, and it was these twelve that were approved by Congress on September 25, 1789, for submission to the states.

Madison may have gotten from Alexander Hamilton the term "due process of law" used in the Fifth Amendment. In any event, here he was following the New York rather than the Virginia language. "Due process of law" represents an important shift from the "law of the land" terminology of Chapter 39 of Magna Carta, because "law of the land" could be construed to mean simply the prevailing customs at the time. In a speech to the New York Assembly on February 6, 1787, Hamilton had emphasized that no citizen could be deprived of rights by a legislative act without due process.[11]

Madison's greatest contribution was his crafting of words in such a way that they would be adaptable to changing conditions in the years ahead. Especially after the addition of the Fourteenth Amendment, the "due process" phrase of the Fifth Amendment allowed for a gradual inclusion of new rights. "Due process," says Schwartz, "expresses more than the restricted views of the eighteenth century; it is an enduring reflection of experience with human nature. The due process concept has enabled

the Supreme Court to serve as a virtual continuing constitutional convention as it has adapted the black letter text
to the needs of later days."[12]

On September 7 the Senate eliminated the amendment
considered by Madison himself to be the most valuable
of all, the provision prohibiting the states from infringing
on freedom of conscience, speech, press, and trial by jury.
As a result, the Bill of Rights limited the powers only
of the federal government, not of the states. This was
confirmed in the 1833 case of *Barron v. Mayor & City
Council*,[13] with the result that many years would pass
before the provisions of the Bill of Rights began to be
interpreted as applying also to the states.

A second provision dear to Madison was weakened by
the House-Senate Conference Committee when it substi-
tuted a weaker religious liberty clause. Madison had
hoped to institute absolute separation of church and state
and the total exclusion of government aid to religion.[14]

Roger Sherman of Connecticut, who opposed a bill of
rights, urged that a series of separate amendments be
appended to the Constitution, if they had to be added at
all, rather than interwoven within the existing articles as
was originally intended. Sherman's motion was defeated
the first time but approved on August 19. If Sherman had
not insisted on a separate cluster of amendments, it is
likely that the Bill of Rights would not have assumed the
prominence it possesses.

On October 2, 1789, President Washington forwarded
the proposed amendments to the states for ratification.
Appropriately, it fell to Thomas Jefferson as secretary of
state to convey official notice to the governors that the
Bill of Rights had been ratified. He did so in a letter of
March 1, 1792, which first mentions two acts concerning
the regulation of fisheries and the establishment of the
post office and postal roads in the United States. Then
Jefferson continues: "Also the ratifications by three
fourths of the Legislatures of the Several States, of certain
articles in addition and amendment to the Constitution
of the United States, proposed by Congress to the said

Legislatures, and of being with sentiments of the most perfect respect, your Excellency's &."

The first two amendments, restricting the size of the House of Representatives to between one and two hundred members and preventing Congress from altering the salaries of senators and representatives until after a session of Congress should have intervened, failed to be ratified by the states.† The remaining ten became part of the Constitution immediately upon ratification by the required number of states on December 15, 1791. Ironically, Virginia was the last state to ratify the Bill of Rights.

The hopes championed by Jefferson in the Declaration of Independence had become—by due process—the law of the land.

THE MEANING OF THE BILL OF RIGHTS

Whereas the Constitution forms the basis of the power of government, the Bill of Rights serves as a check on that power. Both accomplishments are extraordinary, and each complements the other. The Bill of Rights also represents the high point of the transformation of natural law theory to a doctrine of natural rights.

By the time of the American Revolution, what had been begun as essentially a conservative principle had become a liberating one. The doctrine of natural rights was still closely tied with the notion of a fundamental law as the foundation of government, and right reason was still the highest recourse. Now, however, natural law was seen as the source of the fundamental right of human beings themselves to determine which liberties they consider essential to human dignity and what forms of government they would create to assure them.[15]

It should be emphasized that both Federalists and Antifederalists argued their position concerning a bill of rights on the basis of the theory of natural rights. Federalists

---

†The latter provision was ratified as the Twenty-seventh Amendment to the U.S. Constitution on May 19, 1992.

maintained that no specific bill of rights was necessary because everyone took for granted that these rights existed naturally and did not require confirmation in codes devised by human beings. One of the most passionate of the Antifederalists, Elbridge Gerry, argued that "the rights of individuals ought to be the primary object of all government, and cannot be too securely guarded by the most explicit declarations in their favor."[16] Gerry's elaboration of this argument is one that could have been, and often was, expressed by the Federalists in support of natural rights:

All writers on government agree, and the feelings of the human mind witness the truth of these political axioms, that man is born free and possessed of certain unalienable rights—that government is instituted for the protection, safety and happiness of the people, and not for the profit, honour, or private interest of any man, family, or class of men—That the origin of all power is in the people, and that they have an incontestible right to check the creatures of their own creation, vested with certain powers to guard the life, liberty and property of the community.[17]

Both before and after the framing of the Constitution, Americans have engaged in a wide variety of interpretations of natural law.[18] Supreme Court Justice Hugo Black, for example, represents a certain dichotomy of thought about natural rights and constitutional interpretation. Black respects the historical role of natural rights in the development of the Bill of Rights, but he expresses reservations about a thoroughgoing natural rights interpretation of the amendments. Arguing for the right of an individual employee to sue for wages despite a union contract to arbitrate grievances, Black spoke of the contributions to these rights of Magna Carta and other charters of liberty:

At least since Magna Carta people have desired to have a system of courts with set rules of procedure of their own. . . . It was in Magna Carta, the English Bill of Rights, and other such charters of liberty, that there originally was expressed in the English-speaking world a deep desire of people to be able to settle differences according to standard, well-known procedures in courts presided over by independent judges with jurors taken from the public. . . . That right was written into the Bill of Rights of our Constitution and in the constitutions of the states.[19]

On the other hand, in *Adamson v. California* Black expresses his opposition to the "natural law" formula, which in his view the Court had used to expand safeguards already sufficiently laid out in the Bill of Rights:

This decision reasserts a constitutional theory spelled out in *Twining v. New Jersey* that this Court is endowed by the Constitution with boundless power under "natural law" periodically to expand and contract constitutional standards to conform to the Court's conception of what at a particular time constitutes "civilized decency" and "fundamental justice. . . ." I fear to see the consequences of the Court's practice of substituting its own concepts of decency and fundamental justice for the language of the Bill of Rights as its point of departure in interpreting and enforcing the Bill of Rights. . . . Conceding the possibility that this Court is now wise enough to improve on the Bill of Rights by substituting natural law concepts for the Bill of Rights, I think the possibility is entirely too speculative to agree to take that course.[20]

Learned Hand grants that belief in inherent "natural laws" was widely held in the eighteenth century, capping a long history going back to the beginning of our era. The easiest support for such an attitude, he says, was the "will of God," as Thomas Aquinas and also the Deists of the eighteenth century held. Hand proposes that "the Constitution and the 'Bill of Rights' neither proceed from, nor have any warrant in, the Divine Will . . . but on the contrary that they are the altogether human expression of the will of the state conventions that ratified them. . . . This presupposes that all political power emanatcs from the people."[21]

Schwartz classifies in five groups the rights protected under the Bill of Rights: freedom of religion; the rights of expression and association; the right to privacy; the right to due process; and freedom from arbitrary restraint or trial and from cruel and unusual punishment. He concludes that in all cases these rights were insufficiently or not at all protected in late-eighteenth-century England. Libel laws were vigorously enforced, so that anyone who criticized the government was subject to prosecution for sedition. Free association was restricted, as the turbulent history of the Chartist movement demonstrates. Freedom of religion was absent, and due process in the terms of the Fifth Amendment was inconsistent with the supremacy of the parliamentary system. It was, however, in criminal law that the progressive nature of the Bill of the Rights was most manifest. Even when English law recognized similar rights, they did not have the status they have assumed in the American system.[22]

This is due in significant part to the fact that England lacked a written constitution, including a bill of rights, enforceable by the courts against abridgement by Parliament, the Crown, and the common law. The English Bill of Rights of 1689 was hortatory, possessing only the status of a statute. What was "ought not" in the British system became "shall not" in the American. Grammar matters: much depends on whether the mood of the verb is subjunctive ("you may") or imperative ("you must").

Others, however, see a closer connection at least between the Constitution and Magna Carta, especially as interpreted by Sir Edward Coke, with whose works the framers were widely familiar. "Both were written documents," observes A. E. Dick Howard, "both were born of times of crisis in which men believed tyrannical rulers to be threatening their liberties, both were seen by eighteenth-century Americans as embodying natural rights, beyond the reach of positive law."[23] Both, too, were practical solutions to real and urgently felt issues of their times.

Statistically, the Bill of Rights *is* an American innovation. The ten amendments contain a total of twenty-seven separate rights. Only six of these, or about 20 percent, were first stated in Magna Carta. Twenty-one, or about 75 percent, had already been formulated in colonial documents written before the 1689 English Bill of Rights. Only the Ninth Amendment could not be found in several

of the state constitutions written between 1776 and
1787.[24] Only in the case of the Ninth Amendment does
any right receive its first guarantee in the federal Constitution as opposed to earlier enactments by the several
states.

It may therefore be argued that the Bill of Rights is
both an American invention and a further development of
English common law. The Greeks, however, had long
before established the notion of *politeia* and the Romans
the practice of *constitutio* as concepts of self-governance.[25] Britain had a constitution, but it was unwritten,
consisting of traditions and customs so variously embedded that access to it was limited to the educated elite.

Three things were new in the American experience.
Although many experiments of self-governance preceded
the Constitutional Convention, from the Greek leagues
and Swiss cantons to the Mayflower Compact, never before had a group of citizens purposefully come together
on such a scale and with such elaboration to determine
from the start how to govern themselves. Second, their
deliberations resulted in a single written document accessible to everyone. Third, they framed the Constitution,
amplified by the Bill of Rights, in such a way that it
contained the promise of equal treatment before the law
for all citizens. That last is the greatest departure from
Roman law, which always operated with, rather than
without, respect to the economic and social status of
persons.

Most of the provisions contained in the Bill of Rights
reflect issues that had already been raised in some way
in the ancient world. Particularly in matters of judicial
proceedings, many of those issues had been carefully elaborated in Roman law. What remained to be worked out
was a comprehensive belief in the basic rights of all citizens and a written enumeration of those freedoms. That
was the supreme accomplishment of the U.S. Bill of
Rights. It was a revolutionary accomplishment, but it
could not have happened without the earlier revolutions
of theory and practice about human governance first developed by the ancient Greeks and Romans.

The contributions from classical antiquity to the American experience are like two lanes of a long road, now widened and provided with new surfaces and connecting routes, but originating in the assemblies and schools of Athens and the law courts of Rome.

Having traced that road forward, it is time to turn back and examine the antecedents of the American Bill of Rights in the political theories and practices of classical Greece and Rome.

PART TWO

Greek and Roman
Antecedents to the Bill
of Rights

CHAPTER 6

Amendment I: The Basic Freedoms

I. *Congress shall make no law respecting an establishment of religion, or prohibiting the free exercise thereof; or abridging the freedom of speech, or of the press, or the right of the people peaceably to assemble, and to petition the Government for a redress of grievances.*

FOR many people the First Amendment is the heart of the Bill of Rights. Its guarantees of freedom of religion, expression, and political activity reflect the core of the belief in the dignity of the individual. In a letter of 1787, Thomas Jefferson expresses the relationship between the free expression of ideas and successful government by the people: "I am persuaded myself that the good sense of the people will always be found to be the best army. They may be led astray for a moment, but will soon correct themselves. The people are the only censors of their governors: and even their errors will tend to keep these to the true principles of their institution."[1] The good sense of the people, however, will depend on their being fully informed—by a free press, as Jefferson emphasizes subsequently, and by the other freedoms of thought, religion, speech, and association protected by the First Amendment.

Except for freedom of the press, each provision of the First Amendment has antecedents in the classical world. In the discussion that follows, Rome will be the focus of the treatment of religious issues, given its importance for the subsequent history of religion, while Athens will be shown to be the birthplace of freedom of speech and assembly. It must be reiterated, however, that a belief in individual rights was lacking and that individuals had no civic claims in the classical world apart from their membership in the privileged community.

FREEDOM OF RELIGION

It is significant, and perhaps not accidental, that the first right enumerated in the Bill of Rights is freedom from a state-established religion. In a theocracy, where only one religious system is permissible and adherence to it is enforced by the powerful, religious toleration is a contradiction in terms. Fundamentalism of any sort is by definition hostile to the freedom of thought required for a democracy. Freedom from coercion in any respect concerning religion or its absence is thus the necessary precondition for all other freedoms.

The close association between religion and politics is an essential characteristic of the classical Greek and Roman worlds, yet these were not theocracies. They were polytheistic in worship and for the most part tolerant of religious differences. A distinction between gods and state would have been inconceivable in either Athens or Rome in the classical period. We have evidence of decrees by the secular organs of the state in Athens, the council and the assembly, showing that religious practices could be determined by statutory enactment. The decrees of the council and assembly in these matters were a form of legal and political statute.[2] This is also what Edward Gibbon means by the fall of the Roman Empire as the "triumph of barbarism and Christianity," for the triumph of Christianity meant the end of rendering to Caesar what was both Caesar's *and* god's since the two were the same.

While the Romans were obsessed with placating the gods, there is little evidence in the state religion of much connection between religious practice and an individual's behavior. It has been noted that this is puzzling in the modern world, in which religion is somehow "above politics" and, if genuine, should surely have some influence on conduct.[3] Cicero illustrates the character of Roman public religion best when he says, "Jupiter is called Best and Greatest not because he makes us just or sober or wise but safe and secure, rich and prosperous."[4] As R. M. Ogilvie puts it, "Roman religion was concerned with success not sin."[5]

Whereas in modern times religious toleration is a necessary precondition for political liberty, S. L. Guterman suggests that in the ancient world political freedom was the parent of religious liberty. When the Romans persecuted or repressed a religious group, it was for essentially political reasons, whereas medieval opposition to dissenting groups was explicitly religious.[6]

There are two ways to assure freedom of religion in a state. One is to establish no religion, the other is to establish many. One might argue that a compelling reason why a small village on the banks of the Tiber in central Italy became a world power was because of the latter, the plural and permeable character of its religious life. A strong citizen base and a working alliance of patrician and plebeian interests had created a militarily successful state, which was paralleled in its civic and military structures by a variety of religious structures, including strong and diverse priesthoods. Just as new offices were created from time to time, so were new priesthoods, which were held for life by men who also often held secular positions. At Rome, religion and politics were not two separate worlds but intertwined into one.

Rome also demonstrated a remarkable readiness to import new deities. This was not because the existing gods were somehow inadequate, but rather because more gods promised even more success. New divinities were imported as needed, sometimes from certain conquered peoples, such as the Juno of Veii or Juturna of Lavinium, sometimes to accommodate cultural or economic developments, such as the induction of Argentinus when silver money was issued or the association of Neptune with Poseidon as a protection for marine trade. More common was public disaster, which accounts for the importation of Cybele, the Great Mother, from Asia Minor during the Second Punic War.[7]

The Second Triumvirate, yielding to the popularity of Egyptian cults at Rome, built a temple to Isis and Osiris.[8] After the Battle of Actium in 31 B.C., Octavian sought to repress the Egyptian cults reminiscent of Cleopatra by banishing them from the precincts of the city.[9] Later they were restored and sometimes even given special honors.

The establishment of the empire at Rome brought about a new fusion between state and religion, centered in the divine personage of the emperor himself.[10] In the Hellenistic East, this was especially easy to accomplish. At Ephesus, for example, Caesar was considered a manifest god, savior of mankind, descendant of Ares and Aphrodite.[11] Augustus associated himself with Apollo, while Mark Antony was called the New Dionysus in the East, thus forging new fusions between monarchy and traditional religious nationalism. As Arnaldo Momigliano puts it, "If the god was king, would not a king become a god?"[12]

Augustus set about repairing all the temples in the city of Rome—eighty-two of them by his own, perhaps exaggerated, count.[13] He also demonstrated special pride in two deities by dedicating in 29 B.C. a new temple to the Divine Julius, which had been vowed by the triumvirs, and by building a large temple to Apollo on the Palatine as a new imperial cult center. His motives seem patently political in this building program, although Syme allows the possibility that there was more "authentic religious sentiment" in all of this than is sometimes believed.[14]

Jews probably settled in Rome as early as the second century B.C. We know from 2 Maccabees that Jewish slaves came through Roman markets. As these slaves were manumitted, in accordance with established practice they automatically became Roman citizens. Pompey brought others from Palestine in 63 B.C. Cicero's reference to their numbers in the *Pro Flacco* indicates that by 53 B.C. they were well-established in the city. You see, he reminds his audience, how numerous they are, how closely they stay together, and how influential they are in assembly: *scis quanta sit manus, quanta concordia, quantum valeat in contionibus.*[15]

It is a curious question why the Christians were persecuted[16] while Jews were not. Jews, too, were exclusive "atheists." In the first century they also pursued converts, and unlike the Christians, they involved the Romans in three wars of rebellion between the years of A.D. 67 and 132. Robin Lane Fox points out that what saved the Jews was precisely their strength at what the Romans honored most: venerability. As Gibbon noted, "the Jews were a people which followed, the Christians a sect which deserted, the religion of their fathers."[17] Circumcision appeared ridiculous to many Romans, but at least the Jews were not accused of cannibalism or incest as were the Christians. They met in public synagogues, unlike the Christians, who met mysteriously in private houses. Their religious organization was more adapted to the classical notion of religion because of its ethnic character.

The Jews were, in short, familiar to the Romans. Even when the Christians were persecuted in the third century, the Jews were officially tolerated.[18] For example, when Decius demanded in 250 that all subjects of the empire must offer sacrifice to the official gods under pain of death, there is no evidence that this conformity with Roman absolutism was demanded of Jews, who had identical views with Christians concerning the imperial cult.[19] Only for a short period during the reign of Hadrian in the second century was the Jewish religion subject to any disabilities, and this may have been only with regard to circumcision.

One of the earliest Roman accommodations to Judaism was exemption from the ban on the export from the empire of precious metals, notably gold. This exemption was granted to permit the Jewish temple tax to be sent to

Jerusalem from Rome, as it was from throughout the Diaspora. Cicero was critical of this practice, and it had been forbidden when he was consul in 63 B.C.[20] In the *Pro Flacco*, he expanded his tirade against the Greeks to include the Jews, known to congregate by the Aurelian Steps and presumably being pandered to by the witnesses. Cicero says he will speak in a low voice so as not to incite the Jews against him, given their superstitious practice of sending gold to Jerusalem for the temple, since one of the charges against Flaccus was exporting gold. Then he moves into a more general criticism:

Each state, Laelius, has its own religious scruples, we have ours. Even while Jerusalem was standing and the Jews were at peace with us, the practice of their sacred rites was at variance with the glory of our empire, the dignity of our name, the customs of our ancestors. But now it is even more so, when that nation by its armed resistance has shown what it thinks of our rule; how dear it was to the immortal gods is shown by the fact that it has been conquered, let out for taxes, made a slave.[21]

The destruction of the temple at Jerusalem in A.D. 70 ended the payment of the temple tax. At that point Vespasian established the Fiscus Judaicus, a special imperial treasury into which was paid the tax levied on all Jews in the empire over the age of three and their slaves. Funds from this source were used to rebuild the Temple of Jupiter Optimus Maximus in Rome. This tax, which continued into the second century A.D., effectively required Jews to pay a special tribute to the emperor in return for the privilege of practicing their religion.

Augustus and his first successors respected the status of approved religion, *religio licita*, to which Caesar's privileges had raised the Jews in Rome.[22] In the early empire Jews were exempted from service in Rome's legions. In order to become a *religio licita*, however, Judaism at Rome had to lose some of its ethnic character. One way this occurred was through the hegemony of Roman legal institutions. When Rome recognized the legality of a *collegium*, it was as a legal and political grouping no matter what the nature of the association. Thus its members were directly subject to Roman law just as was everyone else. A Roman citizen like Paul could appeal any sentence from a Jewish court to the regular civil tribunal, and the judgment of the latter would always prevail.[23]

Guterman ties much of the Roman treatment of Judaism to the exclusive character of Roman citizenship. Because Roman citizenship was exclusive—that is, Roman citizens normally could not hold citizenship in any other people—the practice of unauthorized foreign cults was forbidden. From the time of the republic the Roman principle was that no one was able to be a citizen of two states under civil law (*duarum civitatium civis noster esse iure civili nemo potest*),[24] although the establishment of the Pax Augusta by Augustus saw the wide extension of citizenship to non-Latin peoples, culminating in A.D. 212 with the grant of the franchise by Caracallus to all or almost all of the free inhabitants of the empire.[25] While these new citizens typically could keep some civic status in their own municipalities, they were now expected to come fully under the Roman *civitas* in both a legal and a religious sense. To be a Roman meant to relate to the gods of Rome as "the highest class of Roman citizens,"[26] but as a freely contracting party, not in the attitude of humility and exclusiveness that was characteristic of both Judaism and Christianity.

There was a major distinction between Judaism as practiced in Rome and in the East. The Jews of Rome, to conform to this pressure, were organized into separate synagogues on the model of *collegia*,[27] which required licensing and authorization. Thus, Judaism was an ethnic cult in Judea, a quasi-ethnic cult in the Hellenistic cities, but an authorized religion in the western parts of the Roman Empire. The Jews at Rome were what de Ste Croix calls "licensed atheists,"[28] that is, officially permitted not to believe in the polytheistic Roman gods.

Pagan Rome, faced with a choice of persecution or toleration of the Jews, chose the latter. From the first century B.C. on, Jewish practices were protected throughout the empire. Traditional Judaism was less dangerous to Rome than Christianity, and therefore treated more tolerantly. Christianity lacked a national basis, and therefore displayed more zeal as a missionary religion. Proselytization was easier because Christianity lacked the liabilities of the unpopular circumcision and other legalistic trammels. It actively repudiated Roman state cults and preached what E. Mary Smallwood calls the "socially disruptive doctrine" of equality.[29]

Then Christianity began to rise over the Roman world, although it held the allegiance of perhaps only 10 percent of the population at the time of the conversion of Constantine in the early fourth century. Tertullian provides a descriptive portrait of a Christian community in Africa. Its features include the election of officers, a treasury filled by monthly assessments, common meals, provisions for funerals for members, and other related activities.[30]

The success of Christianity may be attributed to the crisis in the third century and the loss of confidence in historical Roman values in general. In such circumstances, Christianity could win large numbers of converts. Success was always the measure of Roman religion, and Christianity had brought political success for Constantine. With the help of his imperial patronage, it could now work for everybody else. Liebeschuetz notes the paradox: what began as an association of individuals for private religious purposes ended as a means of political domination as the state religion of an empire.[31]

It is a poignant chapter in religious history that there is some evidence that early Christianity was protected under the wings of its Jewish parent. Christianity was, as Tertullian puts it, "under the umbrella of a well-known religion": *quasi sub umbraculo insignissimae religionis*.[32] Even after he embraced Christianity, Constantine preserved Jewish privileges, and as late as the beginning of the fifth century emperors were still issuing edicts protecting the synagogues.[33] Then the adult child turned on the parent, as successive Christian emperors increasingly restricted Jewish civil and religious liberties. By the middle of the fourth century, legislation forbade mixed marriages between Christians and Jews, and by the early fifth century Jews were barred from service in imperial offices. As Smallwood concludes: "The peace of the Church set the Jews on the road leading to the medieval ghetto."[34]

In summary, religious toleration at Rome worked remarkably well during the era of the republic. Many gods were welcome, even Yahweh, if only the Jews could remember that they were Romans first. With the political crisis of the Roman Empire by the middle of the third century A.D., the way was open for the zealous monotheism of Christianity. When Constantine and Licinius made Christianity a legal entity in A.D. 313 by declaring complete religious freedom, the end to religious toleration was foreshadowed. Christianity, once the persecuted sect, would eventually become the persecutor.

FREEDOM OF SPEECH

For the framers, freedom of speech was the necessary condition of a republic. Speech is intimately tied with action in the civic realm, and both speech and action protect the open space that a society requires for both discourse and citizenship.

The presence of free speech does not ensure good government. Its absence, however, does ensure totalitarianism. Brian Vickers shows that rhetoric has always existed in a symbiotic relationship with society[35] and that an ability to speak effectively is crucial to participation in public life and therefore to freedom in a society. "To Plato, of course," says Vickers, "it was deplorable that the rhetorician, not the philosopher, should have such power, but to the majority of students of rhetoric down to the Renaissance its great attraction was just this promise of success in civic life, and its upholding of liberty."[36] Plato opposed free speech for the same reasons Isocrates praised its virtues, virtues characterized by Vickers as "flexibility, pragmatism in a good sense—working with things as they are—and realism about the existence of conflict in any group, with the need to find a system that will allow it

expression yet contain it by an agreed political procedure."[37] Rhetoric bridges the dichotomy between public
and private discourse, encouraging freedom in both and
therefore in society.

Freedom of speech was invented in ancient Athens.
Isegoria, the "equal right to speak," belonged to every
citizen who wished to address the Boule, Ecclesia, or jury
courts. *Isegoria* is a term with meaning only within an
open society, because freedom of elites to speak as they
wish can be taken for granted.[38] Within certain limits, we
even know when it was invented. Martin Ostwald places
the origin of *isegoria* probably in the era of Cleisthenes
(508–507 B.C.).[39] G. T. Griffith thinks it possible that the
practice was introduced later, somewhere between 487
and 462, or even in the years immediately following, adding that it may not have been introduced by a specific act
of legislation but rather by encroaching usage.[40] A. G.
Woodhead generally agrees with Griffith's dating for the
Ecclesia, but thinks that *isegoria* in the Boule has origins
in the reforms of Cleisthenes. Only gradually between the
time of Solon and 460 B.C. did the people grow confident
enough to believe that they might address their fellow
citizens.[41] J. D. Lewis places the inauguration of *isegoria*
earlier, following the evidence of Aeschines, Lysias, and
Demosthenes that it was Solon who first legislated *isegoria* for the assembly in his reforms of c. 594–593 B.C.[42]

The Athenians never conceived of freedom of speech as
an inherent right possessed by individuals. Rather, public
speaking was, in the words of George Grote, "the standing
engine of government."[43] Freedom of speech was of social
and political rather than individual significance. It was
meant not so much to encourage an individual's free expression as a city's good government. Herodotus emphasized the social significance of this freedom by saying that
because Athens had *isegoria*, free speech enjoyed by all in
a democracy, it had become first in war because each man,
being free, was zealous to achieve for himself.[44] Pericles,
too, insisted on the political character of freedom of
speech:

Here each individual is interested not only in his own affairs but in the affairs of the state as well, and those who are most occupied with their own business are extremely well-informed on general politics. Of all people we alone do not say that a man who takes no interest in politics is a man who minds his own business, but we say that he is useless. We Athenians, in our own persons, take our decisions on policy or submit them to proper discussions, for we do not think that there is an incompatibility between words and deeds; the worst thing is to rush into action before the consequences have been properly debated.[45]

Elsewhere Pericles comments that a person who has good ideas but lacks the ability to express them in public would be of no benefit to the city.[46] Demosthenes argued against restrictions on this freedom not because an individual would suffer but because the city would suffer if orators were not allowed to express their beliefs.[47] Demosthenes characterizes Athenian belief in free speech as opposed to that of the Spartans: "The fundamental difference between the Athenian and the Spartan constitutions is that in Athens you are free to praise the Spartan constitution, whereas in Sparta you are not allowed to praise any constitution other than the Spartan."[48] Demosthenes stated that in Athens, even aliens and slaves could speak with more freedom than citizens could elsewhere.[49] By comparison, for example, in Sparta only about 3 percent of the adult male population possessed full civic rights.

Freedom of speech always presents a dilemma: do opponents of liberal democracy have the right to speak against the system that ensures them freedom of speech, even if their views might lead to the destruction of liberal democracy? The Athenians responded to that paradox on the side of freedom of speech as the lesser danger. Believing that the collective judgment of the people was superior to the views of any one individual, they permitted calumnies lest free speech be eroded by restrictive legislation.[50]

As J. A. O. Larsen concludes, popular government or

isonomia implies not so much equal rights before the law as equal responsibilities under the law.[51] Thomas R. Fitzgerald has shown that there were limitations on the freedom of speech, even in the Athenian assembly.[52] The most obvious is the fact that it was the prerogative only of those admitted to the public assemblies, which omitted all women, slaves, and foreign residents or *metics*. Another was the loss of civic rights or *atimia*. Anyone who had prostituted himself was not permitted by Solon to speak in the assembly,[53] nor was anyone who had squandered his patrimony.[54] Anyone who was condemned three times for unconstitutional motions also lost the right to speak.[55] The most extreme form of silencing was assassination, which happened to Ephialtes, who had made enemies by prosecuting members of the Areopagus on what may have been charges of embezzlement.[56] This also was the fate of Androcles, an adversary of Alcibiades.[57] According to Thucydides, freedom of speech was also suppressed when the oligarchy of the Four Hundred seized power:

Nevertheless the Assembly and the Council chosen by lot still continued to hold meetings. However, they took no decisions that were not approved by the party of the revolution; in fact, all the speakers came from this party, and what they were going to say had been considered by the party beforehand. People were afraid when they saw their numbers, and no one dared to speak in opposition to them. If anyone did venture to do so, some appropriate method was soon found for having him killed.[58]

In meetings of the Athenian Ecclesia, all citizens were entitled to speak, and there were no restrictions on speaking time. The water-clock, called the *klepsydra*, was used to limit the time of speeches only in the law courts, not in the assembly meetings on the Pnyx. After the initial agenda was read, the herald announced, "Who above fifty wishes to speak?" (This practice of allowing older citizens to speak first was apparently discontinued by the time of Demosthenes in the fourth century.) Then the herald would ask simply, "Who wishes to speak?" Any citizen could approach the platform, called the *bema*, to address the people and to move a measure.[59] It was also permitted for a citizen to speak twice on the same item of the agenda.[60]

In addition to libel laws with monetary fines, two other features of Athenian politics, while not limiting freedom of speech, affected the climate in which political participation was conducted. As Jennifer Tolbert Roberts has shown, the Athenian system of accountability was quite severe by modern standards. Even victorious generals might be executed, as in the case of the victors of Arginusae. Those who took leadership roles in public life understood the risks.[61] Further, they did so with no parliamentary or party system and no governmental bureaucracy to support them if they ran afoul of public favor. Individual leaders were on their own.[62]

Another was ostracism, a practice devised apparently by Clesithenes in 508–507 to protect the system of Athenian democracy against politicians who became too powerful.[63] The law was first enforced against Harpokration in 488–487 and remained on the books until the late fourth century.[64] Under this law, the Ecclesia decided once a year whether or not to take a vote, in a following meeting, on whether someone should be banished. Votes were scratched into an *ostrakon* or broken piece of pottery. If such a vote were taken and a total of six thousand votes cast, the person receiving the highest number was banished.[65] This citizen was then expelled from the city for a period of ten years, though without disgrace and without loss of civic rights. It was not necessary to have committed any crime against the state, only to be considered potentially dangerous. Of the nine generally agreed-upon cases of ostracism, all were against politically prominent individuals. Fitzgerald suggests that this practice served a cautionary function in politics, noting that it must have been a cause of some anxiety for Pericles upon entering a public career that both his father and his uncle had been ostracized.[66]

There has been much debate about whether the people had genuine sovereignty over public affairs at Athens.

While there was a certain separation of powers among the assembly, the lawcourts (*dikasteria*), and the legislative commissions (*nomothetai*), the latter two groups were also chosen by lot, so that Aristotle's observation that in a democracy "all citizens deliberate about all matters"[67] was achieved through rotation. All citizens who wished to participate in the Ecclesia could do so simultaneously; as members of the law courts and of the legislative commissions, they took turns. For these offices, about two thousand public officials were chosen by lot for rotating terms of one year. Hansen prefers the term *kyrios* (master) to sovereignty: if a citizen in the fourth century had been asked who was *kyrios* in Athens, he would have answered, the laws (*nomoi*), the people (*demos*), and the jurors in the peoples' courts (*dikasteria*).[68]

Rome differs fundamentally from Athens in regard to freedom of speech. Chaim Wirszubski observes that although citizens had a vote in the Roman assemblies, they had no right to make their voice heard. Freedom of speech, in the sense that any citizen had the *right* to speak, did not exist in the Roman assemblies.[69] A. G. Woodhead also comments on the contrast between Athenians and Romans in this regard; in Rome the aristocracy succeeded in keeping so firm a grip on the "democratic possibilities inherent in the constitution" that citizens in the *comitia* could vote, but nothing more.[70]

With the fall of the republic after what Ronald Syme calls the "Roman revolution," liberty was lost, but it was a liberty that only a minority at Rome had ever enjoyed. No Roman ever conceived of any principle of government other than oligarchy, so that political freedoms for individuals were never present in the Roman mind.[71] So thoroughly was this the case that given a choice in the chaotic last years of the Roman Republic between the old *libertas* and peace, peace was preferred even if it were under a despotism.[72] *Cum domino pax ista venit,* Lucan observed: "Peace came with monarchy."[73]

The democratic traditions of equality of law and equal right to speak, *isonomia* and *isegoria,* were entirely absent from the Roman situation from the beginning. In their place was the guiding principle of authority, *auctoritas*, as exercised by an oligarchy of preeminent citizens—the whole Senate as a body and the senior statesmen, *principes viri*. From an oligarchy of the few to a tyranny of one, the distance is scant. Augustus arrogated to himself all the powers of the Senate, magistrates, and laws[74] through elaboration of his own *auctoritas*.[75] His title was *princeps*—not, as Tacitus notes, king or dictator[76]—but it would not be too many years before Seneca, in counseling the young Nero to practice clemency, would casually use the terms *princeps* and *rex* interchangeably. Princes and kings, he advises, by whatever name, are caretakers of the public realm: *principes regesque et quocumque alio nomine sunt tutores status publici.*[77] Rome turned out after all to be not so far from the monarchy it despised and thought it had ended in 510 B.C.

Senators had possessed the assumed privilege if not the right to speak freely. Cicero in the *Laws* says, "A senator's absence from a meeting of the senate shall be either for cause or culpable. A senator shall speak in his turn and at moderate length. He shall be conversant with public affairs."[78] Tacitus, mourning the loss of public life under the empire, notes that when domestic affairs were debated in the Senate during the Republic, there was freedom of discourse. Among the glories Tacitus attributed to the republic over the listless and oppressive empire was "a free scope for digression," *libero egressu*, in the discussion of domestic politics.[79]

The case of Cremutius Cordus illustrates the loss of freedom of speech under the empire by members of the Senate, for whom alone it had been a prerogative of power, an assumed privilege of their power rather than an inherent or natural right. Cremutius Cordus was a republican historian whose works "proscribed to all eternity the authors of the proscriptions,"[80] Augustus and Marcus Antonius. He glorified Cicero, Brutus, and Cassius while refusing to celebrate Augustus. Surviving the principate of Augustus, Cordus was prosecuted under Tiberius and, after a speech attacking the evils of despotism, anticipated his conviction by committing suicide by starvation in

A.D. 25. His works were burned,[81] a travesty earning the scorn of Tacitus, who uses this episode to deride the stupidity of despots who think they can erase the present from the remembrances of the next generation.[82]

Syme believes that Cremutius Cordus was threatened on various counts, not only because of his writings, and that Tacitus is expressing his own beliefs through his account of Cremutius's eloquent vindication of a historian's rights and freedom of speech.[83] "The speech," declares Syme, is indeed "all Tacitus." The emperor, says Tacitus, listened to the speech with an angry frown. Cremutius proclaims his innocence of having praised Brutus and Cassius by appealing to other panegyrics under Augustus in praise of the latter's enemies, Cicero's praise of Cato, and the harangues of Brutus against Augustus. Yet Julius Caesar and Augustus let these things pass, "whether in forbearance or in wisdom I cannot easily say. Assuredly what is despised is soon forgotten; when you resent a thing, you seem to recognize it."

Then Cremutius closes:

Of the Greeks I say nothing; with them not only liberty, but even license went unpunished, or if a person aimed at chastising, he retaliated on satire by satire. It has, however, always been perfectly open to us without any one to censure, to speak freely of those whom death has withdrawn alike from the partialities of hatred or esteem. Are Cassius and Brutus now in arms on the fields of Philippi, and am I with them rousing the people by harangues to stir up civil war? Did they not fall more than seventy years ago, and as they are known to us by statues which even the conqueror did not destroy, so too is not some portion of their memory preserved for us by historians? To every man posterity gives his due honor, and, if a fatal sentence hangs over me, there will be those who will remember me as well as Cassius and Brutus.[84]

In summary, freedom of speech in the form of *isegoria* in the Athenian Ecclesia approached the status of a right, at least for fully enfranchised citizens. Its purpose, however, was always the well-being of the state, not the freedom of the individual. At Rome, speech was much more severely curtailed and was an assumed privilege only among the members of the senatorial class. With the end of the republic, even the semblance of free speech was lost.

RIGHT TO PEACEABLE ASSEMBLY

In prohibiting Congress from abridging the right of peaceable assembly, the First Amendment refers not to established governmental bodies but to informal gatherings outside politically sanctioned structures. Nevertheless, the Greek and Roman assemblies, together with the Roman suspicion of all private societies, provide historical perspective on the problem of free association of citizens within a state.

The rise of popular assemblies in ancient Athens is a study in the rise of democracy. Unlike the Roman assemblies, which severely and purposefully limited the role of the individual, the Athenian popular assembly was the seedbed of the idea that members of the citizen body have an equal and direct access to the public arena. Until the eighteenth century, the term "representative democracy" would have been considered a contradiction in terms. Until the first mention by Jeremy Bentham in *A Fragment on Government* (1776) and by Alexander Hamilton in a letter of May, 1777, democracy was always taken to mean direct democracy.[85]

The first tear in the aristocratic fabric that bound the early Greek cities seems to lie in the changing nature of military organization. Initially a tyranny was maintained by the well-armed and mounted entourage of a single aristocrat, who gathered members of his family and other dependent nobles into a "phratry" that was a tightly knit military and social unit. Gradually an easier supply of metal and increasing wealth multiplied the number of military champions and the rise of the infantry or hoplite system. While still including cavalry units, the army now depended on the armed infantry soldiers, or hoplites, who fought in close cohesion and were increasingly organized by geographical rather than social units.[86]

This military revolution led in the Greek cities, conspicuously at Athens, to profound political innovations. The law code of Draco, of which we know little except its severity, was established about 620 B.C. Then in 594–593, Solon was appointed "archon and reconciler" to put an end to civil strife. Solon, a man of only moderate wealth although of noble descent, had shrewd political instincts and a radical readiness to make major changes. At that time the nobles not only controlled most of the state but also owned most of the land. In addition, many of the poor had been enslaved for inability to pay their debts. Solon cancelled all existing debts, ended the system of sharecropping that had bolstered the aristocrats and led to personal servitude for defaulting debtors, doubled the number of those eligible for political and military office, provided other guarantees against legal oppression, and encouraged commerce by bringing Athenian coinage and weights and measures into compatibility with those of some other Greek cities.

He also reformed the constitution. Before Solon, a small group of ex-magistrates formed the Council of the Areopagus, the only deliberative body in the state. Although there was a citizens' assembly or Ecclesia, it met only in moments of crisis or to show support for one aristocratic faction or another. Solon instituted a Council or Boule of 400, which prepared the agenda for the Ecclesia, thus freeing it from the domination of the Areopagus. Solon seems also to have established new authority for the assembly, whether by setting regular meeting times, organizing methods of voting, or regularizing the agenda.[87]

Some of Solon's reforms, such as the abolition of debt-servitude, were immediate and lasting. Others took longer to become established. After years of intermittent tyranny, Cleisthenes enacted another set of reforms in 508–507, which greatly increased the share of the common people in the government. Cleisthenes gave Attica a new social and political structure with broad popular support, one that lasted with variations for some two hundred

years until the Athenian democracy was finally abolished
by Antipatros in 322–321 B.C.

Martin Ostwald suggests that Cleisthenes may have
been responsible for the adoption of the term *nomos*, or
statute, to replace the older term *thesmos*, or decree, in
order to signal that laws imposed by a ruling class were
to give way to laws ratified by the will of the people.[88]
Similarly, he may have given rise to the notion of *isonomia* as a term denoting political equality between the
magistrates, who formulate the proposals, and the people,
who approve them.

Further reforms in 462, associated with the names of
Ephialtes and Pericles, increased the power of the Ecclesia
and began to provide pay for the large number of jurors—
some juries consisted of hundreds—which meant that
common people could afford to participate actively in
public affairs by taking time off from their work. In 404
pay was instituted for attending the Ecclesia. Each of the
139 demes, or divisions of the city, supplied a certain
number of council members to the Boule, which had been
enlarged by Cleisthenes to five hundred. There is no evidence that its members were chosen by lot from the
demesmen until 450, nor that its members received pay
before 411, moves that all forwarded the gradual evolution
toward greater democracy.

The primary function of the Boule was to consider in
advance all the matters to be presented to the Ecclesia.
There were some restraints on its power, however, mostly
accomplished by limitations on its membership. Terms
lasted only one year, and, to keep membership from becoming fixed, no one could serve more than twice.

From the perspective of antiquity, participation in the
Ecclesia was broadly inclusive. All adult male citizens
could attend meetings of the assembly. Land ownership
was not a qualification for participation. Only citizens
whose political rights had been removed by law or sentence (*atimoi*) were excluded. The age of majority for
males was eighteen or, in the fourth century, when two
years of military service prevented their attending the
assembly, twenty. Actual participation might also be hin-

dered by the distance one would have to walk[89] or by space in the meeting place on the Pnyx hill (southwest of the Agora), which could seat about 6,000 on benches or cushions on the outcropping rock and, in the latest period, perhaps as many as 13,800.[90]

Only foreigners, resident foreigners (called metics), slaves, and female citizens were excluded from political rights.[91] In 431 B.C. about 45 percent of all adult males were classified as metics and slaves, and by 323 this number had risen to 53 percent. This restriction on participation in public life was tightened in 451 B.C., when a decree was passed limiting citizenship to the offspring of marriages between two Athenian citizens.[92] This exclusion of far more than half the population, when women are included, from public affairs represents no inner contradiction with Athenian democratic theory, since there was no philosophical or religious belief in the full equality of all human beings.[93]

Hansen estimates the number of adult male citizens in the fifth century to be about 40,000, reduced perhaps to 30,000 or fewer after the plague and the defeats in the Peloponnesian War.[94] During the fourth century, the meetings of the Ecclesia were regularly attended by no fewer than 6,000 citizens.

During the last half of the fifth and first half of the fourth centuries, the Ecclesia met in regular mandatory sessions ten times a year, together with a number, perhaps a sizeable number, of other meetings. During the Spartan invasion of Attica in the Peloponnesian War, Pericles arranged that no Ecclesia would be held. Around 355 B.C. the number of meetings was set at forty a year, four in each prytany, of which there were ten of thirty-five or thirty-six days in a normal year. Votes were taken by show of hands. Citizens sat where they pleased rather than according to political groups.[95]

At no point, even in this period of direct democracy, could the people officially issue a call for a meeting. The Ecclesia was usually summoned on four days' notice by the *prytaneis*, the presiding officers. The fifty *prytaneis* were selected by lot from each of the ten tribes that constituted the Boule in turn, and each tribe provided the *prytaneis* for one-tenth of each year. They convened the Ecclesia and arranged the agenda.

Obligatory items for the principal meetings of the Ecclesia included the selection of magistrates, indictments, the defence of the country, and attention to the food supply. Public announcements were also made about important issues such as the confiscation of property, grants of citizenship, religious matters, the bestowal of public honors, and foreign policy. Actions proposed and debated at one meeting could not be voted on until a subsequent meeting.[96]

Since no item could be placed on the agenda for the popular assembly without prior treatment by the Boule, the question arises as to whether the people retained direct sovereignty or whether they merely provided a rubber stamp for measures beyond their control. Hansen finds that the Boule sometimes presented a matter for debate without a specific proposal for action. In those cases, the people themselves determined the consequence. Furthermore, alternative proposals could be moved from the floor during debate. P. J. Rhodes, studying the formulation of decrees passed during the period 403–322, finds that about half of the decrees were ratifications of actions proposed by the council, while half were moved in the Ecclesia.[97] Hansen refines these findings by excluding routine business such as honorific decrees and concludes that although the Boule influenced the people's decisions, the true decision-making rested, both de jure and de facto, with the people.[98]

In summary, in spite of the restricted definition of the citizen body, democratic Athens placed a remarkable value on freedom of assembly. The practice of selection by lot to the Boule from among the citizenry, the direct participation by the people in the proceedings of the Ecclesia, and the ability of the Ecclesia to offer alternate or even new proposals combine to paint a portrait of vigorous public life in democratic Athens.

The case at Rome was quite different. Because they rose later to world prominence, the Romans had the great advantage of being able to feel superior to the Greeks. Rarely is this more evident than in Cicero's comparison of the Greek and Roman assemblies.

In 59 B.C. Cicero defended Lucius Valerius Flaccus on charges of malfeasance in office as governor of Asia. To discredit the testimony of Asian Greeks against his client, Cicero launched a vigorous salvo against the general perfidy of the Greeks and in particular against their untrustworthiness in assembly. After a prefatory disclaimer that no Roman has ever been more sympathetic to the Greeks than he, Cicero grants that the Greek race has literature, art, charm in speaking, keenness of intellect, and rhetorical richness, but that it has never fostered a respect for truth in giving testimony.[99] A Greek witness, he continues, takes the stand only for the purpose of doing harm, *ut laedet*.[100] Cicero admonishes his hearers to remember that when they are listening to a Greek, they are thus listening to a frenzied assembly of the most trivial of nations (*contionem concitatam levissimae nationis*.[101] After expatiating at length on Greek untrustworthiness, he confesses that he will not expand on the subject because if he did his speech would never come to an end.

Then Cicero moves from the hors d'oeuvres to the main course of his argument. The brilliance of our Roman ancestors, he says, was that they gave no power to public assemblies: *Nullam . . . vim contionis esse voluerunt*.[102] The decline of the Greeks, on the other hand, was brought on by their public assemblies. Worse still, the Greeks *sat down* while they deliberated, thus making deliberation more lengthy and considered, instead of standing as Romans did:

But all the states of the Greeks are managed by irresponsible seated assemblies (*sedentis contionis temeritate administrantur*). . . . [T]hat older Greece, which once was so notable for its resources, its power, its glory, fell because of this defect alone—the undue freedom and irresponsibility of its assemblies (*libertate immoderata ac licentia contionum*). Untried men, without experience in any affairs and ignorant, took their places in the assembly and then they undertook useless wars, then they put factious men in charge of the state, then they drove most deserving citizens out of the country.[103]

Cicero's objection to seated assemblies may have stemmed from the platforms such assemblies provided for demagogues. With no controls on their freedom of speech, not even the discomfort of their listeners, they could harangue the people at will and bring about unforeseen and objectionable results. One of the great strengths of Roman political life—and one remarked upon with astonishment by Greeks—was the extent of citizenship. Slaves manumitted by citizens became citizens themselves and after one generation could hold public office. The citizen body was the basis of the military and, in a way much more rigid and pervasive than the Athenian, military considerations in the time of the republic defined Roman civic participation.

From very early times, perhaps the early republic, but ascribed by Roman tradition to the reign of Servius Tullius, the penultimate king toward the end of the sixth century B.C.,[104] Roman citizens were classified into centuries on the basis of wealth. The 193 centuries of the *comitia centuriata* were political units organized to regulate Rome's armed forces by classifying the citizens according to their ability to equip themselves for various military units. At the top were 18 centuries of mounted *equites*, and next came the first class, consisting of 2 centuries of *fabri* (noncombatant armorers) and 80 of the 170 centuries of infantrymen, or *pedites*. The remaining *pedites* were divided into four further classes in descending order of wealth. The fifth class, for example, could afford only javelins and slings. The proletariat (*proletarii*, or "offspring givers," since they had nothing but offspring to contribute to the Roman state), also called *capite censi*, were enrolled by their name alone, since they had no wealth. They constituted one huge century at the bottom. Even though modifications in this system were made with time, the principle remained unchanged that fewer of the wealthier citizens constituted the higher centuries and

classes and that these centuries and classes voted first, so
that the wealthy few always had primacy in the assembly.

Cicero in his *Republic* approves the spirit and effect of
the so-called Servian reforms, which for him enshrined a
basic principle of governance: "He made this division in
such a way that the greatest number of votes belonged,
not to the common people, but to the rich, and put into
effect the principle which ought always to be adhered to
in the commonwealth, that the greatest number should
not have the greatest power (*ne plurimum valeant
plurimi*)."[105]

The growth of the power of the plebeians involved the
creation of plebeian officials, of whom the most important
were the tribunes of the plebs, and of another assembly,
the *concilium plebis* or *comitia tributa*, the plebeians
organized by tribes based originally on the place of domi-
cile. Later a *comitia populi tributa*, to which patricians
were also admitted, was founded, and the earlier *comitia
curiata* persisted in form but was no longer attended by
the people.[106] These assemblies met for the purpose of
voting on magistrates and laws.

The plebeian organization, in creating its assembly, preserved what Michael Crawford calls "one of the most
curious features of existing Roman assemblies,"[107]
namely voting by groups. Indeed, the very word *comitia*
means "goings together," referring to sorting into groups
for the purpose of voting. It was never the case in any
Roman assembly that decisions were reached by a simple
majority of those present and voting. Each group had one
vote, and the decision of the assembly was the decision
of a majority of the groups.

Dionysius of Halicarnassus describes the procedure of
voting. All 193 centuries of the six classes assembled in
the Field of Mars. Standing under their centurions and
standards as in war, they voted in the order of wealth
when called upon by the consuls. There were 98 centuries
in the first class. With one vote per century, if 97 of them
agreed (97 to 96 = 193), then voting proceeded no further
down through the centuries. Dionysius remarks: "The
poorest of the citizens, who were no less numerous than

all the rest, voted last and made but one century; they were exempt from the military levies and from the war taxes paid by the rest of the citizens in proportion to their ratings, and for both these reasons were given the least honor in voting."[108]

In the *contio* (from *conventio*, "gathering"), the people gathered together en masse in unsorted crowds to listen to announcements or speeches, often but not always prior to leaving for voting. Only the magistrates had the right to summon the *contio* and to determine who would address the people. Although the main purpose of the *contiones* was speaking, access to the platform was carefully controlled. It included the presiding magistrates and men from the Senate who were not in office at the time. Sometimes opponents of a measure were also asked to speak, but only to prevent their being given the chance to speak at a *contio* held by an opposing tribune.[109]

Polybius, eager to advance his theory that Rome's greatness resulted from the separation and balance of powers among three equal entities (monarchy = consuls, aristocracy = senate, democracy = people), describes the part left for the people to play since between them the Senate and consuls took care of war, peace, revenues, and all matters foreign and domestic. "But nevertheless there is a part, and a very important part, left for the people. For it is the people which alone has the right to confer honors and inflict punishment, the only bonds by which kingdoms and states and in a word all human society are held together. . . . Thus here again one might plausibly say that the people's share in the government is the greatest, and that the constitution is a democratic one."[110]

In her discussion of the fact that the Romans stood rather than sat in both the *contiones* and the *comitia*, Taylor emphasizes the Roman distrust of having the people deliberate and vote at the same time.[111] She concludes that by the age of Caesar, however, it mattered little anymore. The "Greekling" mobs in the city gave way in importance to the professional soldiers loyal to their generals, and when Caesar won supremacy through his legions, the republic was at an end. "It is significant," says

Taylor," that the only famous *contio* under the dictatorship of Caesar is the one he called on the outskirts of Rome to speak to the soldiers of the Tenth Legion, the speech in which he quelled a mutiny by addressing the soldiers as civilians, *Quirites*."[112]

The republican forms were maintained under the empire, and Augustus, zcalous to appear to keep them, built a fine new rostra or speakers' platform at the temple of the Divine Julius. But the only salient feature of the republican *contio* that was maintained was the tradition of standing rather than sitting. As Taylor wryly notes: "The men who attended did not sit down on the job; instead they stood on their feet, and let the world see the vigor inherent in the Roman race."[113]

The need of the upper classes to control the Roman populace, evident from the very beginning, made any private association outside the established public order cause for suspicion. One example is the funeral associations or burial guilds that were widespread among the lower classes. Caesar banned all private associations as potentially subversive; the burial guilds alone were allowed by Augustus to start up again.

Generally it seems that the funerary colleges (*collegia tenuiorum*) did not require special authorization. Marcian writes: "But it is permitted to the *tenuiores* to contribute a monthly subscription provided, however, that they meet only once a month, lest under a pretext of this kind an unlicensed college arise."[114] An inscription of a *senatus consultum* found at Lanuvinum also seems to indicate that the right of assembly was granted generally to funerary associations.[115] The evidence seems to be that a whole category of *collegia* or associations was thus exempt from compliance with the requirement of special approval, *coire licet*. The Christians found cover under this guise, and it may be that the adherents of Mithraism did so as well.[116] One interpretation of this unusual permissiveness in the Roman state is that the emperors did not fear sedition from the lower classes, among whom these practices were most common. The exemption did not apply to the

middle and upper classes, which alone could have constituted a threat to the emperor.[117]

In summary, the Roman assemblies amounted to carefully contrived forms for maintaining the power of the
oligarchic aristocracy. The Romans, ever scornful of
Athenian democracy, never created even the fiction of
vesting actual political power in the populace. Furthermore, the oligarchy looked with suspicion on private associations of any kind because of the possibility that such
groups might achieve a measure of power.

Ironically, this tenacious resistance to popular power
meant ultimately that the Senate and the Roman people
lacked the ability to prevent the usurpation of supreme
power by the most popular individual of all, Julius Caesar.
Thus came the end of an oligarchic but successful republic, which had lasted nearly five hundred years.

RIGHT TO PETITION

The Roman suspicion of popular assemblies carried over
into the matter of petition. Petitions to the *princeps* for
redress of grievances were common during the empire,
but these were individual petitions handled individually
by the emperor, not expressions of mutually interdepen-
dent relationships in the civic realm.

A great portion of the Roman law that has come down
to us is the product of the first three centuries of the
empire, the period when the emperors were in fact serving
as lawmakers. Once the principate began, the emperor
was expected to assume many of the functions that previously had been held by a variety of officials. He frequently acted as judge and issued opinions on points of
law. At least from the reign of Tiberius if not earlier, the
Roman ruler provided essentially a legal aid service to the
empire. Private citizens, even women and slaves, could
submit a written petition, called a *libellus*, to the emperor
for advice about legal problems. Private petitions—for a
benefit, for legal advice, for some sort of protection—
were generally presented by individuals, although Honoré

reports that groups could petition jointly. Prominent officials of higher status sent letters, *epistula*. The emperor's written replies were called rescripts.[118] The emperors assumed that they were acting in the tradition of private jurists giving legal opinions (*responsa*), for the most part simply declaring that they were operating within existing law rather than actually legislating.[119]

In private cases the rescript was not a judgment and did not constitute a legislative act. As a step in a judicial proceeding, however, it required a governor to apply the law as stated in the rescript. Another important feature of this system was that it contributed to a measure of uniform application of the law by taking account of precedent.[120]

Cicero lists three occasions upon which the opinion of the Roman people could best be assessed: in meetings of the *contio*, the informal gatherings summoned and addressed by the magistrate; in the assemblies; and at the games or gladiatorial contests.[121] Under the empire, even as early as Augustus, the assemblies ceased to have any but the most formal functions. In a long letter to Marcus Aurelius outlining the duties and functions of emperors, Cornelius Fronto states that one of the duties of an emperor is "to address the people on very many matters in public meetings."[122] We gather from this remark that imperial eloquence in the *contiones* seems to have had some value. But the opportunities for confrontation between the emperor and the populace were much more frequent at the Circus Maximus (which held as many as 200,000 spectators) for chariot races, in the amphitheater (which held fewer than 50,000) for gladiatorial shows or wild beast hunts, or in the theatres (that of Marcellus held 10,000, of Balbus 6,000–7,000).[123]

The participation of the emperor on these occasions was marked by elaborate rituals: a formal entry was made, and the emperor was prominently seated where his reactions would be visible to all. He was expected to appear to enjoy the shows. Caesar was resented when he got in some extra reading and writing during the shows, and

Marcus Aurelius was ridiculed for reading and having material read to him while attending the Circus.[124]

On these occasions specific exchanges could take place between the emperor and the people. For example, Claudius sometimes addressed the people at shows or had his messages written on boards, which were paraded around for the spectators to see.[125] The crowds compelled Tiberius to return to the baths a statue by Lysippus, which he had removed to his own bedroom.[126] The execution of individuals was also demanded by the crowds. But larger issues were also addressed, such as the demand of the people in A.D. 15 for the removal of the sales tax. Millar concludes that these occasions were episodic and, though important, were not so important as the communications "endlessly addressed to the emperor in writing and in speech by the communities and associations of Italy and the provinces."[127]

In summary, one of the major devices developed for the administration of the Roman Empire was the written petition to the emperor, whose responses came to form a major body of Roman law. Less formally, the people might demand a favor from the emperor when he appeared at public gatherings. Petition in the Roman world, however, was always centripetal. It signalled the power of the center rather than the power of the petitioner.

A survey of classical culture from the perspective of the First Amendment reveals, at Athens, valiant efforts to develop democratic institutions of assembly and speech, and, at Rome, a capacity for religious toleration that was one of the great strengths of the republic in spite of its oligarchic control of all areas of civic life. Of rights in any of these areas there were none. Of roots, however, there were some. After long centuries of fallow, these roots would prove fruitful in other times and places, for which the innovations of Greece and Rome helped prepare the way.

CHAPTER 7

Amendments II and III: Bearing Arms and Quartering Soldiers

II. A well regulated Militia, being necessary to the security of a free State, the right of the people to
keep and bear Arms, shall not be infringed.

III. No Soldier shall, in time of peace be quartered in
any house, without the consent of the Owner, nor
in time of war, but in a manner prescribed by law.

THE Second and Third Amendments reflect issues acutely felt in America during the armed revolution
against Great Britain. The framers knew from experience
that individual rights are in jeopardy once military control
supplants the civilian rule of law. More generally, these
two amendments of the Bill of Rights speak to the dilemma of regulating the military in any society committed to democracy and the dignity of individuals.

The Second Amendment had its origins in a context
very different from modern controversies over gun control. The wording of the amendment reflects a compromise from the far more radical notion contained in Article
13 of the Virginia Declaration of Rights. That article concedes that a well-regulated militia composed of the people
was "the proper, natural and safe Defence of a free State,"

but goes on to caution that "standing Armies, in Time of Peace, should be avoided, as dangerous to Liberty, and that, in all Cases, the Military should be under strict Subordination to, and governed by, the Civil Power."

The idea shaping the compromise was that even though standing armies in peacetime may be dangerous to liberty, they should not be prohibited. Rather, the Constitution should ensure citizens the right to keep and bear arms so that if state militias needed to be raised under emergency conditions, its members would have their muskets ready at hand.

Alone of the first ten amendments, the Second Amendment has never been construed by the Supreme Court as guaranteeing an inherent right of individuals. In its first decision on the amendment, *United States v. Cruikshank*[1] in 1875, the Court found that the right to keep and bear arms was not an inherent right guaranteed in and of itself by the Constitution, but rather was simply protected against infringement by the federal government. More recently in *Sandidge v. United States*,[2] a case in which an appellant convicted of carrying a pistol without a license argued that the District of Columbia firearms statute violated his constitutional right to bear arms, the appellate court wrote: "We agree with numerous other courts that the Second Amendment guarantees a collective rather than an individual right. . . . The purpose of the second amendment is to preserve the effectiveness and assure the continuation of the state militia. . . . Appellant cannot show that possession of a handgun by an individual bears any relationship to the District of Columbia's desire and ability to preserve a well regulated militia."[3]

The Second Amendment therefore has meaning only in the context of the right of the several states to maintain an organized militia. The right "of the people" means the people as a collective. Guns for personal protection and self-defense or to guard some "right to revolution" are not constitutionally protected as an inherent right of individuals. Roscoe Pound warned of the dangers of the individualistic interpretation: "In the urban industrial society of today a general right to bear efficient arms so as to be enabled to resist oppression by the government would mean that gangs could exercise an extra-legal rule which could defeat the whole Bill of Rights."[4]

Thirty-seven states have constitutional provisions bearing on the right to keep arms.[5] Of those, fifteen states include language that reflects an individual theory of armsbearing.[6] Alabama, for example, provides that "every citizen has a right to bear arms in defense of himself and his state."[7] The Arizona constitution refers to the "right of the individual citizen to bear arms in defense of himself and the state."[8]

Sharply contrasting are those twenty-two states that hold the collective right theory consistent with the federal Constitution.[9] In Ohio, for example, the provision states that "the people have the right to bear arms for their defense and security, but standing armies in time of peace are dangerous to liberty and shall not be kept, and the military shall be kept in strict subordination to the civil power."[10] The Tennessee constitution reads: "The citizens of this state have a right to keep and to bear arms for their common defense; but the Legislature shall have power, by law, to regulate the wearing of arms with a view to prevent crime."[11]

It is therefore tragically ironic that possession of handguns has been argued so vociferously as "a constitutional right."[12] Congressman Edward F. Feighan of Ohio points out that lobbying groups opposing gun control fail to say that this supposedly unassailable constitutional right is solely directed to maintaining a "well-regulated Militia" and that any statutory regulation of gun sales does not necessarily infringe upon a constitutional right to bear arms.[13]

In sum, the Second Amendment, unlike the others, proposes an entitlement that is at most a privilege, not an inherent and protected right of individuals. As we turn to ancient Greece and Rome, however, we find armsbearing at the very center of the definition of citizenship.

ARMSBEARING IN GREECE AND ROME

The heroic age of Greek culture reflected in Homer's *Iliad* was one in which war *was* politics. War and success in fighting were also the source of individual identity—for men, certainly, but also for women as they acted or re-acted in response to male heroism.[14] It is significant that Achilles revealed his true identity by reaching for armor while he was hidden in disguise.

The taming of the Homeric warrior into a citizen of the Greek polis has been compared with the taming of the individualist cowboy ethic in the American mythic tradition. Jean Bethke Elshtain assesses the movie *Shane* in that context. Shane, who has put away the gun that was his identity, reluctantly arms himself one last time when the settlers face a "hired gun" brought in by a leader of the ranchers. Once Shane has done what he must do, he realizes that his continued presence would represent a threat to the peace of the community. Elshtain concludes: "Shane *must* ride away at the film's conclusion. He is as out of place in the placid, settled kingdom of a tamed town as was Achilles' gory glory in Aristotle's list of civic virtues."[15]

Plato and Aristotle are the leading Greek theorists on armsbearing and civic life. But they *are* theorists—the one more than the other but both essentially armchair politicians. The material out of which they construct their theories, however, is the historical experience of the Athenian polity.

For the conservative Plato, an armed citizenry is a threat to the oligarchy he prefers and might even lead to that dangerous offspring of the rabble, democracy. When former members of the elite who have lost their power begin to long for a revolution, "these drones are armed and can sting."[16] Eventually, whether by force of arms or terrorism, the poor majority would establish a democracy that grants the people "an equal share in civil rights and government," and then "liberty and free speech will be rife everywhere."[17]

In the later and even more conservative *Laws*, Plato would require compulsory military training for all citizens, both male and female.[18] It is not clear whether the citizens would own their own arms or would be issued them for the monthly training exercises.[19] In both the

Republic and the *Laws*, the assumption is that citizens would never use arms to free themselves from a tyranny in their own state but only against external enemies of the tyranny: "All citizens shall regard a friend or enemy of the state as their own personal friend or enemy."[20]

Aristotle, although critical of the authoritarian and elitist state proposed by Plato, also raises the question of armsbearing. Aristotle would prefer a middle ground between oligarchy and democracy composed of a populace of armsbearers: "Finally, when the masses govern the state with a view to the common interest, the name used for this species is the generic name common to all constitutions (or polities)—the name of 'Polity . . .' What we can expect particularly [in a Polity] is the military kind of excellence, which is the kind that shows itself in a mass. This is the reason why the defence forces are the most sovereign body under this constitution, and those who possess arms are the persons who enjoy constitutional rights."[21]

Aristotle cites the issue of armsbearing also in his criticism of the ideal state proposed by Hippodamas of Miletus, who was, he says, "the first man without practical experience of politics who attempted to handle the theme of the best form of constitution."[22] Hippodamas had proposed a state of 10,000, divided into thirds: one of farmers, one of skilled artisans, and the third of armsbearers.[23] The problem is the restriction of armsbearing to one class alone. The farmers and the artisans, not possessing arms, become the virtual slaves of the groups possessed of arms, in which case the offices of the state cannot be truly shared, and discontent will erupt.[24] Since armed cavalry and hoplites would tend to come from the wealthier classes, it was ideal to have as much of the population as possible possessed of light arms so they would be able to overcome oligarchy and enjoy citizens' rights: "When, however, states began to increase in size, and infantry forces acquired a greater degree of strength, more persons were admitted to the enjoyment of political rights."[25]

Aristotle would include arms among the basic requirements, along with food and tools, of the democratic or

mixed polity because arms are required against both civil
and external enemies. For Aristotle possession of arms is
thus required for free citizens in such a state, since they
are the persons who decide whether or not a constitution
may continue.

One myth-making episode in early Athenian history,
the slaying of the tyrant Hipparchus by Harmodius and
Aristogiton, involves the question of whether, how, and
when citizens were armed within the city in the late sixth
century B.C. In the middle of his account of the disastrous
Sicilian expedition during the Peloponnesian War in 415,
Thucydides pauses to offer a lengthy account of the tyrannicides Harmodius and Aristogiton. What motivates this
digression is not clear. The best judgment is that it results
from "the temptation before which all historians and
commentators are by their very nature weak," that is, the
temptation to take any available opportunity to correct
misinformation about a famous event.[26]

Thucydides describes the events leading up to the slaying of Hipparchus, brother of the tyrant Hippias, by the
two lovers Harmodius and Aristogiton, taking care to
explain that they planned their attack for the day of the
Panathenaic procession because this was "the only day
on which the citizens, who were taking part in the procession, could gather in arms without exciting suspicion."[27]
When the surviving brother, the tyrant Hippias, learned
what had happened, he approached the armed men in
the procession, ordered his bodyguards to take their arms
away, picked out the men he suspected of being guilty,
and found that all were carrying concealed daggers even
though shields and spears were the only arms customarily
carried during the annual procession.[28]

The *Athenian Constitution* contradicts the story Thucydides tells, holding that a procession with arms was an
innovation of the later democracy.[29] The Parthenon frieze
shows men with shields and helmets, and it is probably
impossible to discern what armament was permissible
when. The matter is of some moment, because if the
Athenians in the procession were all bearing arms, a great
foe of tyranny might properly ask why all the armed peo-

ple did not rush to the aid of the tyrannicides—who both
were killed, but were given credit by the popular tradition
(but not by Thucydides, who laid it to the pressure of the
Spartans[30]) for the eventual downfall of the tyranny three
years later and the subsequent reforms of Cleisthenes.[31]

We can conclude from this episode two things: that in
the late sixth century the Athenian people were generally
not armed within the city except on special yearly occasions, and that the legitimate carrying of arms (whether
Pisistratean or an innovation of the democracy at a later
period) was productive of ridding the city of tyrants.
Whether that is a good thing or not depends on whether
one is a Platonist or an Aristotelian.

Or a Roman. As we turn to armsbearing at Rome, it is
revealing that the first word in Vergil's *Aeneid*, the defining epic of the Roman experience, is "arms"—*Arma vi-
rumque cano*. The basis of Roman civic organization from
the times of Servius Tullius was fundamentally military,
as we saw in the preceding chapter, with the classes determined according to the degree citizens could afford to arm
themselves.

The militaristic character of Roman society was never
at issue, but the problem of professionalized standing armies was. During the Civil Wars in Rome in the first
century B.C., Gaius Marius began admitting people into
the army who had no property qualifications. This practice of arming the *capite censi*, or persons outside the
economic classes determined by the census, was a radical
break with Roman tradition in which the citizens with
the most to lose formed the core of the army. From the
time of Marius's reforms, the Roman armies became increasingly professionalized, permanent, and independent
of civilian influence. They still took their oath to the
populus Romanus, the Roman people, but it was to their
generals that they looked for benefits.

Gone was the ideal of Cincinnatus returning to his plow
after serving or saving the republic.[32] Now soldiers who
had come from nothing had nothing to go back to after
their service and no source of support nor center of loyalty
except their general. It may reasonably be argued that this

was the beginning of the end of the Roman Republic, for it was troops personally loyal to him who made possible Caesar's successful challenge to the power of the Senate, and eventually it was the armies who determined who the emperor would be. The citizen-soldier of the republic had been replaced by the soldier-for-pay, the mercenary and emperor-maker.

But even before Caesar, the rupture had occurred. The Senate did not permit soldiers within the city unless the city was under outside attack. From the time of Servius, the procedure was that in such an emergency the consul would proclaim an emergency levy. Although this had been misused in 133, 100, and 67 B.C., the first time in which an act of the Senate invited serving soldiers into the city occurred in 52 B.C.. As A. W. Lintott observes: "In 52 at last the logic of the Roman tendency to political violence in a state which had no proper police force led to the inevitable solution, professional troops in Rome, summoned on the senate's recommendation in support of law and order."[33]

Once Pompey had been invited in with his proconsular army to quell domestic violence, it was a small step for Caesar to cross the Rubicon.

One important feature of Roman law demonstrates the limits on armsbearing that the ideal of the armed citizen-soldier might suggest. This was the legislation against armed domestic violence in the late republic, legislation that, like the Second Amendment of the Bill of Rights, was predicated by the prevailing political conditions of the times.

The transition from armies fighting in the field to gangs fighting in the streets is one of scale only. This transition was disastrous for the Roman Republic, but it is not difficult to understand how it occurred.[34] Until about 133 B.C., the era of the Gracchi brothers, Rome's mixed constitution of monarchic, aristocratic, and popular elements, together with military domination of the Italian peninsula and the foreign wars with Carthage, Greece, and beyond, had largely succeeded in maintaining at least the facsimile of domestic tranquility in the city. Then Rome's age-old tradition of tolerating, even encouraging violence, in the settlement of public and private disputes began increasingly to define the way of life at home, with urban violence reaching its highest pitch in the decade 59–49 B.C.

Cicero's speeches reflect the extreme civil unrest of the first century B.C. and the ambivalence about armed violence in the civic sphere. In his attack on Catiline, Cicero praises the brave men of earlier days, who did not lack the courage to strike at conspirators who were even more dangerous than foreign foes.[35] But it was criminal to carry arms specifically for the purpose of assassination:

For you must realize that, out of all these men seated here, not one single person is unaware how during the consulship of Lepidus and Tullus, when you took your place in the Assembly on the last day of December, you were illegally carrying arms. You had got together a group determined to strike down the leading men of the state, including the two consuls themselves; and what prevented this mad crime from being carried out was no sanity or nervousness of yours, but the good fortune that favors the people of Rome.[36]

In his defense of Milo, Cicero reiterated the Roman law that carrying arms with intent to kill is criminal, while carrying or using arms in self-defense is justifiable.[37]

Two further developments in this period require mention. In 56 B.C. the Senate extended the legislation against violence to apply to membership in a private association, *sodalitas* or *decuria*, which might serve as the foundation for a gang. This may have been a precedent for the clause in the *Lex Julia* outlawing membership in *collegia*, discussed under freedom of assembly in the preceding chapter. Second, we know from Pliny the Elder that an edict of Pompey's third consulship "prohibited any weapon in the city."[38] This order was more far-reaching than the clause of the *Lex Plautia* forbidding appearance in public with a weapon. It may have led to the additional clause in the *Lex Julia*, which prohibited the possession of any weapons except for hunting, voyages, and journeys.[39]

Given the extent of the unrest, laws against political

violence rose rather late in the republican period. Cicero mentions a law brought by Q. Catulus, *quam . . . Q. Catulus . . . tulit*,[40] which has been identified as the *Lex Lutatia*, a consular law passed in 78 B.C. and therefore the earliest legislation against public violence in Rome.[41] Another important statute was the *Lex Plautia*, datable perhaps to 70,[42] under which Catiline was prosecuted by L. Aemilius Paulus. Publius Cornelius Sulla[43] was indicted under this law in 62, and it was also within its provisions that Vettius informed on Caesar.[44] Pompey passed a related law in 52 to deal with the murder of Clodius on the Appian Way and with the riots that ensued. The *Lex Lutatia* set up a perpetual investigating board (*quaestio perpetua*), which could be used whenever there was sedition. The *Lex Plautia* increased the occasions in which the courts could function in matters of sedition.[45]

It is difficult to identify these early laws in clear outline, however, because all were subsumed under a Julian law on violence, the *Lex Julia de vi*, for which alone we have evidence in the *Digest*. In his study of the *Lex Julia*, Duncan Cloud concludes that the Julian laws on violence were twofold, one passed by Caesar and the other by Augustus, probably between 19 and 16 B.C., but that the material in the *Digest* (48.6 and 7) styled *ad legem Iuliam de vi publica* derives from the same Augustan *vis* statute as the *de vi privata*.[46] There was thus a unitary Augustan measure on violence.[47] Cloud suggests that it is possible that Augustus introduced the phrase *vis publica* to designate the "one important newcomer" under his law against violence, namely "state" or "institutional" violence.[48]

Among its provisions, of which there were at least eighty-eight, the *Lex Julia* forbade carrying an offensive weapon in certain public places (*in publico*), blockading the senate, making violent physical attacks on magistrates, occupying temples and city gates with armed men, and gathering gladiators, citizens, and slaves for riotous purposes, murder, or arson.[49] Many but not all of these reiterated provisions of the earlier *Lex Plautia*,[50] which prohibited the carrying of weapons with the intent to commit murder or theft.

Roman tradition had always encouraged violence, which the Roman constitution was unable to control. By the time the Senate passed legislation to control the bearing of arms for violent purposes in the public realm, it was too late. Armsbearing citizens would prove fatal to the constitution.

QUARTERING SOLDIERS

The Third Amendment, which, like the Second, arose from experience with the British during the Revolutionary War, protects property rights by ensuring freedom from involuntary billeting of soldiers on private property during peacetime or even during times of war unless by due process. While this amendment was shaped by recent American history, the more general problem it addresses was not unfamiliar to the ancient Romans and in fact formed one Roman strategy for dealing with the problem of administration of its far-flung empire.

This had to do with the quartering of Roman soldiers in cities around the empire, and whether such quartering was to be assumed as a right of the Roman armies or withheld as a sign of the conqueror's favor. For example, the city of Termessus in Asia Minor sided with Sulla and Rome during the war with Mithridates, suffering dire consequences as a result. When peace was restored, the Romans promulgated the *Lex Antonia de Termessibus Maioribus* in about 71 B.C., which restored to the inhabitants of Termessus the ownership of their property and included a provision that prohibited the billeting of Roman soldiers in private quarters in the town: "No magistrate or promagistrate or legate or any other person shall introduce soldiers into the town or land of the people of Greater Termessus in Pisidia for the object of winter billeting, or shall allow another so to introduce them, or shall cause soldiers to be billeted in the said town, unless the Senate shall have expressly declared that soldiers be brought into winter quarters with the people of Greater Termessus in Pisidia."[51]

In contrast, Sulla made a point of billeting his troops in

the Asian cities that had supported the uprising led by Mithridates. In one case an actors' guild appealed to him for exemption from this and other penalties. As dictator in 81 B.C., Sulla, perhaps like other politicians solicitous of actors, granted them these immunities and ordered a huge stele erected to announce his benevolence. Among its provisions are these: "You shall be exempt from all public and military service, you shall not pay any tax or contribution, you shall not be troubled by anyone for provisions or billets, and you shall not be compelled to receive any lodger in your homes against your will."[52]

Later, even greater favor was bestowed upon Aphrodisias, a city in Caria, modern western Turkey, which had early emphasized its connections with Venus/Aphrodite, mother of Aeneas and matriarch of the Julian clan, to establish its deference to Julius Caesar. Called by Octavian "the one city from all Asia I have selected to be my own," a *senatus consultum de Aphrodisiensibus* was passed in 39 B.C. to restore Aphrodisias as a free city or *civitas libera*. This measure was supported by Octavian because of the friendliness of the city to his cause in the aftermath of Caesar's assassination. The *senatus consultum de Aphrodisiensibus*, inscribed on a wall of the theater building, granted the city freedom from taxation, preferential treatment of embassies to Rome, non-interference with its magistrates, and freedom from the billeting of Roman soldiers in the city.[53]

When Cicero spoke in favor of the Manilian Law, the abuse of billeting was one of his themes: "Who then does not know how great is the ruin which, owing to this avarice on the part of our generals, is caused by our armies in every place to which they go? . . . Which do you think have been more frequently destroyed during late years— the cities of your enemies by your soldiers' arms or the territories of your friends by their winter quarters?" Cicero then contrasts the avaricious generals with Pompey, who is superior to other generals in part because he does not allow the communities where his soldiers are billeted to incur any costs on their account: "And further, the way in which our soldiers behave in winter quarters is shown by the tidings and the letters which reach us daily: so far from any man being compelled to incur expense on a soldier's account, no man is allowed to do so even if he would. For our forefathers desired that the roofs of their allies and friends should be a shelter against the winter, not a refuge for avarice."[54]

Later in a letter to Atticus, Cicero had occasion to refer to his own restraint from billeting when he served as governor of Cilicia in 51–50 B.C. Though not thrilled with being posted to such a backwater, he determined to govern the province according to the high principles he had established in his *Republic*.[55] In a letter to Atticus of February 13, 50 B.C., he writes:

During the six months of my administration there have been no requisitions and not a single case of billeting. Before my time this season had been devoted each year to the pursuit of gain. The richer towns used to pay large sums to escape from having soldiers billeted on them for the winter. The people of Cyprus, for example, used to pay 200 Attic talents, but under my administration they will appropriate, in literal truth, not a penny. I will accept no honors except speechifying in return for these kindnesses which have so amazed people.[56]

In 42 B.C. the Munatian-Aemilian law was passed, giving the triumvirs power to grant dual Roman citizenship and other privileges to provincials who helped them in their war against Caesar's assassins. This was a great variance from the fundamental Roman law that Roman citizens could not hold any other citizenship, but it demonstrates the Roman inclination to follow Hellenistic institutions where possible. In an edict of 41 B.C., Octavian granted a certain Seleucus of the Asian city of Rhosus, in return for his "devotion and fidelity to the Republic and ... to our safety," Roman citizenship and various privileges thereof, including exemption from taxation and from billeting soldiers.[57]

That the exemption from billeting was one means of exerting or withholding imperial favor is evident also in an edict of Octavian on the privileges of veterans, dated to 31 B.C.:

Likewise, just as I desired the veterans to be privileged in the said respects, I grant permission that they possess, use, and enjoy also whatever priesthoods, offices, prerogatives, privileges, and emoluments they possessed. Neither the other magistrates nor a legate nor a procurator nor a farmer of the tribute shall be in their homes for the purpose of lodging or wintering, nor shall anyone be conducted to winter quarters therein[58] against their will.[59]

In summary, the origins of both the Greek and Roman cultures were essentially military. Bearing arms was a way of life for the aristocratic males who eventually came to constitute the citizen classes. Both classical Athens and republican Rome attempted to regulate armsbearing, but, especially in the case of Rome, violence was so ingrained in the civic ethos that legislative countermeasures came too late to prevent the destruction of the republican constitution.

For a militaristic society, especially one that administered an empire stretching from Scotland to Iraq, the quartering of soldiers was a necessary corollary to imperialism. For the hapless peoples subject to the power of Rome, relief from the quartering of soldiers was occasionally granted as a favor and sign of special status conferred from above. But it was only that, a favor conferred, not a right assured. The American framers insisted that freedom from such measures be included among the rights of all free citizens.

CHAPTER 8

Amendment IV: Search and Seizure

IV.   The right of people to be secure in their persons,
      houses, papers, and effects, against unreasonable
      searches and seizures, shall not be violated, and
      no Warrants shall issue, but upon probable cause,
      supported by Oath or affirmation, and particularly
      describing the place to be searched, and the per-
      sons or things to be seized.

MR. Justice Brennan stated in a Supreme Court
decision that the issue of illegal search and seizure was the
"single immediate cause of the American Revolution."[1]
Protection against such violations of individual rights had
been claimed in Chapter 39 of Magna Carta: "No free man
shall be taken or imprisoned or disseised or outlawed or
exiled or in any way ruined, nor will we go or send against
him, except by the lawful judgement of his peers or by the
law of the land." In insisting on constitutional guarantees
guarding the privacy of one's person and home, however,
the framers were continuing a legal tradition far older
than Magna Carta.

ROMAN RULES OF SEARCH

While the details of its origins are obscure, the notion of private property was well established in Rome by the time of the Twelve Tables in 451 B.C.[2] Private ownership of house and garden arose first, followed by that of arable land. Table VII of the Twelve Tables, for example, entitles an owner to enter the grounds of his neighbor to collect any of his fruit that had fallen there.[3] In Roman society the home was considered to be under the special protection of the household gods. The Twelve Tables did not constitute the public political system but rather codified the civil law, *ius civile*, which dealt with the rights and duties of individual citizens. In general, this meant that the humbler classes were safeguarded against arbitrary behavior from the wealthier patricians.[4]

Safeguards against illegal search in cases of suspected theft are as old as the provision in the Twelve Tables for *lance et licio*, a practice that must date back even earlier among Indo-Germanic people since parallels have been found among the Greeks, Germans, and Slavs.[5]

Under this provision, anyone whose goods had been stolen could demand to search, together with witnesses, any premises on which he suspected his stolen goods were hidden. First, the accuser had to describe to a court in detail the goods he was seeking. If the accused refused the search, the accuser could exact a penalty from him. If the search were allowed and the goods were found, then the owner of the premises was liable to a penalty even if he knew nothing about the theft—for instance, if a guest had brought in stolen goods and left them there concealed.

To enter the premises, the searcher could be clad only in a loincloth (*licium*) and had to carry a platter (*lanx*) in his hands. The purpose of the loincloth is obvious. If the searcher were nearly naked, he would be unable to smuggle anything into the house under his clothing and pretend that he found it there. The purpose of the platter is more obscure. Gaius offers two explanations without accepting either: that it was to put the stolen items on, or that it kept the accuser's hands occupied so that he could not smuggle anything into the house. Mommsen suggests that the platter was a symbol of the intended seizure and carrying away of the goods.[6] Another possibility is that it contained some sort of reward or caution money. In any event, this unusual practice offered to suspects remarkable protection against illegal searches.[7]

The ritual of *lance et licio* was probably not in practice in classical times. By the time of Gaius it was certainly obsolete but still subject to much speculation. By Justinian's time search was a public matter, and no special provision was needed for the knowing receipt of stolen goods. In the common Roman conception of theft, the receiver of stolen property was likewise simply a thief.[8]

EVIDENCE IN CRIMINAL CASES

In criminal cases, a body of law eventually grew up to regulate procedures for gathering evidence. The complainant had to gain a warrant stating the names of the accused and the nature of the accusation. Such a warrant instructed all officials and other individuals to assist in the gathering of evidence and summoning of witnesses. Once he had such a warrant, the complainant seems to have possessed a general power of search for documentary evidence. In order to take away any such evidence, the accuser had to seal the documents in the presence of a witness and deliver the seized evidence to a court within a specified period of time.[9]

Cicero's prosecution of Verres in 70 B.C. provides a number of insights into Roman procedures regulating searches for evidence. Verres had been for three years the rapacious provincial governor of Sicily. Upon retirement from that office (governors could not be prosecuted while in their post) he was accused of extortion by the Sicilian people before the *quaestio de pecuniis repetundis*—"the court of inquiry into moneys claimed back." While this was technically a civil suit, the case was in effect a criminal prosecution for misgovernment and oppression.

In a survey of Verres's earlier crimes as assistant governor in Asia, Cicero mentions his thefts from the island of

Samos of paintings and statues, which Cicero himself saw when he went to Verres's house for the purpose of sealing his evidence (*cum obsignandi gratia venissem*).[10] Later Cicero describes finding incriminating papers during a surprise visit to one Lucius Vibius, who had been a magistrate in the year under question, papers which contained lists of goods exported by Verres from Sicily with no export tax. These, he says, he put under seal at once: *itaque obsignavi statim.*[11]

Some scholars have proposed that until the nineteenth century, the criminal systems of England and all other modern states were less humane than that of the Romans.[12] It is remarkable that the earliest recorded laws of Rome—a hierarchical society supremely conscious of class and privilege—provided a measure of security for common persons, even those suspected of theft, against illegal searches of their homes. Further, evidence had to be gathered under legal constraints even when the powerful were being investigated.

CHAPTER 9

Amendments V, VI, VII, and VIII: Judicial Process

V. *No person shall be held to answer for a capital, or otherwise infamous crime, unless on a presentment or indictment of a Grand Jury, except in cases arising in the land or naval forces, or in the Militia, when in actual service in time of War or public danger; nor shall any person be subject for the same offence to be twice put in jeopardy of life or limb, nor shall be compelled in any criminal case to be a witness against himself, nor be deprived of life, liberty, or property, without due process of law; nor shall private property be taken for public use, without just compensation.*

THE Fifth Amendment, most commonly known for its prohibition of self-incrimination, also contains the assurance of two other rights, the right to indictment by a grand jury before standing trial in serious cases and the right to freedom from double jeopardy for the same offence. A brief history of the jury system will be reserved for discussion of the Sixth and Seventh Amendments, except to say here that in England the origins of the grand jury were earlier than those of the trial jury.[1] Following the clause that "no person shall be compelled in any criminal case to be a witness against himself" is the addition that no person shall "be deprived of life, liberty, or property, without due process of law." The Fifth Amendment ends with an oddly placed clause not pertaining to criminal procedures, forbidding that "private property be taken for public use, without just compensation."[2]

The Fifth Amendment assures first that no person shall be held to answer for a "capital or otherwise infamous crime" (presently construed to mean a crime for which one can lose the right to vote if convicted) without having first been indicted by a grand jury. In other words, probable cause has to be determined by a grand jury before a person can be taken to trial. This feature of the judicial process would have seemed superfluous to the ancient Romans, who took for granted the authority or *imperium* of the magistrate to decide which cases would be heard. From the modern point of view, we would say that the Roman magistrate functioned as the grand jury but without the check of a jury of peers of the accused and without constitutional constraints on the arbitrary power of the magistrate.

Under the *Lex Acilia*, the Gracchan jury law passed in 123–122 B.C., an action was initiated by bringing a written indictment, *nominis delatio*, before the praetor. The praetor then required an oath to ensure that the accuser was not acting out of malice, *calumnia*. In later *iudicia publica*, where there might be several accusers, a more complicated procedure called a *postulatio* required an application for permission to bring an accusation. The praetor might refuse to grant this permission for several reasons: the charge might be against some law or the accused might be legally immune from prosecution. For example, the *Lex Acilia* specifically exempted magistrates from prosecution during their year's term of office, an exemption that saved Clodius from an accusation of violence or *vis* by Milo by his getting elected aedile just in time. Sometime before 113 B.C. another law, the *Lex Memmia*, provided exemptions for persons absent from Rome *rei publicae causa*, so that to get oneself nominated as a legate might prove a useful dodge from prosecution.[3] The magistrate, however, had wide discretion in the application of the *Lex Memmia*.

These provisions indicate some protection for the accused against capricious prosecution. The essential difference from the American system, however, is the discretion left in the hands of the magistrates as to what cases they would hear and the absence of a jury of peers in voting a true bill and presenting an indictment before a person could be brought to trial.

The next provision of the Fifth Amendment reads, "Nor shall any person be subject for the same offence to be twice put in jeopardy of life or limb." In Roman law it was also true that a person could not be tried twice for the same offense in the same criminal court. These courts, called *iudicia publica* or synonymously *quaestiones*, were in Cicero's day permanent courts, presided over by a praetor with a large jury, which gave its verdicts by majority vote.[4] Here the Romans had at least the principle of protection against double jeopardy for the same offense. The *Lex Acilia* provided that a person could not be accused on a matter that had already been adjudicated, whether the accused was condemned or acquitted. A. H. M. Jones thinks the same provision against double jeopardy was probably included in the laws setting up other criminal courts.[5]

There were, however, different courts for different offenses, and a person could be tried for the same charge under more than one statute. For example, three laws against *vis* were in force at the time that Milo was charged with violence: the *Lex Pompeia*, which applied only to disturbances of the year 52 B.C.; the *Lex Lutatia*; and the *Lex Plautia*. Milo was condemned under the *Lex Pompeia* and, shortly thereafter, under one of the other two laws, probably the *Lex Lutatia*. Milo's follower Saufeius was acquitted under the *Lex Pompeia*, and then, for the same offense, again accused and again acquitted under the *Lex Plautia*.[6]

This protection against double jeopardy in the Bill of Rights is a cornerstone of American criminal law. A prosecutor does not have two chances to convict a defendant of the same crime in the same court.[7] Nevertheless, in the American as in the Roman system, a defendant can be tried for the same crime in two different sovereignties, which generally means on the state and federal levels.

The third clause of the Fifth Amendment holds that persons in criminal cases shall not be compelled to witness against themselves. The principle is a simple one, namely, that governments must prove their cases themselves; defendants cannot be forced to do it for them. Leonard Levy sees this provision as an embodiment of American political morality, namely, that citizens are the masters of government, not its subjects. He quotes with approval the words of Mr. Justice Fortas: "The principle that a man is not obliged to furnish the state with ammunition to use against him is basic to this conception."[8]

In some ways, however, the Romans went even further than their American heirs in protecting against self-incrimination. Not only was the accused protected from having to testify against himself, but neither could any relative by blood or marriage, or any freedman testify against him except in cases of *maiestas*, adultery, or fiscal improprieties. The *Lex Julia* provides that no one who is unwilling should be summoned to give evidence in court against his father-in-law, son-in-law, stepfather, stepson, cousin, or cousin's child, or those nearer in degree; and likewise no one's freedman should be summoned nor the freedman of his child, parent, husband, wife, patron, or patroness. Further, a patron or patroness cannot be compelled to give evidence against a freedman nor a freedman against a patron.[9]

VI.   *In all criminal prosecutions, the accused enjoy the right to a speedy and public trial, by an impartial jury of the State and district wherein the crime shall have been committed; which district shall have been previously ascertained by law, and to be informed of the nature and cause of the accusation; to be confronted with the witnesses against him; to have compulsory process for obtaining witnesses in his favor, and to have the assistance of counsel for his defence.*

VII. *In Suits at common law, where the value in controversy shall exceed twenty dollars, the right of trial by jury shall be preserved, and no fact tried by a jury shall be otherwise re-examined in any Court of the United States, than according to the rules of common law.*

Amendments VI and VII further explicate the rights of the accused in criminal cases and of litigants in civil cases. In criminal cases, the Sixth Amendment ensures the right to a speedy public trial by an impartial jury in the district where the crime occurred, the right of the accused to be informed of the charges, the right to confront hostile witnesses, the right to obtain witnesses in one's behalf, and the right of assistance to counsel for the defense. The Seventh Amendment preserves the right of jury trial also in civil cases.[10]

The jury system in America, valued by Jefferson as the anchor of constitutional government, has two origins: the practice of trial by jury invented by the ancient Athenians, and the concept of judgment by peers, which grew up with feudalism in the Middle Ages.

JURY TRIAL IN CLASSICAL ATHENS

The lawgiver Solon (c. 638–c. 558 B.C.) introduced the right of appeal of magistrates' decisions to the people convened in a judicial assembly called the Heliaea, as distinguished from the Ecclesia, or political assembly.[11] Apparently a quorum consisted of six thousand persons; certain kinds of actions, including ostracism, required that six thousand persons vote. In the time of Pericles the juries or dicasteries consisted of ten panels of jurors, five hundred each, selected annually from six thousand citizens. These jurors had to be male, over thirty years of age, free and full citizens, and free of debt.

The body before which a case was tried was selected by lot from one of these panels. A magistrate presided, but the dicasts were the judges of both law and fact. The number of dicasts varied according to the amount at stake.[12] Verdicts were by majority vote, and they were final, not subject to appeal or review.[13] The ballots, which were black and white stones, were put in urns for secrecy. Pericles is credited with instituting pay for jury service in about 460–450 B.C. *The Athenian Constitution*[14] suggests that his motive was to curry favor by bribing the people with their own money, although this work is not an unbiased witness in this instance. More likely, some pay was necessary to induce the poorer citizenry to participate.[15] In some cases the prosecutor needed to get one-fifth of the votes or be subject to a large fine.

Draco's homicide law, which was passed about 620 B.C. and remained in force at least until the fourth century, advanced the transition from voluntary to compulsory procedures. After an initial public proclamation stating the name of the accused, the accused could immediately go into exile, stand trial, or ignore the proclamation. If he chose the latter, he could be killed or arrested immediately. Following the initial proclamation, three preliminary hearings were held before a magistrate before the trial itself took place. The penalty for homicide was exile, even in the case of an unintentional murder. Draco's law also provided protections for the accused against self-help retaliation and for reconciliation of the killer with the victim's family.[16]

The Athenian jurors took an oath, which predates the dicasteries and may date back to the time of Solon. The oath has been reconstructed[17] as follows:

I shall vote according to the laws and the decrees of the Athenian people and the Council of the Five Hundred, but concerning things about which there are no laws, I shall decide to the best of my judgment, neither with favor nor enmity. I shall judge concerning those things which are at issue and shall listen impartially to both the accusation and the defense. I swear these things by Zeus, by Apollo, by Demeter. May there be many blessings on me if I keep my oath, but if I break it may there be destruction on me and my family.[18]

Unlike all the other Athenian officials, the dicasts were not required to submit to scrutiny at the end of their year of service. The reason for this is that they were not like the other servants of the people because they *were* the people.[19] Jurors were selected by lot, submitting wooden or bronze nameplates called *pinakia*, which were inserted into a chest or *kleroteria* from which the nameplates were drawn randomly.[20] This process demonstrates the Athenian confidence that ordinary citizens were qualified to judge as final authorities.

Aeschylus's trilogy, the *Oresteia*, reflects in drama the events taking place politically in contemporary Athens. In order to put an end to a seemingly endless series of revenge murders, Athena establishes a jury of twelve of the finest citizens to hear the case of matricide against Orestes. Before they vote, she tells them that her vote, if she should be forced to break a tie, would be for acquittal. The jury is nevertheless independent enough to vote its conscience. The result is a six-six tie, and Athena does indeed cast the deciding vote.[21] In discharging the jury she declares: "In all goodwill toward these citizens I establish in power spirits who are large, difficult to soften. To them is given the handling entire of men's lives."[22]

David Luban assesses the trial in the *Eumenides* from a legal perspective and asks whether Athena stood as a fair judge in the matter of Orestes' matricide. He concludes that she did not, ruling instead from her stated biases in favor of the male. Aeschylus's motives, he suggests, stem from social control rather than legal fairness:

A shallower playwright than Aeschylus would not have composed the trial scene as he did. . . . Aeschylus, however, like Homer before him, understood that the civil peace and stability that he implicitly elevated to the highest-ranked social value must be purchased at a high price. . . . For Aeschylus, the price of order is that we abandon legal justice in favor of social control.[23]

A more generous reading of the *Oresteia* suggests that the "self-help justice" of personal revenge for crimes leads only to more crimes. A jury of citizen "outsiders" can restore order in society and end the chain of retributive justice. Aeschylus celebrated through his poetry the possibility for a peaceful rule of law in the civic realm.

ROMAN CRIMINAL PROCEDURES

Of the eight provisions of the Sixth Amendment, the most fully elaborated in Roman law had to do with the role of the compulsory process of witnesses in criminal trials. Callistratus holds that the reliability of witnesses must be carefully assessed and that the question prior to all the others is the witnesses' *condicio,* that is, economic and social status: are they decurions (town counselors of minimal status) or plebeians? Only then is it to be determined whether they lead an honest and blameless life and whether they are wealthy or needy (*locuples an egens*), the inference being that if they are needy they are likely to be motivated by personal gain. Potential witnesses are also to be queried as to whether they are enemies of those against whom they give evidence or friends of those for whom they give it. Evidence can be admitted, Callistratus concludes, if the witness is free from suspicion on all these counts.[24]

There are also several references in the *Digest* to rules for summoning witnesses, for example the following: "Witnesses should not lightly be summoned from long distances, still less soldiers called away from their military duties. In a rescript, Hadrian wrote 'So far as summoning witnesses is concerned, the careful judge should find out what the practice is in the province in which he is judge.' "[25] The only witnesses who can be summoned under compulsion, however, are witnesses for the accusers, not for the defendants.

Before Sulla's redesign of the legal system in 81 B.C.

there was no regular jury system in criminal cases. Defendants could, however, if condemned by a magistrate, appeal to the people in a *iudicium populi*. By definition these trials were public, and once set in motion, they were also speedy. The first step in this procedure, which Cicero believed to have been enacted in 509 B.C., was the setting by the magistrate of the day (*dicere diem*) on which the trial could begin. Then there would be three successive hearings or *contiones* with a day between each hearing. No more than a month later came the formal judgment of the magistrate and the vote of the people.[26]

After the Sullan reforms, jury trials in criminal cases were regularized, and an upper-class Roman man, if asked whether he considered that he could expect a trial by jury, would probably say yes.

The last provision of the Sixth Amendment protects the right of the defendant to counsel in criminal cases. The Roman criminal system, again in contrast with the American, takes more care to see that the accusers have lawyers than the defendants. In civil cases, however, the urban praetors would provide the defendant with an *advocatus* if the defendant did not have one.

FEUDALISM AND THE JUDGMENT OF PEERS

In this chapter it is appropriate to consider the evolution of the jury system in medieval England because of the particular impact of feudal institutions upon its development and the remarkable marriage of Roman and feudal law it represents.

An English judge emphasizes that the jury system grew up in England not because some lawgiver decreed it as a promising theory but because it worked in practice. The English excel, he says, in working things out as they go and in the "art of knowing where to place their feet."[27]

It was the Normans, however, who brought with them into England the practice of swearing oaths to the king, who used such promises of veracity to gain information (such as that compiled in the Domesday book) that assisted his administration. The oathtaker was called a "juror" from the Latin verb *iurare*, to swear. Imported from the Continent, too, was the informal understanding of "judgment by peers" (*iudicium parium*), the peers understood to be the principal military tenants of various fiefs. By 1066 the underlying doctrine of judgment by peers had been promulgated by edicts of the emperors in Italy, attached to the *Corpus* of Justinian, and annotated by jurists. The *Libri feudorum* carried Roman law all over Europe, and although Roman law was never valid in England, it exerted great influence on medieval English thought.[28]

Barnaby Keeney attributes the revival of legal studies in northern Italy to the Carolingian conquest and the importation of Frankish ideas favorable to feudalism. This created an Italian context for bringing Roman law to bear on solving problems in feudalism. The edict of Conrad the Salic, issued in Lombardy in 1037, documents several features of feudalism and contains the first explicit reference to judgment by peers as a way of resolving disputes between lords and their vassals.[29]

Keeney shows, too, that the idea of the "twelve peers of France" was of long standing, even though the number does not appear in official sources until late in the thirteenth century. One scholar argues that the number comes from the first half of the twelfth century, when the total of twelve was composed of the dukes of Normandy, Aquitaine, and Burgundy; the counts of Flanders, Champagne, and Toulouse; the archbishop of Rheims; and the bishops of Langres, Laon, Châlons, Beauvais, and Noyon.[30] Only in epic poetry, however, does the number twelve appear as significant during that period.[31] Keeney concludes that the chivalric legends either reflected the existence of a peerage of twelve or influenced the adoption of that number.[32]

Thus the invaders with William the Conqueror were familiar with the idea that a person should be judged by his peers. The issue was not a burning one, however, until the time of King John and Magna Carta.

Keeney emphasizes that the practice of judgment by peers was feudal and existed only where feudalism did.

"It was Germanic only in so much as feudalism was Germanic; it was not one of the immemorial liberties of the Teuton, if indeed he ever had any. Nor was it Roman, although the rationalization of feudal custom under the influence of Roman law seems to have played some part in its definition and development."[33]

Later, King Henry II (1154–1189) established the Grand Assize, a court of four knights and twelve neighbors, who ruled on challenged claims to land. This extended to settlement of disputes the practice of information-gathering under oath. This procedure could occur only in royal courts because only the king had sufficient authority to compel anyone to take an oath. In land disputes, for example, the local landowners who might be expected to be most aware of all the facts could be bound under oath to swear who had the best claim to the land in question. The first disputant to get twelve oaths, including his own, in his favor won.

Henry II has been described as a man of powerful will, administrative genius, and reforming spirit. In increasing greatly the power of the royal courts, he regarded as of public consequence the kinds of breaches of the peace and threats that formerly had been considered private matters. "What was once only an administrative inquiry became the foundation of the jury of accusation and the jury of trial in both civil and criminal matters."[34]

The Church also added a major thrust toward the establishment of trial by jury in England. In November 1215, in the early years of the reign of Henry III, Pope Innocent III prohibited church officials from taking part in trial by ordeal, whereby a person's innocence was determined by subjecting the person to horrible physical torture. If he survived, then he was innocent. Trial by ordeal included such practices as walking barefoot over hot iron plowshares, carrying hot iron weights barehanded, or reaching into a pot of boiling water. Although technically Pope Innocent's prohibition applied only to the clergy, in effect it ended the practice altogether. On the Continent, where legal theory was more advanced, a new system was quickly devised. In England, the itinerant judges mostly improvised. If a prisoner wanted to be judged by his neighbors, he could "put himself upon his country" by pleading not guilty and accepting the jurors' verdict.

Gradually the character of the jurors changed from the neighbors most likely to know the facts firsthand to those bound to attend only to the evidence as presented in court and to ignore everything they might know about the case from other sources. As this expectation has evolved in the present day, those who confess to prior knowledge about the case or acquaintance with the parties or their attorneys are likely to be dismissed from service on the jury for that trial.

WHY TWELVE?

Many theories have been offered to explain the number twelve in a jury. Among these are the twelve apostles, the twelve tribes of Israel, and the twelve patriarchs. One Englishman explains it much more simply: that in addition to wanting a number sufficient to pose an overwhelming preponderance of evidence, the British simply had an early abhorrence of the decimal system, as evidenced by the fact that until recently there were twelve pence to the shilling.[35]

In 1970 the U.S. Supreme Court ruled in the case of *Williams v. Florida*[36] that the defendant's rights under the Sixth Amendment as applied through the Fourteenth Amendment had not been violated because Mr. Williams had been convicted of robbery by a Florida jury of only six members. In that decision, the Court considered at length whether the constitutional guarantee of trial by jury required trial by exactly twelve persons. It held that it did not, offering extensive documentation to suggest that the precise size of juries was no more than an historical accident.

One source cited in the opinion[37] notes that in the Frankish Empire juries are recorded with the numbers of 66, 41, 20, 17, 13, 11, 8, 7, 53, 15, and many others. Among the Normans the number varied also, so that twelve does not prevail even there. "It seems to have been the recognitions under Henry II that established twelve as the usual number; even then the number was not uniform." Then the opinion avers:

Some have suggested that the number 12 was fixed upon simply because that was the number of the presentment [grand] jury from the hundred, from which the petit [trial] jury developed. Other, less circular but more fanciful reasons for the number 12 have been given, "but they were all brought forward after the number was fixed,"[38] and rest on little more than mystical or superstitious insights into the significance of "12." Lord Coke's explanation that the "number of twelve is much respected in holy writ, as 12 apostles, 12 stones, 12 tribes, etc.," is typical.

One of the ancient kings of Wales, Morgan of Gla-Morgan, is said to have adopted trial by a jury of twelve in A.D. 725, "For as Christ and his twelve apostles were finally to judge the world, so human tribunals should be composed of the king and twelve wise men."[39] King Morgan apparently did not consider whether this implies that there will be a Judas on every jury.

"In short," the Court concludes, "while sometime in the 14th century the size of the jury at common law came to be fixed generally at 12, that particular feature of the jury system appears to have been a historical accident, unrelated to the great purposes which gave rise to the jury in the first place." The Court then determines that this "accidental feature" had not been immutably codified into the Constitution. The opinion addresses also the question of whether a 12-person jury is more advantageous that a smaller one to the defendant and concludes that it is not necessarily so. "We conclude, in short, as we began: the fact that the jury at common law was composed of precisely 12 is a historical accident, unnecessary to effect the purposes of the jury system and wholly without significance 'except to the mystics.' "[40]

THE VALUE OF THE JURY SYSTEM

In 1968 the U.S. Supreme Court in *Duncan v. Louisiana*[41] affirmed the right of criminal defendants to jury trial "in order to prevent oppression by government," even if the sentence were only sixty days and a fine of $150. That decision offered an eloquent defense of the jury system laced with historical references.

The Court noted that many trace the history of trial by jury back to Magna Carta and quoted with approval Blackstone's *Commentaries on the Laws of England* (349–350). Blackstone compares the English jury system with the power of the Crown, who might, "as in France or Turkey, imprison, dispatch, or exile any man that was obnoxious to the government, by an instant declaration that such is their will and pleasure." The founders of English law, by contrast, contrived that "the truth of every accusation, whether preferred in the shape of indictment, information, or appeal, should afterwards be confirmed by the unanimous suffrage of twelve of his equals and neighbours, indifferently chosen and superior to all suspicion."

This right came with the English to the colonies, and the colonists resented any royal interference with it. As early as the Stamp Act Congress on October 19, 1765, among the resolutions stating "the most essential rights and liberties of the colonists" was the declaration that trial by jury was an inherent and invaluable right of every British subject in the colonies. The First Continental Congress, in its resolve of October 14, 1774, objected to trials conducted before judges of the Crown alone and to trials held in England for crimes alleged to have occurred in the colonies: "That the respective colonies are entitled to the common law of England, and more especially to the great and inestimable privilege of being tried by their peers of the vicinage, according to the course of that law." The Court also quotes the Declaration of Independence with its objections to the king's making "judges dependent on his will alone" and to his "depriving us in many cases of the benefits of Trial by Jury."

The Court noted that jury trial was protected by Article III, Section 2, of the Constitution, almost immediately bolstered by the Bill of Rights. Then it offered its own eloquent defense:

The guarantees of jury trial in the Federal and State Constitutions reflect a profound judgment about the way in which law should be enforced and justice administered. A right to jury trial is granted to criminal defendants in order to prevent oppression by the government. Those who wrote our constitutions knew from history and experience that it was necessary to protect against unfounded criminal charges brought to eliminate enemies and against judges too responsive to the voice of higher authority. The framers of the constitutions strove to create an independent judiciary but insisted upon further protection against arbitrary action. Providing an accused with the right to be tried by a jury of his peers gave him an inestimable safeguard against the corrupt or overzealous prosecutor and against the compliant, biased, or eccentric judge. If the defendant preferred the common-sense judgment of a jury to the more tutored but perhaps less sympathetic reaction of the single judge, he was to have it. . . . Fear of unchecked power, so typical of our State and Federal Governments in other respects, found expression in the criminal law in this insistence upon community participation in the determination of guilt or innocence.[42]

The value of the jury may be seen also in a more immediate and personal perspective. In addition to affording ordinary citizens the occasion to express their faith in government and to protect their fellow citizens, the jury system may also protect oneself. In remarks to prospective jurors, one judge observes: "It is an assurance of your guarantee that if chance or design brings you into a court of law in any civil or criminal entanglement, your rights and liberties will be regarded in the same light of justice and protected by the same manner of consideration that you administer here in the faithful discharge of your duty as jurors."[43]

The use of a jury introduces flexibility into the legal system and may bring the law into closer accord with justice in the context of one's own community. This can be double-edged. In 1735 John Peter Zenger, a New York newspaper publisher, was accused of seditious comments against the British colonial governor, William Cosby, including charges that Cosby was limiting the right of the colonists to trial by jury. A jury of Zenger's peers ignored the British judge's insistence that it was to determine only the fact of publication, while he, the judge, would determine whether or not Zenger's expression was seditious. Persuaded by Zenger's attorney, Andrew Hamilton, the jury ignored the judge's instructions and acquitted Zenger.[44] On the other hand, after the Supreme Court overturned the first convictions in the famous Scottsboro case, a second trial in Alabama found one of the defendants, Haywood P. Patterson, guilty. Judge Horton, disagreeing with the jury's verdict, set it aside and ordered a new trial. Judge Horton was soundly defeated in his next election, while Patterson was convicted in a third trial in 1933.[45]

Generally, however, a judge's powers to set aside a jury's verdict are wider in civil cases than in criminal cases, in which it is a fundamental principle that a verdict of not guilty is final and cannot be set aside.[46]

As imperfect a system as the jury is, as imprecise its approximations of an abstract ideal of justice, it nevertheless helps preserve the accountability of judges to the people and to the law. Perhaps sometimes it also enlivens judicial sensitivities calloused by the constant parade of horrors through the courts. Certainly the jury provides a safeguard against unjust laws and, finally, against tyranny. As one jurist observes, any revolutionary bent on overthrowing a country would first abolish the legislative body and second trial by jury, because "no tyrant could afford to leave a subject's freedom in the hands of twelve of his countrymen."[47]

Alexis de Tocqueville compared the American jury system favorably with the British. The British jury, he noted, is selected from the aristocratic portion of the population, while in America, every citizen is eligible. De Tocqueville saw the jury as a powerful school for citizenship and attributes the practical intelligence and political good sense of the Americans to their long use of the jury in civil cases. He concludes: "The jury is both the most effective way of establishing the people's rule and the most efficient way of teaching them how to rule."[48]

VIII.   Excessive bail shall not be required, nor exces-
sive fines imposed, nor cruel and unusual pun-
ishments inflicted.

The last of the amendments of the Bill of Rights providing protection from judicial encroachment prohibits excessive bail, excessive fines, and cruel and unusual punishment.

In most Athenian legal procedures the accused was not
held prior to trial, even in homicide cases prosecuted
under normal circumstances, so there would have been
no need for bail. In one case described by Antiphon, the
defendant protests that he was not allowed to provide
sureties for getting out of jail where he was being held for
trial, which may imply that this possibility would have
been normal in such cases.[49] For the most part, however,
the idea of bail has its origins in Anglo-Saxon practice and
to some extent among Germanic tribes on the Continent.[50]

In matters of cruel and unusual punishment, the Romans were masters. In the Roman world we know that
slaves were examined under torture, since it was supposed
that they were so lowly or so unable to distinguish truth
from falsehood that only torture could extract true testimony from them. Later, perhaps by the second half of the
second century of this era, torture was legally extended
from slaves to free persons of low degree. In cases of
maiestas, all free persons, and not just those of rank,
could be tortured. Jones observes that *maiestas* "always
remained an exception to any rules exempting the upper
classes."[51]

In one respect, however, Roman practices of criminal
punishment may have been more advanced than American. Ulpian writes in the *Digest*, "Governors are in the
habit of condemning men to be kept in prison or in chains,
but they ought not to do this; for punishments of this type
are forbidden. Prison indeed ought to be employed for
confining men [before trial], not for punishing them."[52]

Amendments V through VIII of the Bill of Rights constitute what some people consider "technicalities" by which

criminals escape punishment. These "technicalities," however, are another term for the elaborate procedures, hard won over a period of more than two thousand years, that are meant to protect the innocent as well as to convict the guilty. It is these often cumbersome practices that ensure the rule of law instead of the tyranny of whim in human governance.

In the case of the jury system, we see in the American Bill of Rights a return to the faith of classical Athens, that ordinary citizens[53] are capable in orderly ways of governing their own affairs and settling their own disputes. Now, however, that capacity is dignified as a right of human beings as individuals and not just as members of a community. The notion has come full circle, amplified by the gradual evolution of a belief in individual rights.

CHAPTER 10

Amendments IX and X: Retained Rights and Reserved Powers

IX.   The enumeration in the Constitution of certain
      rights shall not be construed to deny or disparage
      others retained by the people.

X.   The powers not delegated to the United States by
      the Constitution, nor prohibited by it to the
      States, are reserved to the States respectively, or
      to the people.

BY happenstance, the last two amendments in
the Bill of Rights return us to the initial discussions of
Greek philosophy and Roman law in Chapter 1. The
Ninth Amendment raises issues originating in Greek philosophy, while the Tenth recalls the Roman gift for administration.

These two amendments are a tribute to the political
canniness and vision of the framers. The Ninth Amendment mollified critics who feared that enumerating rights
in a set of amendments to the Constitution would imply
that no other rights were protected. Having come this
far toward freedom and representative government, the
framers were reluctant to place limits on other individual

rights that might come later into focus. The Tenth Amendment affirms the role of the states and the people[1] in their federal relationship with a strong central government.

THE NINTH AMENDMENT AND UNENUMERATED RIGHTS

Because there was no doctrine of inherent individual rights in the classical world, the Ninth Amendment lacks analogies in ancient Greece and Rome. Indeed, the idea of protecting undefined rights would have been the worst nightmare of the Romans, who labored assiduously in their legal documents to specify every possible application and exception. The Romans were married to the "black letter law."

Even as a part of the United States Constitution this provision lay dormant for nearly 175 years. In recent times, however, the Ninth Amendment has become the center of a swirl of controversy about whether other rights not presently delineated by the government are "retained by the people"—and if so, how and by whom they are to be determined. Hence it is more closely connected than any other provision of the Bill of Rights with the doctrine of natural law doctrine, which originated in Stoic philosophy and evolved into the theories of rights of John Locke and the Enlightenment.

A belief in natural rights clearly lay behind the amendment in the first place. If they had not believed in a doctrine of natural rights, the framers would probably have enumerated many more rights than those contained in the present ten amendments, as evidenced by the much longer list of rights proposed by the state ratification conventions.

James Wilson of Pennsylvania was an impassioned opponent of a bill of rights because he was so strong a believer in natural rights. The fundamental purpose of government, he held, is to protect and expand the natural rights of its members. If a government does not have this view, then it is not a legitimate government.[2] It is therefore unnecessary to provide a list of particular rights that it is the responsibility of government to protect. "Enumerate all the rights of men!" exclaimed Wilson. "I am sure, sirs, that no gentleman in the late Convention would have attempted such a thing."[3]

In his speech to the House explaining his proposed amendments, James Madison took care to respond to the concern that enumerating some rights would imply that there are no others:

It has been objected also against a bill of rights, that, by enumerating particular exceptions to the grant of power, it would disparage those rights which were not placed in that enumeration; and it might follow, by implication, that those rights which were not singled out, were intended to be assigned into the hands of the General Government, and were consequently insecure. This is one of the most plausible arguments I have ever heard urged against the admission of a bill of rights into this system; but, I conceive, that it may be guarded against. I have attempted it, as gentlemen may see by turning to the last clause of the fourth resolution.[4]

For contemporary observers who are skeptical of such a theory of rights, the Ninth Amendment thus poses both a philosophical and a political dilemma. Randy E. Barnett asks whether the Ninth Amendment was a philosophical mistake, pointing out that until quite recently, many—if not most—modern philosophers insisted that there is no such thing as natural rights. In this view, government, not "nature," is the ultimate source of all rights.[5]

Given a philosophical skepticism about rights, the reference in the Ninth Amendment to unspecified retained rights is no different from a constitutional prohibition of discrimination against ghosts. . . . If rights antecedent to government are mere illusions or ghosts, then judicial enforcement of these alleged "rights" can only be wholly subjective and arbitrary. . . . Decisions that are unavoidably based on subjective preferences, the argument continues, ought to be made by the representative branch of government so as to reflect the preferences of the majority.[6]

Modern skeptics about the possibility of discerning rights independent of those already defined by government—which presumably means by the will of the majority—are therefore left in some quandary about where to base their arguments. Barnett notes that it is doubtful that all rights retained by the people could be specified in advance:

In a classical liberal theory of rights, rights define a sphere of moral jurisdiction that persons have over certain resources in the world—including their bodies. This jurisdiction establishes the boundaries within which persons are free to do what they wish. As long as people are acting within their respective jurisdictional spheres, their acts are deemed to be "rightful" (as distinguished from "good"), and others may not use force to interfere.[7]

To define is therefore to limit. A theory of natural rights establishes parameters, not particulars—and those parameters are seen to be somehow independent of the current will of the majority. In a letter to Thomas Jefferson, Madison wrote of his sense of the dangers to individual rights from governments acting by the will of the majority or popular causes:

Wherever the real power in a Government lies, there is the danger of oppression. In our Governments the real power lies in the majority of the Community, and the invasion of private rights is chiefly to be apprehended, not from acts of Government contrary to the sense of its constituents, but from acts in which the Government is the mere instrument of the major number of its Constituents.[8]

Madison thus considered the Bill of Rights a way of constraining, by means of an independent judiciary, abuses by the legislature and the executive. That is, the Bill of Rights was not designed to protect the majority or the powerful.[9]

The Ninth Amendment has been interpreted as a cautionary or even redundant means of constraining government power, both by reinforcing the limitations on the delegated powers of government, and by placing additional restrictions on the ways by which government may pursue its delegated ends.[10] In this view, the conflict between natural or individual rights and government power will expand as the power of government increases. According to Mr. Justice Brennan, the "possibilities for collision between government activity and individual rights will increase as the power and authority of government expands."[11]

Many unenumerated rights have already been acknowledged by the courts over the past two hundred years. Among these are the right to vote, subject only to reasonable restrictions, and the right to cast a ballot equal in weight to those of other citizens; the right to associate with others; the right to marry or not to marry; the right to travel in the United States; the right to receive equal protection not only from the states but also from the federal government; the right to make one's own choice about having children; the right to attend and report on criminal trials.[12] Others have been acknowledged and established by constitutional amendment. In 1865, seventy-four years after the Bill of Rights was ratified, the Thirteenth Amendment abolished slavery. Fifty-five years after that, the Nineteenth Amendment in 1920 assured the right of women to vote.

One way to avoid a limitless theory of rights is to view the Ninth Amendment as generally "presumptive," that is, that it establishes a constitutional presumption in favor of individual liberty.[13] This would resemble the specific presumption of the First Amendment in favor of free speech, even though constraints such as fraud, copyright, and defamation might provide limits or boundaries on that presumption.

Under the formal limits of the presumptive approach to the Ninth Amendment, the judiciary would be confined to enforcing only whatever unenumerated rights are comparable to substantive and procedural rights that were enumerated, so long as they are consistent with the constitutional principles of due process and equal protection.

Respect for those procedural constraints, as Barnett notes, is the price of using public as opposed to private institutions to achieve social goals.[14]

One may, however, take a more thoroughgoing natural rights approach to the Ninth Amendment. Bennett B. Patterson, for example, emphasizes its close connection with the Declaration of Independence, which does not state that rights and liberties are contrived by governments but rather are "inalienable" and are "endowed" by a "Creator." Jefferson carefully prefaced his list of the rights of life, liberty, and the pursuit of happiness by the words "among these," implying that such a list is not complete. Governments, he adds, are instituted "to secure these Rights."

Patterson would see the Declaration of Independence as a legal as well as philosophic document and looks for the day when the courts will cite it as a legal authority for a doctrine that individual liberties are natural and inherent rather than deriving from the U.S. Constitution. The Constitution, says Patterson, echoing Jefferson, was never intended to be the creator but only the protector of these rights.[15]

This view understands the Ninth Amendment as opening the door to a wider range of rights, wider than the Constitution and, for Patterson, wider also than the Declaration of Independence. It recognizes a spectrum of individual rights more inclusive than those consistent with presently enumerated constitutional principles.

Prior to 1965 the Supreme Court had never used the Ninth Amendment as a basis for a decision. Then, in *Griswold v. Connecticut,* which concerned the legality of making information about contraceptives available to married couples, the majority opinion, written by Justice Douglas, used the Ninth Amendment as support for the existence of a "penumbra" of privacy surrounding certain specific rights in the first eight amendments.[16] In a concurring opinion, Justice Goldberg elaborated on the language and history of the Ninth Amendment, which reveal "that the Framers of the Constitution believed that there are additional fundamental rights, protected from govern-

mental infringement, which exist alongside those fundamental rights specifically mentioned in the first eight
constitutional amendments."[17] This reinforced the view
that further individual rights may inhere in the notion of
"liberty" or in the nexus of the Bill of Rights, and that it
is the obligation of the Constitution to protect them.

Griswold began a new era in the expansion of individual
rights. In its wake the courts decided such cases as those
having to do with schoolboys and long hair, fundamental-
ists and schoolbooks, felons and maximum security, and
healthful environment in the work place.[18] Then, in 1970,
a Texas district court in the case of *Roe v. Wade*,[19] citing
a "Ninth Amendment right to have an abortion," struck
down a state statute prohibiting abortions unless necessary to save a mother's life.

The U.S. Supreme Court upheld *Roe v. Wade* in 1973
by a vote of seven to two. It based its judgment, however,
not on the Ninth but the Fourteenth Amendment: "This
right of privacy, whether it be founded in the Fourteenth
Amendment's concept of personal liberty and restrictions
upon state action, as we feel it is, or, as the District Court
determined, in the Ninth Amendment's reservation of
rights to the people, is broad enough to encompass a wom-
an's decision whether or not to terminate her preg-
nancy."[20]

The last time the Supreme Court mentioned the Ninth
Amendment in a majority opinion was the 1980 case
of *Richmond Newspapers v. Virginia*.[21] In that decision,
which upheld the right of public access to criminal trials,
the Court wrote: "Notwithstanding the appropriate caution against reading into the Constitution rights not explicitly defined, the Court has acknowledged that certain
unarticulated rights are implicit in enumerated guarantees." In a footnote it cited the Ninth Amendment as
supporting evidence.[22]

References to the Ninth Amendment are absent from
two subsequent controversial cases decided by the Court.
By a vote of five to four in 1986, the Court in *Bowers v.
Hardwick*[23] reversed a lower court decision to strike down
a Georgia law criminalizing sodomy, whether between

homosexual or heterosexual, married or unmarried persons. Hardwick had claimed that private sexual activity was protected by the constitutional right to privacy. The dissenting opinion stated: "This case . . . is about 'the most comprehensive of rights and the right most valued by civilized men', namely, 'the right to be let alone.' "[24] Then in 1989 in *Webster v. Reproductive Health Services*[25] the Court upheld state restrictions on abortions. These two cases in particular leave grave doubt about the future protection by the Supreme Court of a right to privacy.

Griswold v. Connecticut, Roe v. Wade, Bowers v. Hardwick, and *Webster v. Reproductive Health Services* illustrate the controversial nature of arguments about rights and point to the kinds of issues the courts will yet be called upon to decide. Even if the framers did not foresee such rights as a right to privacy, it was for just such arguments as these that Madison and supporters of the Ninth Amendment consciously opened the door. In their insistence on the wider scope of a natural law basis for human rights, they meant to ensure that the new nation would keep its doors open to new as well as established ideas of the dignity of the individual.

THE TENTH AMENDMENT: POWERS RESERVED TO THE STATES OR THE PEOPLE

A consideration of the Tenth Amendment turns us from political philosophy to practical problems of political administration. By reserving to the states or the people powers not delegated to the federal government, nor prohibited by the Constitution to the states, the framers addressed the issue of how to reconcile a strong central government with government on the state and local levels.

Here again we look to the Romans. The Tenth Amendment, *mutatis mutandis*, recalls one of the greatest strengths of the Roman Empire: the ability of the Romans to govern a vast array of provinces stretched over three continents with notable success for hundreds of years. Seldom has the government of the world been conducted in so orderly a fashion for so long a time. The rules of administration, laid out by Caesar and elaborated by Augustus, were maintained with remarkable continuity for three centuries and, when appropriated by the Catholic Church and other European institutions, far longer.

This success was due in part to the Roman genius for organization, but it was due also to the Roman willingness to permit local control to the provinces in certain respects. That flexibility helps account for the longevity of the empire, which in turn assured the establishment of Roman law and customs which have played so large a role in the present story.

Paradoxically, Greek precedents rather than Roman were preferred during much of the earlier period in colonial America. The Greek concept of a colony was preferred over the more tightly organized Roman system, since the former by and large lived free from domination from the mother city. Of special interest as the framers wrestled with the question of a strong central government versus the Articles of Confederation were the Greek Amphictyonic leagues, organized around religious centers of worship, and the other more political federations such as the Achaean, Lycian, and Aetolian leagues.[26]

Once the United States was established, however, the Roman model offers a closer analogy. There are fundamental differences, of course, between the genuinely federal system in America and the highly centralized monarchy of the Roman Empire. Nevertheless, a look at Roman provincial administration, particularly in the case of Gaul, will demonstrate the Roman genius for imposing new order on a profusion of existing orders and combining centralized power with at least the semblance of local control.

Until the time of Augustus there was no well-developed bureaucracy for administering the provinces, even though Rome had been in the business of extending its Italian domain almost from the beginning and beyond Italy after the wars with Carthage in the third century B.C. Governors ran Italy and the provinces with the help of quaestors. Tax collecting was conducted by means of contracts let out to tax-farming companies. The reward of holding office in Rome was that it served as admission to the imperial service, perhaps the governorship of a province where wealth was available for the taking. As one observer puts it, the provinces were the *praeda* or booty of the Roman people, to be exploited at will.[27]

It was Augustus, serving as emperor from 31 B.C. to A.D. 14, who created the machinery of Roman imperial administration. His accomplishments are due, no doubt, to the sheer force of his intellect and political instincts, but it was to his advantage that, unlike his predecessor, Julius Caesar, he lived long enough to pay attention to details. A close look at Gaul will be instructive both because of Augustus's personal role in developing the provincial administration and because the Romanization of Gaul had such long-term consequences for the European West.[28]

Mommsen observes that the Roman policies for retaining mastery over the provinces were a greater feat than gaining the dominion in the first place.[29] Before Julius Caesar's Gallic war, the rule of the Romans already extended as far as Toulouse and Geneva; afterward, as far as the Rhine and the Atlantic. While Caesar won the military victories, Augustus made permanent the gains.

Turning over the previously occupied Roman territory of Gaul (called Gallia Narbonensis after the city of Narbo) to the control of the Senate, Augustus kept New Gaul (called Gallia Comata) under his own administration. The Romanization of the older province of southern Gaul in language and customs was already extensive by the Augustan age; many of the cities such as Avennio (Avignon) and Aquae Sextiae (Aix) had Latin rights, with the leading citizens of those towns having acquired for themselves and their descendants the privilege of holding office in the imperial administration.

Augustus divided New Gaul into three administrative districts, each with its own imperial governor. These were attached to the threefold division of the old Celtic territories according to national distinctions, divisions already recognized by Caesar: Aquitania, Lugdunensis, and Belgica. In the year 27 B.C., still early in his reign, Augustus went to Gaul and at Lyons (Lugdunum) instituted a census of the Gallic province that became the basis for land registry and for the payment of tribute to Rome. Later in his career he spent three years, 16–13 B.C., at Lyons to lay out further the imperial organization of Gaul. Other key members of his staff and family, including Agrippa, Tiberius, Drusus, and Germanicus, were sent at various times for the same purpose.

Only Lyons of the three provinces of New Gaul already possessed Roman or Latin rights by the time of the arrival of Augustus. These dated from the year 43 B.C., during the civil wars, when the town was established by Italians who had been expelled from Vienne. The site of Lyons, in the far southern region of the imperial province at the confluence of the Rhône and the Saône, was auspicious for both military and commercial purposes. Since Lyons did not grow out of a previously existing Celtic community but from the very beginning was founded by Italians with full Roman franchise, it occupied a unique position in New Gaul. The three provinces did not have a common chief authority. Nevertheless, when emperors or their designates stayed in Gaul, it was usually at Lyons. The city was the site of the only mint for imperial money in the western empire during the earlier period, and it was the headquarters for collection of transit dues for all of Gaul.

Furthermore, Lyons was the converging point for the extensive road system throughout all of Gaul. Some 50,000 miles of major roads crisscrossed the Roman Empire at its height, all measured in standard Roman miles of 1.48 km. Only in Gaul was the local measure of the *leuga* maintained, equivalent to one and a half Roman miles or 2.22 km. Probably it was Augustus who formally decreed the Roman mile for the measure of the entire imperial road system but in reality tolerated in Gaul its more familiar road measurement. This became official at the time of Severus at the end of the second century, a concession to local tradition.

A certain forbearance was also maintained for Gallic

religious traditions. Worship of non-Roman deities continued, as attested by the discovery of numerous altars to the Druidic gods of the Celtic pantheon. Perhaps as a countermeasure, Augustus instituted an annual religious festival of a strictly Roman character at Lyons, where his representative Drusus consecrated on August 1, 12 B.C., an altar to Roma and the genius of the ruler. Each of the Gallic districts was to choose each year a priest to conduct the annual sacrifices at this altar and the festival games associated with it. Augustus also prohibited Roman citizens from taking part in the Gallic cults, but beyond that he does not seem to have taken any further measures against the national religion. Tiberius outlawed Druidism, a move that Claudius after him had to reiterate. By the third century a Gallo-Roman flavor predominated in the religion of the area, and both components eventually gave way to Christianity.

While national traditions in Gaul were respected in other areas insofar as they were compatible with Roman imperial administration, this was not the case with the Celtic language. Celtic continued to be spoken and written, but it was the design of Roman administration that provincial government throughout the empire should be conducted entirely in Latin. The church father Jerome, who had travelled in Galatia in Asia Minor as well as in Gaul, commented that the spoken Latin was roughly the same in both places—a testament to the spread if not the elegance of the language. No coins were struck or monuments raised in Gaul with Celtic inscriptions. The final coup to the Celtic dialect came, however, not through the designs of Roman imperial administration but through the Christianizing of Gaul with a Gospel preached in Latin.

The granting or withholding of citizenship privileges was historically Rome's master stroke for maintaining control of the provinces. In the case of Gaul, Augustus withdrew the privileges of candidacy for the imperial magistracies and thus to the imperial Senate from those native Gauls—the inhabitants of Lyons always excepted—who might have gained them one way or another, perhaps through a grant from Julius Caesar. It is not clear whether this was to limit the intrusion of foreign elements into the Roman system or to promote a continuation of Gallic traditions of governance. In any case, these restrictions on Italian rights were removed by Claudius (emperor in A.D. 41–54), who was born in Lyons.

The Roman capacity for appropriating from the peoples it appropriated is nowhere more evident in the case of Gaul than in military matters. With the disappearance of the old citizen cavalry of the Roman Republic, the cavalry of the imperial armies became essentially Gallic—not only because it was largely recruited from Gaul but also because the cavalry maneuvers and even technical terms were taken from the Celts when Caesar and Augustus reorganized the cavalry.

Gaul was a wealthy province, with extensive natural resources including wine, agriculture, and livestock, especially cattle and sheep. Roman rule enhanced this prosperity; Roman taxation prodded it on. Evidence both of the prosperity of the region and of its increasing Romanization still survives in such imposing monuments as the amphitheater at Arles, the theater of Orange, and the temples and bridges near Nîmes. Gallic wealth was so remarkable that, as Josephus reports, King Agrippa put to the Jews the question of whether they imagined themselves to be richer than the Gauls, stronger than the Germans, or more sagacious than the Hellenes.[30] In Lyons the wealth was so extensive that when Rome suffered the catastrophic fire in A.D. 64, which destroyed much of the city, the Gallic city sent relief of four million sesterces to the Romans who had suffered losses.

It was wealth such as this that inspired Roman attention to its provinces. Rome managed its empire through an ad hoc mix of mechanisms combining intentional design with pragmatic accommodation to local institutions. By the time of the empire this combination had been evolving for over two hundred years in the wake of Roman expansion throughout the Mediterranean, but the case of Gaul is instructive because of the newly centralized and ongoing role of the emperor at the center of the show.

In the imperial provinces of Gaul, administrative strategies included strict control of access to the magistracies and other privileges of citizenship; special favors granted to certain cities; toleration of local religious practices together with the institution of elaborate Roman rituals in honor of the emperor, rituals that also enticed the native elite into the Roman sphere; the pragmatic appropriation of military expertise; deference to certain local institutions such as the proper length of a mile; and insistence on Latin as the language of empire. This combination of strategies worked for the most part because it was gradual enough, and the preferments enticing enough, that the Gauls themselves came to want to be Romans. Throughout its history Gaul remained a monument to the success of Romanization.

The great similarity between the Roman Empire and America in regard to the powers reserved to local government lies in the pragmatism with which the systems were developed and the flexibility that made both so workable for so long. Rome's practical capacity for imposing new patterns on old traditions maintained the semblance of continuity and smoothed the transition from regional autonomy to the centralized Roman order.

The difference between the Roman and American experiences is, of course, greater than the similarities. That difference is federalism and the direction of the flow of power. Rome conquered and created its provinces. In America, the states created the Union. In Rome, power was always located at the center, with privileges conferred on the provinces and imperial administration flowing in one direction only: out from the center. In America, the Constitution, ratified by the states, created a federal system with rights and powers specifically delegated to the national government and others continuing to reside with the states. Privileges conferred can always be withdrawn. A constitution establishes mutuality.

The federal system in the United States was established not by the Tenth Amendment but by Article I of the Constitution. Sections 1 through 7 define the organization of Congress and the functions of each of its houses.

Section 8 details the positive powers of Congress, while Section 9 enumerates prohibitions. The tenth and final section of Article I lists actions that are prohibited to the states.

Some issues related to the Tenth Amendment, like those of the rest of the Bill of Rights, still have not been permanently settled. The greatest point of conflict has arisen in relation to the commerce clause of Article I, Section 8: "The Congress shall have Power. . . . To regulate Commerce with foreign Nations, and among the several States." The question of whether the federal government can also regulate commerce *within* and not just *among* states falls into an open space between Article I and the Tenth Amendment.

That space was the battleground for several cases related to the imposition of federal child labor and minimum wage laws on local municipalities and businesses that do not engage in interstate commerce. In 1918 in *Hammer v. Dagenhart*,[31] the Supreme Court struck down the Child Labor Law as "repugnant to the Constitution." It continued, "If Congress can thus regulate matters entrusted to local authority, all freedom of commerce will be at an end, the power of the States over local matters may be eliminated, and thus our system of government may be practically destroyed."[32]

In 1941 the Supreme Court in *United States v. Darby*[33] overruled *Hammer v. Dagenhart*. Here the Court held that the power of Congress over interstate commerce is complete in itself and may be exercised to the fullest. Both of those cases involved private employers, however, leaving unresolved the question of whether the federal can regulate the commercial activities of state and local governments.

In 1976 in *National League of Cities v. Usery*,[34] the Supreme Court struck down an act of Congress that extended a federal minimum wage law to most state employees, asserting that "there are attributes of sovereignty attaching to every state government which may not be impaired by Congress"[35] because the Tenth Amendment of the Constitution prohibits it. Only nine years later, however, the Court reversed itself in *Garcia v. San Antonio Metropolitan Transit Authority.*[36] Decisions in both *National League of Cities* and *Garcia* were reached by votes of five to four, illustrating how controversial the issues related to federalism continue to be.[37]

In 1957 Edward Dumbauld wrote that the Ninth and Tenth Amendments were dead letters in practice, not because conditions have changed but because of the "intrinsic nature" of the amendments themselves. He terms the Ninth Amendment a "simply technical proviso," which was not intended to add "anything of meaning" to the Constitution. "Similarly," he continues, "the Tenth Amendment really adds nothing to the rest of the Constitution," since it states only that powers not granted to the federal government are reserved but fails to clarify what powers have or have not been granted.[38]

Much has changed in the intervening years to alter such an assessment of the last two amendments of the Bill of Rights. The rights of citizens and the best mechanisms for power-sharing are two of the most crucial questions for any political system. By fashioning the Ninth and Tenth Amendments as they did, the framers left open a spacious plain that would allow for future expansions of civic consciousness, just as the amendments themselves stand as a measure of the evolution of issues first addressed in the classical world.

Conclusion

THE ideas and practices that formed the Bill of Rights are older than we thought. They are older than two hundred years. They are older even than eight hundred years. When traced to their earliest origins, they represent the yearnings of people over a period of two and a half millennia for better ways of living together and for civic arrangements that bring those hopes to reality.

For individuals to live together happily in communities requires a compromise between freedom and order. The Bill of Rights achieved this balance because of the two intellectual traditions that combined to give it birth: the natural law tradition, with its earliest origins among the Greeks, and the positive rule of law that is the gift of Rome.

It was a belief in natural law that undergirded the claims of the framers to the rights articulated in the first ten amendments. Although there was no theory of inherent individual rights in antiquity, that idea originated in the doctrine of natural law first articulated by the Greek philosophers, especially the Stoics, and then mediated through the political traditions of the Continent and England.

The framers were also committed to the rule of law as

the basis of civil society. The civic and legal institutions of Greece and Rome underlie almost all the provisions of the Bill of Rights. While the Roman contributions are greater in the matters of criminal and civil procedure, the Athenian genius endures in such practices as freedom of speech, freedom of assembly, and trial by jury.

The early political achievements of Athens and Rome reflect their recognition of basic problems of society and politics. The ancient Athenians were capable of innovation because they were more interested in equity (*epieikeia*) than in strict applications of law. Their tolerance for "legal uncertainty" contrasts with the *ius strictum* of the Romans, the preference for tying down all the details in "black letter law."

The American framers wanted it all: equity, freedom, and a written constitution in which to make those things secure. The Bill of Rights, stitched together out of a host of experiences, ideas, and beliefs, was the enduring piecework by which they established those values as the law of the land.

An understanding of the long heritage of the Bill of Rights helps us realize that in terms of its defining documents, the United States is founded on traditions stretching back to Greece and Rome rather than to Jerusalem. In our civic infrastructure we are a secular nation.

The Constitution is the glue that holds American society together. It is the only defining document that applies to everyone and to which, by virtue of citizenship, the assent of everyone is implied. It provides the foundation for what has been called "constitutional faith," that is, an attachment to the Constitution as the basis of political life for both individuals and the nation.[1] In an odd way, Homer's poetry provided a similar glue for the diverse communities of ancient Greece. Homer was the *biblos*, the secular "book," that provided a common frame of reference for diverse peoples and communities without requiring conformity.

In ancient Rome, where there was no separation between church and state, not to believe as the majority believed was seen as a political lapse or unpatriotic deviance. When Americans engage in making a religion out of nationalism, or nationalism out of religion, we are behaving more like Romans than the secular citizens that the Constitution establishes. In a liberal democracy, where freedom of thought is valued, attitudes toward any issue may vary widely with impunity. The Bill of Rights preserves the possibility that we do not all have to be the same to get along.

Knowing the longer story of which our own story is an episode engages us more actively as caretakers of its claims. An awareness of the long heritage behind the Bill of Rights enlivens us to the values it represents. These are important ideas with a long history, not lightly to be discarded even in times of great pressures, when the temptation to do so may be strong.

Understanding the political origins of civic identity in the ancient world may also lead to another kind of awareness. From a contemporary perspective, Athens and Rome placed too heavy an emphasis on the state as the definer of civic identity. Now, however, we may be in danger of the opposite emphasis, on the individual at the expense of the common good.[2] If excessive individualism has replaced the excessive corporatism of ancient societies, then an appreciation for the history of rights may be a salutary reminder that we are formed by our communities as well as by our natures. In that way the story of the Bill of Rights places us in the rich sphere of interplay between the private and the public good.

The framers brought to the new American nation all the traditions of governance to which they were heir. Combining the Athenian fearlessness of innovation with the political pragmatism of the Romans, they wrote into the Constitution their belief that the civic rights of human beings are so basic that they cannot be restricted by government. The Bill of Rights makes explicit the constitutional guarantees of liberal democracy. In part because of its long parentage, it has been both enduring and adaptable as a safeguard of free society.

Notes

INTRODUCTION

1. *Dialogues of Alfred North Whitehead, As Recorded by Lucien Price* (Boston: Little, Brown and Company, 1954), pp. 203, 161.
2. Plato, *Laws* 923a (tr. Taylor).
3. Aristotle, *Politics* 1337a28–29 (8.1.4) (tr. Barker).
4. A. P. d'Entrèves, *Natural Law: An Introduction to Legal Philosophy,* 2d ed. (London: Hutchinson, 1970), p. 18, proposes that there would have been no American or French Revolution, and no ideas of freedom or equality under the law, without the influence of natural law.

CHAPTER 1

1. William V. Harris, *Ancient Literacy* (Cambridge, Massachusetts, and London: Harvard University Press, 1989), p. 46.
2. Harris, *Ancient Literacy*, p. 328, estimates on the basis of the rules of ostracism that from the 480s on, probably only about 15 percent of male citizens or 5 percent of the total adult population, including women and slaves, were literate. Alfred Burns, "Athenian Literacy in the Fifth Century B.C.," *Journal of the History of Ideas* 42 (1981), p. 371, concludes that from the end of the sixth century B.C., the "vast majority" of Athenian citizens were literate.
3. Harris, *Ancient Literacy*, p. 47. The complete text of the inscription, with translation and an extended discussion, is given by Michael Gagarin, *Early Greek Law* (Berkeley: University of California Press, 1986), pp. 81–86.
4. Harris, *Ancient Literacy*, p. 51.
5. Gagarin, *Early Greek Law*, pp. 132–33.

6. Gagarin, *Early Greek Law*, p. 141. R. K. Sinclair, in *Democracy and Participation in Athens* (Cambridge: Cambridge University Press, 1988), acknowledges the importance of legislative sovereignty as the underlying assumption of Athenian democracy (pp. 1, 67–68), but locates the compelling cause of democratic government in the victories of the Athenians, virtually unaided, against the Persians at Marathon in 490 B.C. and Salamis in 479: "These remarkable military successes engendered in the Athenians in general a high confidence in their polis and in themselves, and also a recognition of the contribution of all Athenians to the security and safety of their polis" (p. 5).

7. Robert J. Bonner, *Lawyers and Litigants in Ancient Athens* (Chicago: University of Chicago Press, 1927), pp. v, 1, 135.

8. Roscoe Pound, *The Lawyer from Antiquity to Modern Times* (St. Paul: West Publishing, 1953), pp. 28–34.

9. Bonner, *Lawyers and Litigants*, p. 110.

10. Lionel Casson, "Imagine, if you will, . . ." *Smithsonian* 18 (October 1987), p. 122: "Imagine, if you will, a time without any lawyers at all; civilization flourished in Egypt and ancient Greece with little help from lawyering, but then came Rome and our troubles began."

11. Edward E. Cohen, *Ancient Athenian Maritime Courts* (Princeton: Princeton University Press, 1973), p. 3.

12. Eric A. Havelock, *The Greek Concept of Justice* (Cambridge, Massachusetts: Harvard University Press, 1978), pp. 13–14.

13. Heraclitus, fragment 220 in G. S. Kirk and J. E. Raven, *The Presocratic Philosophers* (Cambridge: Cambridge University Press, 1971), p. 199.

14. Kirk and Raven, *Presocratic Philosophers*, pp. 214–15.

15. See Martin Ostwald, *From Popular Sovereignty to the Sovereignty of Law: Law, Society, and Politics in Fifth-Century Athens* (Berkeley: University of California Press, 1986), pp. 260–273.

16. Aristotle, *Politics* 1294a7–9 (4.8.6).

17. Aristotle, *Nicomachaean Ethics* 1098a7–8, b2–4 (1.7.14).

18. John Locke, *Essays on the Law of Nature*, ed. Wolfgang von Leyden (Oxford: Clarendon Press, 1954), pp. 112–13. Locke's early notebooks show that he recommended Aristotle's *Nicomachaean Ethics* to his students. See Wolfgang von Leyden, *Aristotle on Equality and Justice: His Political Argument* (New York: St. Martin's Press, 1985), p. 35, n. 3.

19. Von Leyden, *Aristotle*, p. 87: "In my opinion, this fact provides firm evidence that Aristotle's doctrine, in addition to his analysis of the concept of conventional law, contains part of an authoritative formulation and one of the original sources of natural-law theory." Other scholars, however, deny that Aristotle was an early proponent of natural law. See D. N. Schroeder, "Aristotle on Law," *Polis* 4 (1981), pp. 17–31.

20. E.g., Aristotle, *Nicomachaean Ethics* 1144b4–6 (6.13) and 1151a18 (7.8).

21. Plutarch, *De Alexandri magni fortuna aut virtute* 329a–b.
22. A. A. Long, *Hellenistic Philosophy: Stoics, Epicureans, Sceptics* (London: Gerald Duckworth, 1974), pp. 144–45.
23. Long, *Hellenistic Philosophy*, p. 147.
24. Long, *Hellenistic Philosophy*, pp. 164–65.
25. Long, *Hellenistic Philosophy*, p. 165.
26. Cicero, *De natura deorum* 1.14.36.
27. Brad Inwood, *Ethics and Human Action in Early Stoicism* (Oxford: Clarendon Press, 1985), pp. 198–99.
28. Robert Drew Hicks, *Stoic and Epicurean* (New York: Charles Scribner's Sons, 1910), p. 82.
29. David E. Hahm, *The Origins of Stoic Cosmology* (Columbus: Ohio State University Press, 1977), p. 202. See entire ch. 7, pp. 200–215.
30. Inwood, *Ethics and Human Action*, p. 107.
31. I. G. Kidd, "Moral Actions and Rules in Stoic Ethics," in *The Stoics*, ed. John M. Rist (Berkeley: University of California Press, 1978), p. 248.
32. Long, *Hellenistic Philosophy*, p. 192.
33. Margaret Reesor, *The Nature of Man in Early Stoic Philosophy* (New York: St. Martin's Press, 1989), p. 8.
34. Benjamin Fletcher Wright, Jr., *American Interpretations of Natural Law: A Study in the History of Political Thought* (Cambridge, Massachusetts: Harvard University Press, 1931), pp. 4–5.
35. Joseph Declareuil, *Rome the Law-Giver* (London: Kegan Paul, Trench, Trubner; New York: Alfred A. Knopf, 1927), p. 3.
36. Barry Nicholas, *An Introduction to Roman Law* (Oxford: Clarendon Press, 1962), p. 1.
37. Nicholas, *An Introduction to Roman Law*, pp. 1–2.
38. *Digest* CXL, 84–101. Given the nature of the compilation of the *Digest*, the absence of the phrase from earlier texts does not mean that it had not been used previously.
39. Declareuil, *Rome the Law-Giver*, pp. 28–29.
40. Declareuil, *Rome the Law-Giver*, p. 4. This "astonishing second life of Roman law," as Nicholas calls it, provided Europe with a common stock of legal thought and many common legal rules. There are therefore to this day "two great families of law" of European origin: the common law of England, predominant in the English-speaking world, and Roman or civil law, embracing almost all the countries of Europe and the state of Louisiana. See Nicholas, *Introduction to Roman Law*, p. 2.
41. Robert Mark Wenley, *Stoicism and Its Influence* (New York: Longmans, Green, 1927), p. 130.
42. Gerard Watson, "The Natural Law and Stoicism," in *Problems in Stoicism*, ed. A. A. Long (London: Athlone Press, 1971), p. 225.
43. Edward Gibbon, *The Decline and Fall of the Roman Empire*, ch. 44, first paragraph.
44. D'Entrèves, *Natural Law*, p. 32.

45. Quirinus Breen, *Christianity and Humanism: Studies in the History of Ideas*, ed. Nelson Peter Ross (Grand Rapids: William B. Eerdmans Publishing, 1968), p. 211.

46. D'Entrèves, *Natural Law*, p. 33.

47. D'Entrèves, *Natural Law*, p. 33.

48. Robert N. Wilkin, *Eternal Lawyer, A Legal Biography of Cicero* (New York: Macmillan, 1947), p. 227.

49. D. H. Van Zyl, *Cicero's Legal Philosophy* (Roodepoort: Digma Publications, 1986), p. 21.

50. Long, *Hellenistic Philosophy*, p. 231. Also Watson, "Natural Law and Stoicism," p. 228.

51. Cicero, *De re publica* 3.22.33 (tr. Keyes).

52. Hicks, *Stoic and Epicurean*, p. 338.

53. Van Zyl, *Cicero's Legal Philosophy*, p. 99.

54. Cicero, *De legibus* 1.6.18: *Lex est ratio summa insita in natura . . . eadem ratio cum est in hominis mente confirmata et confecta, lex est.*

55. Chaim Wirszubski, *Libertas as a Political Idea at Rome during the Late Republic and Early Principate* (Cambridge: Cambridge University Press, 1950), p. 85.

56. Paul MacKendrick (with the collaboration of Karen Lee Singh), *The Philosophical Books of Cicero* (New York: St. Martin's Press, 1989), p. 63.

57. Henry Sumner Maine, *Dissertations on Early Law and Custom* (New York: H. Holt and Company, 1886), p. 365.

58. Herbert Felix Jolowicz, *Roman Foundations of Modern Law* (Oxford: Clarendon Press, 1957), pp. 66–67.

59. Sophocles, *Antigone* 450–457.

60. D'Entrèves, *Natural Law*, p. 34.

61. Cicero, *De legibus* 1.10.29; 12.33 (tr. Keyes).

62. Occasionally slavery is defined as an institution of the *ius gentium* contrary to Nature and resulting from war, e.g. *Institutes* 1.2.2: "Slavery is contrary to natural law, because by nature all men are born free at the beginning": *Servitutes, quae sunt iuri naturali contrariae (iure enim naturali ab initio omnes homines liberi nascebantur).*

63. Aristotle, *Nicomachaean Ethics* 1134b18–19 (5.7.1).

64. Herbert Felix Jolowicz, *Historical Introduction to the Study of Roman Law* (Cambridge: University Press, 1932), p. 105.

65. Jolowicz, *Roman Foundations of Modern Law*, p. 113.

66. *Digest* 25.4.1.1; 35.2.9.1. But n.b. 50.16.153. See also Jolowicz, *Roman Foundations of Modern Law*, p. 109.

67. Declareuil, *Rome the Law-Giver*, p. 190.

68. Nicholas, *Introduction to Roman Law*, p. 98.

69. Geoffrey Samuel, "Epistemology, Propaganda, and Roman Law: Some Reflections on the History of Subjective Right," *The Journal of Legal History* 10 (September 1989), p. 164.

70. Samuel, "Epistemology, Propaganda, and Roman Law," p. 164.

71. Samuel, "Epistemology, Propaganda, and Roman Law," pp. 172–74.

72. Watson, "Natural Law and Stoicism," pp. 231, 232.

CHAPTER 2

1. D'Entrèves, *Natural Law*, p. 42.
2. Marcia L. Colish, *The Stoic Tradition from Antiquity to the Early Middle Ages*, vol. 2 (Leiden: E. J. Brill, 1985), p. 302.
3. Wenley, *Stoicism and Its Influence*, pp. 158–59.
4. James Lorimer, *The Institutes of Law, a Treatise of the Principles of Jurisprudence As Determined by Nature* (Edinburgh: T. & T. Clark, 1872), pp. 150, 151.
5. At least in the view of Gerard Verbeke, *The Presence of Stoicism in Medieval Thought* (Washington: Catholic University of America Press, 1983), p. 3. There is some disagreement about the status of women in Stoic thought. Sarah Pomeroy emphasizes the Stoic reinforcement of women's traditional roles; see *Goddesses, Whores, Wives, and Slaves: Women in Classical Antiquity* (New York: Schocken Books, 1975), pp. 131–32, 230.
6. See Harald Hagendahl, *Augustine and the Latin Classics* (Stockholm: Almqvist & Wiksell, 1967), pp. 245–49.
7. *Quid Athenae Hierosolymis?* Tertullian, *De praescriptione haereticorum* 7.
8. Ambrose, *De fuga saeculi* 3.15; *Corpus scriptorum ecclesiasticorum Latinorum* 32.2.
9. Colish, *Stoic Tradition*, vol. 2, pp. 50, 51.
10. Verbeke, *Presence of Stoicism*, p. 44.
11. Verbeke, *Presence of Stoicism*, pp. 55–56.
12. Seneca, *De ira* 3.36.
13. Wenley, *Stoicism and Its Influence*, p. 150.
14. Ernst Troeltsch, *The Social Teaching of the Christian Church*, tr. O. Wyon, 2 vols. (London: Allen & Unwin, 1931; reprint 1950). After World War I, Troeltsch came to believe that natural law, both as a law common to humanity and as an assertion of the fundamental human rights, was the distinguishing mark of political thought in Western Europe. He proposed that the German world broke away from that belief in the age of romanticism, perhaps earlier, with the consequence that force became glorified over reason and the state over the individual as the embodiment of moral life. See "The Ideas of Natural Law and Humanity in Western Politics," 1922 (Appendix 1 in Otto Friedrich von Gierke, *Natural Law and the Theory of Society, 1500, with a Lecture on the Ideas of Natural Law and Humanity by Ernst Troeltsch*, translated with an introduction by Ernest Barker (Cambridge: Cambridge University Press, 1934).
15. Watson, "Natural Law and Stoicism," p. 235.

16. D'Entrèves, *Natural Law*, pp. 38–39.

17. The *Decretum Gratiani* is contained in the *Corpus iuris canonici*, which is the name given by the Council of Basel in 1441. Gratian was an Italian monk working at Bologna. The *Decretum* is also called the *Concordia discordantium canonum*, and it recalls the *Digest* of Justinian, as the rest of the collection recalls the *Code*.

18. Isidore, *Decretum Gratiani*, I pars, dist. I, proem.

19. D'Entrèves, *Natural Law*, p. 40.

20. Verbeke, *Presence of Stoicism*, p. 5.

21. Thomas Aquinas, *Summa theologica* 1 2ae, 91, 1 and 2.

22. Thomas Aquinas, *Summa theologica* 1a 2ae, 95, 2.

23. Thomas Aquinas, *Summa theologica* 1a 2a, 94, 2.

24. D. J. O'Connor, *Aquinas and Natural Law* (London: Macmillan, 1967), p. 84.

25. Walter Ullmann, *Law and Politics in the Middle Ages: An Introduction to the Sources of Medieval Political Ideals* (Ithaca: Cornell University Press, 1975), p. 272.

26. D'Entrèves, *Natural Law*, p. 45.

27. D'Entrèves, *Natural Law*, p. 46.

28. D'Entrèves, *Natural Law*, p. 48.

29. Ullmann, *Law and Politics*, pp. 30–32.

30. Walter Ullmann, *The Individual and Society in the Middle Ages* (Baltimore: Johns Hopkins Press, 1966), p. 5.

31. Ullmann, *Individual and Society*, p. 9.

32. Platonism also flourished in the Middle Ages. See Endre von Ivanka, *Plato Christianus: Übernahme und Umgestaltung des Platonismus durch die Väter* (Einsiedeln: Johannes Verlag, 1964); also Raymond Klibansky, *The Continuity of the Platonic Tradition during the Middle Ages* (London: Warburg Institute, 1950).

33. Ullmann, *Law and Politics*, pp. 34–37. Constantine's decree is preserved in Lactantius, *De mortibus persecutorum*, c. 48, in *Corpus scriptorum ecclesiasticorum Latinorum* 27, 2, 228f.

34. Ullmann, *Law and Politics*, p. 32.

35. All biblical references are to the Revised Standard Version.

36. Ullmann, *Individual and Society*, p. 19.

37. John Chrysostom, *In epistolam ad Romanos* homil. 23 (*Patr. Graeca* lx. 615).

38. Ullmann, *Law and Politics*, p. 33.

39. Augustine, *The City of God* 5.17 (tr. Walsh, Zema, Monahan, and Honan).

40. Brian Tierney, *The Crisis of Church and State 1050–1300* (Englewood Cliffs, New Jersey: Prentice-Hall, 1964), p. 10.

41. Ullmann, *Law and Politics*, p. 42.

42. Hans Julius Wolff, *Roman Law: An Historical Introduction* (Norman: University of Oklahoma Press, 1951), p. 192.

43. Paul Vinogradoff, *Roman Law in Medieval Europe* (Oxford: Clarendon Press, 1929), p. 43.

44. A medical school had been started at Salerno in the tenth century.

45. Ullmann, *Law and Politics*, p. 77.
46. Vinogradoff, *Roman Law in Medieval Europe*, pp. 56–57.
47. Ullmann, *Law and Politics*, pp. 47, 49–50.
48. Ullmann, *Law and Politics*, p. 41.
49. One of the continuing problems between the East and West was that these letters did not have binding force at Constantinople, which did not acknowledge the legal sovereignty of the papacy. See Ullmann, *Law and Politics*, p. 122.
50. Ullmann, *Individual and Society*, p. 38.
51. Gregory I, *Moralia* xxi. 15.22 (*Patrologia Latina* lxxvi 203): *Omnes namque homines natura aequales . . . omnes homines natura aequales genuit, sed variante meritorum ordine, alios aliis dispensatio occulta postponit.*
52. Ullmann, *Individual and Society*, p. 14.
53. Peter N. Riesenberg, *Inalienability of Sovereignty in Medieval Political Thought* (New York: Columbia University Press, 1956), p. 3.
54. Riesenberg, *Inalienability of Sovereignty*, p. 47.
55. Ullmann, *Law and Politics*, p. 78.
56. Wenley, *Stoicism and Its Influence*, p. 139.

CHAPTER 3

1. Catullus, *carmen* 11, 11–12.
2. Ullmann, *Individual and Society*, pp. 53–62.
3. Sidney Painter was one of the first to point out the contributions of feudalism to individual liberty, which he tied to the practicality of feudal arrangements. See *Feudalism and Liberty*, ed. Fred A. Cazel, Jr. (Baltimore: Johns Hopkins Press, 1961), p. 253.
4. Ullmann, *Individual and Society*, p. 66.
5. Ullmann, *Individual and Society*, p. 68.
6. Ullmann, *Law and Politics*, pp. 299–300.
7. Ullmann, *Individual and Society*, p. 97.
8. Anthony Babington, *The Rule of Law in Britain from the Roman Occupation to the Present Day* (Chichester and London: Barry Rose Publishers, 1978), pp. 59–61.
9. Wolff, *Roman Law*, p. 198.
10. Wilkin, *Eternal Lawyer*, pp. 228–29.
11. Vinogradoff, *Roman Law in Medieval Europe*, p. 97.
12. M. M. Knappen, *Constitutional and Legal History of England* (Hamden, Connecticut: Archon Books, 1964), p. 202.
13. Wolff, *Roman Law*, p. 197.
14. Vinogradoff, *Roman Law in Medieval Europe*, p. 101.
15. Vinogradoff, *Roman Law in Medieval Europe*, pp. 35–36.
16. *Guardian*, June 1, 1956, on the 750th anniversary of Magna Carta.
17. *Nullus miles . . . sine certa et convicta culpa suum beneficium perdat nisi secundum constitucionem antecessorum nostrorum et*

iudicium parium suorum. (*Monumenta Germaniae Historiae, Const.* 1, 90.)

18. *Unusquisque per pares suos judicandus est, et eiusdem provinciae. Leges Henrici Primi,* cap. 31.7; *Gesetze,* I, 564.

19. William F. Swindler, *Magna Carta: Legend and Legacy* (Indianapolis: Bobbs-Merrill, 1965), pp. 96–97.

20. Ullmann, *Individual and Society,* p. 75.

21. Ullmann, *Individual and Society,* p. 72.

22. J. C. Holt, *Magna Carta* (Cambridge: Cambridge University Press, 1965), p. 68.

23. See J. W. Gough, *Fundamental Law in English Constitutional History* (Oxford: Clarendon Press, 1955), pp. 30–31, 44–45.

24. Swindler, *Magna Carta,* pp. 226–27.

25. The other thirty-three were repealed between 1828 and 1969 as English law became more simplified. Remaining in force are Clauses 1, 9, 29, and part of 37. Clause 1 establishes freedom for the English Church from interference by the monarchy in matters of ecclesiastical governance and control of church property. Clause 9 limits the Crown's remedies in the satisfaction of debts. Clause 29 protects due process. The first part of Clause 37, having to do with the feudal practice of *escuage* or "shield money," became obsolete with the abolition of feudal tenures in 1660 and was formally abolished in 1863. The remainder of Clause 37 remains in force as a general policy statement and summary of the guarantees of the foregoing clauses. It reads: "[Moreover,] AND all these customs and liberties aforesaid, which we have granted to be held in this our realm, as much as appertaineth to us and our heirs, we shall observe; and all men of this our realm, as well spiritual as temporal, as much as in them is, shall observe the same against all persons, in like wise." In 1225, this clause meant only that, just as the king granted these liberties to his tenants, they were in turn to grant them to their subtenants. With the abolition of the tenurial system, the benefits of Magna Carta gradually came to be interpreted as applying to all persons. See Swindler, *Magna Carta,* p. 346.

26. Henry Parker, *Animadversions Animadverted* (1642), p. 3.

27. Chatham, speech during the debate on the state of the nation (1770), in William Cobbett, *The Parliamentary History of England from the Earliest Period to the Year 1803,* vol. 16 (London: T. C. Hansard, etc., 1806–1820), p. 148.

28. Cobbett, *Parliamentary History,* vol. 16, p. 177.

29. James Mackintosh, *Vindiciae Gallicae: Defence of the French Revolution and its English Admirers* (Dublin: Printed by W. W. Corbet for R. Cross, et al., 1791), pp. 305–6.

30. Anne Pallister, *Magna Carta: The Heritage of Liberty* (Oxford: Clarendon Press, 1971), p. 77.

31. Some observers argue that Burke maintained a strong belief in natural law, even though he scorned a theory of natural rights. See for

example Peter J. Stanlis, *Edmund Burke and the Natural Law* (Ann Arbor: University of Michigan Press, 1965), especially pp. 14–28.

32. Paul E. Sigmund, *Natural Law in Political Thought* (Cambridge, Massachusetts: Winthrop Publishers, 1971), p. 56.

33. Michel Villey, "La genèse du droit subjectif chez Guillaume d'Occam," *Archives de philosophie du droit* 9 (1964), pp. 97–127. See also Brian Tierney, "Villey, Ockham and the Origin of Individual Rights," in John Witte, Jr., and Frank S. Alexander, eds., *The Weightier Matters of the Law: Essays on Law and Religion* (Atlanta: Scholars Press, 1988), pp. 1–31.

34. Ockham, however, does not mention the term "natural law" in his ethical or theological writings. See Kilian McDonnell, "Does William of Ockham Have a Theory of Natural Law?," *Franciscan Studies* 34 (1974), pp. 383–92.

35. This is the view of Sigmund, *Natural Law in Political Thought*, p. 56.

36. Richard Tuck, *Natural Rights Theories: Their Origin and Development* (Cambridge: Cambridge University Press, 1979), pp. 22–24.

37. Ullmann, *Law and Politics*, pp. 293–94.

CHAPTER 4

1. This discussion largely follows Ullmann, *Individual and Society*, pp. 104–45.

2. Otto of Freising, in *Monumenta Germaniae historiae, scriptores rerum Germanicarum* [1912] i. 47, 65: *Nos non tragediam, sed iocundam scribere proposuimus hystoriam.*

3. Ullmann, *Law and Politics*, p. 270.

4. See Edward Rosen, "The Invention of Eye Glasses," *Journal of the History of Medicine and Allied Sciences* 11 (1956), pp. 12–46, 183–218.

5. Ullmann, *Individual and Society*, p. 121.

6. Dante, *De Monarchia* 1.12.

7. Ullmann, *Individual and Society*, p. 134.

8. Walter Ullmann, *The Medieval Idea of Law* (New York: Barnes and Noble; London: Methuen, 1946; reprint 1969), p. 47.

9. Ullmann, *Medieval Idea of Law*, p. 184.

10. Ernst Cassirer, *The Individual and the Cosmos in Renaissance Philosophy*, tr. Mario Domandi (New York: Harper and Row, 1963), p. 81.

11. Cassirer, *Individual and the Cosmos,*, p. 140.

12. Ullmann, *Law and Politics*, p. 269.

13. Ullmann, *Law and Politics*, p. 271.

14. Cassirer, *Individual and the Cosmos*, p. 191, describes the dilemma this way: "The man of the Renaissance confronts the divinity

and the infinite universe as both 'captor' and 'captive'. The philosophy of the Renaissance never resolved the dialectical antinomy that is enclosed in this double relationship."

15. See Richard Tuck, "The Recovery and Repudiation of Grotius," ch. 8 in *Natural Rights Theories*, pp. 156–73.

16. Hugo Grotius, *Laws of War and Peace* I, i, x.

17. Grotius, *Laws of War and Peace* I, i.

18. Sigmund, *Natural Law in Political Thought*, p. 62.

19. H. A. Rommen, *The Natural Law: A Study in Legal and Social History and Philosophy*, tr. Thomas R. Hanley (St. Louis and London: B. Herder, 1947), p. 74.

20. D'Entrèves, *Natural Law*, pp. 53–55.

21. Grotius, *Laws of War and Peace*, Prolegomena, 58. Jean Domat, in his preface to *The Civil Law in its Natural Order: Together with the Public Law* (1722), also cites the analogy of geometry as a way to learn about self-evident truths.

22. Tuck, *Natural Rights Theories*, pp. 161–62.

23. Rommen, *Natural Law*, p. 82.

24. E.g., D'Entrèves, *Natural Law*, p. 58.

25. See W. K. C. Guthrie, *The Sophists* (Cambridge: Cambridge University Press, 1971), ch. 5, "The Social Compact," pp. 135–47.

26. D'Entrèves, *Natural Law*, p. 59.

27. Peter Stein, *The Character and Influence of the Roman Civil Law: Historical Essays* (London and Ronceverte: Hambledon Press, 1988), p. 62.

28. D'Entrèves, *Natural Law*, p. 58.

29. Sigmund, *Natural Law in Political Thought*, p. ix.

30. Sigmund, *Natural Law in Political Thought*, p. 89.

31. Rommen, *Natural Law*, p. 86.

32. Andrzej Rapaczynski, *Nature and Politics: Liberalism in the Philosophies of Hobbes, Locke, and Rousseau* (Ithaca and London: Cornell University Press, 1987), p. 6.

33. Rapaczynski, *Nature and Politics*, pp. 6–7.

34. Rapaczynski, *Nature and Politics*, p. 8.

35. Philip Abrams, ed., *John Locke: Two Tracts on Government* (Cambridge: Cambridge University Press, 1967), p. 77.

36. Rapaczynski, *Nature and Politics*, p. 124.

37. George W. Carey, "The Separation of Powers," in George J. Graham, Jr., and Scarlett G. Graham, eds., *Founding Principles of American Government* (Chatham, New Jersey: Chatham House Publishers, 1977, 1984), p. 109.

38. Thomas Erskine, *The Trial of Thomas Hardy for High Treason ... Taken Down in Shorthand*, vol. 3, (London, 1794), p. 243.

39. Early in his career Locke wrote that people take on ideas as they do spouses and, left to their own devices, probably find divorce of the latter easier than of the former: "Truth is seldom allowed a fair hearing, and the generality of men conducted either by change or advantage take to themselves their opinions as they do their wives, which when

they have once espoused them think themselves concerned to maintain, though for no other reason but because they are theirs, being as tender of the credit of one as of the other, and if 'twere left to their own choice, 'tis not improbable that this would be the more difficult divorce." Abrams, *John Locke*, p. 117.

40. Locke, *An Essay Concerning Human Understanding*, vol. 1, ch. 3, section 13.

41. Sigmund, *Natural Law in Political Thought*, p. 81.

42. James Tully, *A Discourse on Property: John Locke and His Adversaries* (Cambridge: Cambridge University Press, 1980), pp. 53, 54.

43. Quentin Skinner, *The Foundations of Modern Political Thought*, vol. 1 (Cambridge: Cambridge University Press, 1978), p. xiv.

44. Skinner, *Foundations of Modern Political Thought*, vol. 2, p. 122.

45. Locke, *Two Treatises of Government, The Second Treatise*, sections 19 and 4.

46. Locke, *Two Treatises of Government, The Second Treatise*, section 190.

47. Rapaczynski, *Nature and Politics*, p. 14.

48. Rapaczynski, *Nature and Politics*, pp. 120, 121.

49. C. B. Macpherson, *The Political Theory of Possessive Individualism* (Oxford: Clarendon Press, 1962) takes the opposite view, that Locke wrote not to justify private ownership as a means of assuring individual rights but to justify a transition to the unrestrained acquisitiveness of a new capitalism. From the other side of the political spectrum, Leo Strauss in *Natural Right and History* (Chicago: University of Chicago Press, 1953) takes a similar position, arguing that Locke was really a hidden Hobbesian. Rapaczynski counters these arguments persuasively in *Nature and Politics*, ch. 4, "Locke on Property," pp. 177–217.

50. Rommen, *Natural Law*, p. 233.

51. Sigmund, *Natural Law in Political Thought*, p. 86.

52. Skinner, *Foundations of Modern Political Thought*, vol. 2, p. 153, points out that the Levellers and the Anabaptists assumed that the rights of property holders could be abrogated without any affront to natural justice. Locke's way out of this dilemma was to take the interpretation of the jurists rather than that of the theologians, arguing directly that the right to hold property is a law of nature, not a privilege granted by positive law.

53. Locke himself was aware of this. In a letter to Rev. Richard King of August 25, 1703, he compares his *Two Treatises* with Aristotle's *Politics*.

54. Rapaczynski, *Nature and Politics*, p. 117.

55. Tuck, *Natural Rights Theory*, p. 15.

56. Tully, *Discourse on Property*, p. 176.

57. John Locke, *The Educational Writings*, ed. James Axtell (Cambridge: Cambridge University Press, 1968), pp. 213–15.

58. Rapaczynski, *Nature and Politics*, p. 279.

59. Rommen, *Natural Law*, p. 89.

60. Von Gierke, *Natural Law and the Theory of Society*, p. 113.

61. Tuck, *Natural Rights Theories*, pp. 175, 177.

62. Macpherson, *Political Theory of Possessive Individualism*, p. 262 passim.

63. John Dunn, *The Political Thought of John Locke* (Cambridge: Cambridge University Press, 1969; reprint, 1975), p. xi.

64. Dunn, *Political Thought of John Locke*, p. 263. Dunn draws a sober conclusion on p. 267: "We have, it seems, come to accept in the broadest of terms the politics of Locke but, while doing so, we have firmly discarded the reasons which alone made them acceptable even to Locke. It is hard to believe that this combination can be quite what we need today."

65. Skinner, *Foundations of Modern Political Thought*, vol. 2, p. 174.

66. Troeltsch, "Ideas of Natural Law and Humanity," p. 208.

67. James Gordon Clapp, "John Locke," *Encyclopedia of Philosophy*, ed. P. Edwards, vol. 4 (New York: Macmillan, 1967), p. 502.

68. Abrams, *John Locke*, p. 78.

69. See the discussion of Babington, *Rule of Law in Britain*, pp. 157–58.

70. For a complete text and notes, see E. S. Creasy, *The Rise and Progress of the English Constitution* (London: Richard Bentley and Son, 1892), pp. 317–26.

71. E.g., Michel Villey, *La formation de la pensée juridique moderne* (Paris: Montchrestien, 1968). See also Tuck, *Natural Rights Theories*, pp. 7–8, 13: "Consequently, although linguistic evidence is necessary, it is never going to be sufficient to establish that the classical Romans possessed the concept of a right; and the evidence of their theory suggests that they did not."

72. Thomas Hobbes, *Leviathan* (London and Toronto: J. M. Dent & Sons; New York: E. P. Dutton, 1914; reprint, 1934), part 1, ch. 14, pp. 66–67.

73. Wolff, *Roman Law*, pp. 214–15.

74. Wolff, *Roman Law*, p. 215.

75. Christian Wolff, *Ius naturae methodo scientifica pertractatum* (1741) I, Prol. 3.

76. Wolfgang Kunkel, *An Introduction to Roman Legal and Constitutional History*, tr. J. M. Kelly, 2d ed. (Oxford: Clarendon Press, 1973), p. 189. For a critical examination of the role of Locke in the thought of the framers, see John Dunn, "The Politics of Locke in England and America in the Eighteenth century," in John W. Yolton, ed., *John Locke: Problems and Perspectives* (Cambridge: Cambridge University Press, 1969), pp. 45–80, and Oscar Handlin, "Learned Books and Revolutionary Action, 1776," *Harvard Library Bulletin* 34 (1986), pp. 362–79.

CHAPTER 5

1. Bernard Schwartz, *The Great Rights of Mankind: A History of the American Bill of Rights* (New York: Oxford University Press, 1977), p. x.

2. Julian P. Boyd et al., eds., *The Papers of Thomas Jefferson*, vol. 1 (Princeton: Princeton University Press, 1950), p. 292.

3. Schwartz, *Great Rights of Mankind*, p. 70.

4. Brent Tarter, "Virginians and the Bill of Rights," in Jon Kukla, ed., *The Bill of Rights: A Lively Heritage* (Richmond: Virginia State Library and Archives, 1987), p. 7.

5. Robert Allen Rutland, *The Ordeal of the Constitution* (Boston: Northeastern University Press, 1983; Norman: University of Oklahoma Press, 1966), pp. 33–34.

6. Wright, *American Interpretations of Natural Law*, pp. 124–25.

7. Max Farrand, ed., *Records of the Federal Convention of 1787*, rev. ed., vol. 2 (New Haven: Yale University Press, 1966), pp. 637–40.

8. Robert Allen Rutland, *The Birth of the Bill of Rights* (Chapel Hill: University of North Carolina Press, 1955), p. 119.

9. *The Papers of Thomas Jefferson*, vol. 12, pp. 440, 558.

10. Gaillard Hunt, ed., *The Writings of James Madison*, vol. 5 (New York: G. P. Putnam's Sons, 1900–1910), pp. 389–90.

11. Harold C. Syrett, ed., *The Papers of Alexander Hamilton*, vol. 4 (New York: Columbia University Press, 1962), p. 35.

12. Schwartz, *Great Rights of Mankind*, p. 202.

13. *Barron v. Mayor & City Council*, 32 U.S. (7 Pet.) 243 (1833). See ch. 9, n. 2, for discussion.

14. Irving Brant, *James Madison: Father of the Constitution* (Indianapolis: Bobbs-Merrill, 1950), p. 272.

15. D'Entrèves, *Natural Law*, p. 62.

16. Paul Leicester Ford, ed., *Pamphlets on the Constitution of the United States* (New York: Da Capo Press, 1968; originally published in Brooklyn, 1888), p. 13.

17. Ford, *Pamphlets on the Constitution*, p. 6.

18. Wright, *American Interpretations of Natural Law*, p. 327 passim.

19. *Republic Steel Corp. v. Maddox*, 379 U.S. 650, 669 (1965), J. Black, dissenting.

20. *Adamson v. California*, 332 U.S. 46, 69, 89, 90 (1947), J. Black, dissenting. For further discussion of this issue, see Gerald T. Dunne, *Hugo Black and the Judicial Revolution* (New York: Simon and Shuster, 1977), pp. 182–83, 258–59.

21. Learned Hand, *The Bill of Rights: the Oliver Wendell Holmes Lectures, 1958* (Cambridge, Massachusetts: Harvard University Press, 1958), pp. 2–3.

22. Schwartz, *Great Rights of Mankind*, p. 197.

23. A. E. Dick Howard, *The Road from Runnymede: Magna Carta*

and Constitutionalism in America (Charlottesville: University Press of Virginia, 1968), p. 280.

24. See Donald S. Lutz, *The Origins of American Constitutionalism* (Baton Rouge: Louisiana State University Press, 1988), p. 62.

25. Lutz, *Origins of American Constitutionalism*, p. 9. See also Charles H. McIlwain, *Constitutionalism Ancient and Modern* (Ithaca: Cornell University Press, 1947; reprinted 1958), especially ch. 3, "The Constitutionalism of Rome and Its Influence," pp. 41–66. McIlwain writes: "The oftener I survey the whole history of constitutionalism the more I am impressed with the significance and importance of the republican constitution of Rome in that development" (p. 41).

CHAPTER 6

1. Thomas Jefferson to Edward Carrington (January 16, 1787), in Merrill D. Peterson, ed., *The Portable Thomas Jefferson* (New York: Viking Press, 1975), p. 414.

2. Martin Ostwald, *From Popular Sovereignty to the Sovereignty of Law*, p. 97.

3. J. H. W. G. Liebeschuetz, *Continuity and Change in Roman Religion* (Oxford: Clarendon Press, 1979), p. 3.

4. Cicero, *De natura deorum* 3.36.

5. R. M. Ogilvie, *The Romans and Their Gods* (London, 1969), p. 17.

6. Simeon L. Guterman, *Religious Toleration and Persecution in Ancient Rome* (London: Aiglon Press, 1951), pp. 159–60.

7. Guterman, *Religious Toleration*, pp. 27–28.

8. Dio Cassius 47.15.4.

9. Dio Cassius 53.2.4; 54.6.6.

10. On the divinization of the emperor, see Lily Ross Taylor, *The Divinity of the Roman Emperor* (Middletown, Connecticut: American Philological Association, 1931). See also J. Rufus Fears, *Princeps a Diis Electus: The Divine Election of the Emperor As a Political Concept at Rome* (Rome: American Academy, 1977), and S. R. F. Price, *Rituals and Power: The Roman Imperial Cult in Asia Minor* (Cambridge and New York: Cambridge University Press, 1984).

11. *Sylloge inscriptionum Graecarum* 3.760. See also Taylor, *Divinity of the Roman Emperor*, pp. 267ff. for other cities.

12. Arnaldo Momigliano, *On Pagans, Jews, and Christians* (Middletown, Connecticut: Wesleyan University Press, 1987), p. 88.

13. Augustus, *Res gestae* 20; see also Livy 4.20.7.

14. Sir Ronald Syme, *The Roman Revolution* (Oxford: Oxford University Press, 1960), p. 448.

15. Cicero, *Pro Flacco* 66.

16. For persecution of the Christians, see G. E. M. de Ste Croix, "Why Were the Early Christians Persecuted?" in M. I. Finley, ed., *Studies in Ancient Society: Past and Present Series* (London:

Routledge and Kegan Paul, 1974), pp. 210–49, and response by A. N. Sherwin-White following.

17. Edward Gibbon, *The Decline and Fall of the Roman Empire* 2.16.80.

18. Robin Lane Fox, *Pagans and Christians* (San Francisco: Harper and Row, 1986), pp. 428–30.

19. E. Mary Smallwood, *The Jews under Roman Rule* (Leiden: Brill, 1976), p. 540.

20. Cicero, *Pro Flacco* 67.

21. Cicero, *Pro Flacco* 69 (tr. Lord).

22. Smallwood, *Jews under Roman Rule*, p. 539.

23. Guterman, *Religious Toleration*, p. 92.

24. A. N. Sherwin-White, *The Roman Citizenship*, 2d ed. (Oxford: Clarendon Press, 1973), p. 245.

25. Sherwin-White, *Roman Citizenship*, p. 280.

26. Guterman, *Religious Toleration*, p. 25.

27. Guterman, *Religious Toleration*, p. 76.

28. De Ste Croix, "Why Were the Early Christians Persecuted?," p. 240.

29. Smallwood, *Jews under Roman Rule*, p. 543.

30. Tertullian, *Apologeticus* 39.

31. Liebeschuetz, *Continuity and Change*, pp. 305–6.

32. Tertullian, *Apologeticus* 21, 1.

33. E.g., Constantinus, *Codex Theodosianus* 16.8.2 (a. 330), 3 (a. 321), 4 (a. 331 *vel* 330).

34. Smallwood, *Jews under Roman Rule*, p. 545.

35. Brian Vickers, *In Defence of Rhetoric* (Oxford: Clarendon Press, 1988), p. 5.

36. Vickers, *In Defence of Rhetoric*, p. 7.

37. Vickers, *In Defence of Rhetoric*, p. 124.

38. G. T. Griffith, "Isegoria in the Assembly at Athens," in *Ancient Society and Institutions* (*Studies Presented to Victor Ehrenberg*) (New York: Barnes and Noble, 1967), p. 115.

39. Ostwald, *From Popular Sovereignty*, p. 203.

40. Griffith, "Isegoria," pp. 125, 131.

41. A. G. Woodhead, "*Isegoria* and the Council of 500," *Historia* 16 (1967), p. 140. Woodhead also says that the ordinary Athenian people came to see *isegoria* as "an inherent right."

42. J. D. Lewis, "Isegoria at Athens: When Did It Begin?" *Historia* 20 (1971), p. 139.

43. George Grote, *A History of Greece*, 2d ed., vol. 2 (London: John Murray, 1888), p. 19.

44. Herodotus 5.78.

45. Thucydides 2.40.2 (tr. Warner).

46. Thucydides 2.60.6.

47. Demosthenes 3.11–12; 6.3.

48. Demosthenes 20.106.

49. Demosthenes 9.3.

50. Thomas R. Fitzgerald, "Limitations on Freedom of Speech in the Athenian Assembly" (Ph. D. diss., University of Chicago, 1957), pp. 189–91.
51. J. A. O. Larsen, "The Judgment of Antiquity on Democracy," *Classical Philology* 49 (1954), p. 2.
52. Fitzgerald, "Limitations on Freedom of Speech."
53. Aeschines 1.19. See also discussion of K. J. Dover, *Greek Homosexuality* (London: Duckworth, 1978), pp. 33–34.
54. Aeschines 1.30.
55. Antiphanes in Athenaeus, *Deipnosophistae* 10.451a.
56. Aristotle, *The Athenian Constitution* 25.2–4.
57. Thucydides 8.65.2.
58. Thucydides 8.66 (tr. Warner).
59. Thucydides comments on the loquacity of the Athenians at 3.38.2–7 and 3.40.3.
60. Mogens Herman Hansen, *The Athenian Assembly in the Age of Demosthenes* (Oxford: Basil Blackwell, 1987), p. 171, n. 584, questions the authenticity of the law inserted in Aeschines 1.35 prohibiting the same speaker from speaking twice on a measure, observing also that Euryptolemos was not prevented from speaking twice during the debate after the battle of Arginousai (Xenophon, *Hellenica* 1.7.12, 16).
61. Jennifer Tolbert Roberts, *Accountability in Athenian Government* (Madison: University of Wisconsin Press, 1982), pp. 180–82.
62. See M. I. Finley, "Athenian Demagogues," *Past and Present* 21 (1962), pp. 15–16.
63. This is the view of Rudi Thomsen, *The Origin of Ostracism* (Copenhagen: Gyldendal, 1972), especially p. 114.
64. Aristotle, *The Athenian Constitution* 43.5. Hansen, however, points out that it was never used during the fourth century: *The Athenian Assembly*, p. 144, n. 141.
65. There is confusion in the ancient sources about whether this meant one person had to receive 6,000 votes against him or whether 3,001 of a total of 6,000 votes was sufficient. See Thomsen, *Origin of Ostracism*, pp. 66–67, n. 23, for a discussion of the evidence.
66. Fitzgerald, "Limitations on Freedom of Speech," p. 42.
67. Aristotle, *Politics* 1298a29.
68. Hansen, *Athenian Assembly*, p. 130.
69. Wirszubski, *Libertas As a Political Idea at Rome*, p. 18.
70. A. G. Woodhead, "Isegoria," p. 130.
71. Here the emphasis is on the political or public realm. As Wirszubski puts it in *Libertas As a Political Idea at Rome*: "Under the principate the ruling law which had been the basis of libertas was in fact replaced by the will of the Princeps. Within the Roman community itself, the possession of libertas became a gift rather than a right and, ceasing to be a right, lost what had been its essential quality" (p. 171). In the personal realm, Roman citizens continued to enjoy certain protections under the legal system even under the empire.
72. Syme, *Roman Revolution*, pp. 2, 9.

73. Lucan, *Pharsalia* 1.670.

74. Tacitus, *Annals* 1.2: *Munia senatus magistratum legum in se trahere.*

75. Wirszubski, *Libertas as a Political Idea at Rome*, p. 116, explains the difference between *potestas* (power) and *auctoritas* (authority): "The practical implications of supremacy by virtue of auctoritas are far-reaching. Unlike potestas, auctoritas is not defined, and therefore, whereas potestas is confined within certain limits, there is, in theory at least, no limit to the scope of auctoritas: it can be brought to bear on any matter. This fact may explain the peculiar character of the Augustan Principate. His auctoritas enabled Augustus to perform functions for which, strictly speaking, he had no legal warrant."

76. Tacitus, *Annals* 1.9: *Non regno tamen neque dictatura sed principis nomine constitutam rem publicam.*

77. Seneca, *De clementia* 1.4.3.

78. Cicero, *Laws* 3.4 (tr. Keyes).

79. Tacitus, *Annals* 4.32.

80. Syme, *Roman Revolution*, p. 487.

81. We are told by Dio Cassius, 57.24.4, that his daughter preserved copies. These were later reissued by Gaius.

82. Tacitus, *Annals* 4.35.

83. Sir Ronald Syme, *Tacitus*, vol. 2 (Oxford: Clarendon Press, 1958), p. 517. Tacitus may be telling us something about himself, too, through those he describes, with whom he seems to identify, including Cremutius (so Syme, *Tacitus*, vol. 2, p. 546).

84. Tacitus, *Annals* 4.35 (tr. Church and Brodribb).

85. Hansen, *Athenian Assembly*, p. 5.

86. George Forrest, "Greece: The History of the Archaic Period," in John Boardman, Jasper Griffin, and Oswyn Murray, eds., *The Oxford History of the Classical World* (Oxford: Oxford University Press, 1986), pp. 28–30.

87. Forrest, "Greece," pp. 31–32. This is disputed by Mogens Hansen, who holds that the only Solonian law affecting the Ecclesia was an enactment regulating the conduct of speakers: Hansen, *Athenian Assembly*, p. 135, n. 19.

88. Ostwald, *From Popular Sovereignty*, p. 27.

89. Hansen, *Athenian Assembly*, pp. 9–10.

90. Hansen, *Athenian Assembly*, pp. 12–14.

91. Hansen, *Athenian Assembly*, p. 7. "Only an eccentric like Plato [*Republic* 451C–7B] or a mocker like Aristophanes [*Ecclesiazusae*]," says Hansen, "could take it into their heads to enfranchise women."

92. Fitzgerald, "Limitations on Freedom of Speech," p. 181.

93. Fitzgerald, "Limitations on Freedom of Speech," p. 182. Chester G. Starr, *The Birth of Athenian Democracy* (New York: Oxford University Press, 1990), pp. 34–35, shows by way of comparison with American society in the nineteenth century that of the total census returns of 31,443,321 in the year 1860, only about 6,300,000 would have been adult white males who were eligible to vote—about 20 percent of the

total population, which is close to the 18.5 percent of the total Athenian population who could participate in the assembly. Starr points out wryly that in actuality in the election of 1860 only about 4,700,000 votes were cast, and voting requires much less time and effort than attendance at the Athenian assembly.

94. Hansen, *Athenian Assembly*, p. 8.

95. Hansen, *Athenian Assembly*, p. 127.

96. Hansen, *Athenian Assembly*, pp. 26–30.

97. P. J. Rhodes, *The Athenian Boule* (Oxford: Clarendon Press, 1972), pp. 78–81.

98. Hansen, *Athenian Assembly*, p. 37.

99. Cicero, *Pro Flacco* 9: *Nam si quis umquam de nostris hominibus a genere isto studio ac voluntate non abhorrens fuit, me et esse arbitror. . . . Verum tamen hoc dico de toto genere Graecorum: tribuo illis litteras, do multarum artium disciplinam, non adimo sermonis leporem, ingeniorum acumen, dicendi copiam, denique etiam, si qua sibi alia sumunt non repugno; testimoniorum religionem et fidem numquam ista natio coluit.*

100. Cicero, *Pro Flacco* 11.

101. Cicero, *Pro Flacco* 19.

102. Cicero, *Pro Flacco* 15.

103. Cicero, *Pro Flacco* 16 (tr. Lord).

104. Naphtali Lewis and Meyer Reinhold, eds., *Roman Civilization*, 3d ed., vol. 1 (New York: Columbia University Press, 1990), p. 98.

105. Cicero, *Republic* 2.22.39 (tr. Keyes).

106. Lily Ross Taylor, *Roman Voting Assemblies* (Ann Arbor: University of Michigan Press, 1966), pp. 3–8.

107. Michael Crawford, "Early Rome and Italy," in *The Oxford History of the Classical World*, edited by John Boardman, Jasper Griffen, and Oswyn Murray (Oxford: Oxford University Press, 1986), p. 395.

108. Dionysius of Halicarnassus, *Roman Antiquities* 7.59.6 (tr. Cary).

109. Taylor, *Roman Voting Assemblies*, pp. 15–16, 18.

110. Polybius, *Histories* 6.14.3–4, 12 (tr. Paton).

111. Taylor, *Roman Voting Assemblies*, pp. 29–33.

112. Taylor, *Roman Voting Assemblies*, p. 32.

113. Taylor, *Roman Voting Assemblies*, p. 33.

114. Marcian, *Digest* 47.22: *Sed permittitur tenuioribus stipem menstruam conferre dum tamen semel in mense coeant ne sub praetextu hujusmodi illictum collegium coeat.*

115. *Corpus inscriptionum Latinarum* 14.2112, I, 11–12: *Quib[us coire co]nvenire collegium—[que] habere liceat.*

116. Franz Cumont, *Les mystères de Mithra* (Bruxelles: H. Lamertin, 1913), p. 86, however, takes the view that Mithraism received protection through its association with the cult of Magna Mater.

117. Guterman, *Religious Toleration*, p. 140.

118. Tony Honoré, *Emperors and Lawyers* (London: Gerald Duckworth, 1981), pp. vii–ix.

119. Honoré, *Emperors and Lawyers*, p. 6.

120. Honoré, *Emperors and Lawyers*, p. 33.

121. Cicero, *Pro Sestio* 106.

122. Cornelius Fronto, *Ad M. Antoninum de eloquentia* 2.7. The entire passage, quoted in Fergus Millar, *The Emperor in the Roman World* (Ithaca: Cornell University Press, 1977), p. 203, gives an insight into at least one contemporary's view of imperial duties:

> Therefore consider whether in this second category of duties the study of eloquence should be included. For the duties of the emperors are: to urge necessary steps in the senate; to address the people on very many important matters in public meetings; to correct the injustices of the law; to send letters to all parts of the globe; to bring compulsion to bear on kings of foreign nations; to repress by their edicts the faults of the provincials, give praise to good actions, quell the seditious and terrify the fierce ones. All these are assuredly things to be achieved by words and letters. Will you therefore not practice a skill which you can see will be of great service to you on so many and such important occasions?

123. See Zvi Yavetz, *Plebs and Princeps* (Oxford: Oxford University Press, 1969), pp. 18–24.

124. Suetonius, *Augustus* 45; *Historia Augusta, Marcus Antoninus* 15.1.

125. Millar, *The Emperor in the Roman World (31 BC–AD 337)*, (Ithaca: Cornell University Press, 1947; reprint, 1958), p. 371.

126. Pliny, *Natural History* 34.19.62.

127. Millar, *Emperor in the Roman World*, p. 375.

CHAPTER 7

1. *United States v. Cruikshank*, 92 U.S. 542 (1875).

2. *Sandidge v. United States*, 520 A.2d 1057 (D.C. Cir. 1986), certiorari denied, 484 U.S. 868 (1987).

3. *Sandidge*, at 1058. For the full argument, see Warren Freedman, *The Privilege to Keep and Bear Arms: The Second Amendment and Its Interpretation* (New York: Quorum Books, 1989), pp. 22–25.

4. Roscoe Pound, *The Development of Constitutional Guarantees of Liberty* (New Haven: Yale University Press, 1957), p. 91.

5. States *without* an armsbearing provision are California, Delaware, Iowa, Maryland, Minnesota, Nebraska, Nevada, New Hampshire, New Jersey, New York, North Dakota, West Virginia, and Wisconsin.

6. States subscribing to the individual right theory include Alabama, Arizona, Colorado, Connecticut, Illinois, Louisiana, Maine, Michigan, Mississippi, Missouri, Montana, New Mexico, Oklahoma, Texas, and

Washington. (See Freedman, *Privilege to Keep and Bear Arms*, pp. 28–29.)

7. Alabama constitution, Article I, Section 26.

8. Arizona constitution, Article II, Section 26.

9. States subscribing to the collective right theory are Alaska, Arkansas, Florida, Georgia, Hawaii, Idaho, Indiana, Kansas, Kentucky, Massachusetts, North Carolina, Ohio, Oregon, Pennsylvania, Rhode Island, South Carolina, South Dakota, Tennessee, Utah, Vermont, Virginia, and Wyoming. (See Freedman, *Privilege to Keep and Bear Arms*, pp. 29–30.)

10. Ohio constitution, Article I, Section 4.

11. Tennessee constitution, Article I, Section 26.

12. The arguments against handguns need no reiteration here. In a speech to an annual meeting of the American Bar Association in August 1988, former justice Lewis Powell of the United States Supreme Court clarified the danger posed by possession of handguns. He said that the FBI reported 20,613 murders in 1986, 60 percent of which were committed with firearms. In England and Wales, by contrast, where firearms are strictly regulated, there were only 662 homicides in 1986, of which only 8 percent were committed with firearms. *American Bar Association Journal* (October 1, 1988), p. 30.

13. Edward F. Feighan, "A Way to Control Handguns," *New York Times* (April 15, 1987), p. A27.

14. Jean Bethke Elshtain, *Women and War* (New York: Basic Books, 1987), pp. 49–50.

15. Elshtain, *Women and War*, p. 53.

16. Plato, *Republic* 8.555D (tr. Cornford).

17. Plato, *Republic* 8.557A–B (tr. Cornford).

18. Plato, *Laws* 7.813–14 (tr. A. E. Taylor).

19. Plato, *Laws* 8.830 (tr. Taylor).

20. Plato, *Laws* 12.955B (tr. Taylor).

21. Aristotle, *Politics* 1279a37–b4 (tr. Barker).

22. Aristotle, *Politics* 1267b29–30 (tr. Barker).

23. Aristotle, *Politics* 1267b31–33.

24. Aristotle, *Politics* 1268a17–20.

25. Aristotle, *Politics* 1297b23–24 (tr. Barker).

26. A. W. Gomme, A. Andrewes, and K. J. Dover, *A Historical Commentary on Thucydides*, vol. 4 (Oxford: Clarendon Press, 1970), p. 329.

27. Thucydides 6.56.2 (tr. Warner).

28. Thucydides 6.58.

29. Aristotle, *Athenian Constitution* 18.4. This document is generally attributed to one of his students rather than to Aristotle himself. See discussion in P. J. Rhodes, trans., *Aristotle, The Athenian Constitution* (Harmondsworth: Penguin Books, 1984), pp. 9–13.

30. Thucydides 6.53.3.

31. Gomme, Andrewes, and Dover, *Historical Commentary on Thucydides*, vol. 4, p. 336.

32. For the extent to which George Washington consciously emulated this tradition, see Garry Wills, *Cincinnatus: George Washington and the Enlightenment* (Garden City, New York: Doubleday, 1984).

33. A. W. Lintott, *Violence in Republican Rome* (Oxford: Clarendon Press, 1968), p. 200.

34. Lintott, *Violence in Republican Rome*, p. 1.

35. Cicero, *Catilinarian* 1.3.

36. Cicero, *Catilinarian* 6.15 (tr. Grant).

37. Cicero, *Pro Milone* 9–11.

38. Pliny, *Natural History* 34.39.139; cf. *Digest* 48.6.1.

39. Lintott, *Violence in Republican Rome*, p. 123.

40. Cicero, *Pro Caelio* 70.

41. Lintott, *Violence in Republican Rome*, p. 111.

42. So Lintott, *Violence in Republican Rome*, p. 123. Aulus Plautius was still active in that year, and it would have been a good time to reinforce the earlier laws against violence, given the restitution of full powers to the tribunes.

43. Sallust, *Catilinarian War* 31.4.

44. Suetonius, *Julius Caesar* 17.

45. Lintott, *Violence in Republican Rome*, p. 121.

46. Duncan Cloud, *"Lex Iulia de vi*: Part 1," *Athenaeum* 66 (1988), p. 587.

47. Cloud, *"Lex Iulia de vi*: Part 1," p. 592: "The distinction lay in the sanction: *vis publica* constituted forms of *vis* meriting interdiction and later deportation, *vis privata* less grave forms of *vis* meriting loss of a third of one's property and the disabilities which, at any rate later, formed *infamia*."

48. Duncan Cloud, *"Lex Iulia de vi*: Part 2," *Athenaeum* 67 (1989), p. 456.

49. Cloud, *"Lex Iulia de vi*: Part 2," pp. 437, 443, 444, et passim.

50. For *cum telo esse* in the *Lex Plautia*, see Cicero, *In Vatinium* 24; *Letter to Atticus* 2.24.3; and Sallust, *Catilinarian War* 27.2.

51. *Corpus inscriptionum Latinarum* 1, 2d ed., 589. Text and translation in E. G. Hardy, *Roman Laws and Charters* (Oxford: Clarendon Press, 1912), pp. 100–101. Also adapted by Lewis and Reinhold, *Roman Civilization*, vol. 1, p. 370.

52. The stele is discussed by Mario Segre, "Due lettere di Silla," *Rivista di filologia* 66 (1938), pp. 253–63. Text given by Lewis and Reinhold, *Roman Civilization*, vol. 1, p 371.

53. Kenan T. Erim, *Aphrodisias, City of Venus Aphrodite* (London: Muller, Blond & White, 1986), pp. 1 and 83. See also J. M. Reynolds, *Aphrodisias and Rome, Journal of Roman Studies*, Monograph 1 (London, 1982).

54. Cicero, *Pro lege Manilia* 38–39 (tr. Hodge).

55. Cicero, *Letters to Atticus* 6.1.

56. Cicero, *Letter to Atticus* 5.21 (tr. Winstedt, adapted by Lewis and Reinhold, *Roman Civilization*, vol. 1, pp. 398–99.)

57. Salvatore Riccobono et al., eds., *Fontes iuris Romani Antejustini-*

ani, 2d ed., vol. 1 (Florence: S. a. G. Barbera, 1941), p. 55. See Lewis and Reinhold, *Roman Civilization,* vol. 1, pp. 421–22.

58. Or possibly "no one is to be dispossessed against his will."

59. Berlin papyrus 628=*Fontes iuris Romani antejustinani* 1.56; see Lewis and Reinhold, *Roman Civilization,* vol. 1, pp. 423–24.

CHAPTER 8

1. *Lopez v. United States,* 373 U.S. 427, 454 (1963) J. Brennan, dissenting).

2. György Diósdi, *Ownership in Ancient and Preclassical Roman Law* (Budapest: Akadémiai Kiadó, 1970), pp. 40–42, 132.

3. *Tabula* VII.9.a; Ulpian (71 *ad edictum*), *Digest* 43.27.1.8. Also Pliny, *Natural History* 16.5.15: *Cautum est praeterea lege XII tabularum, ut glandem in alienum fundum procidentem liceret colligere.*

4. Kunkel, *Introduction to Roman Legal and Constitutional History,* pp. 24–25.

5. For references, see Egon Weiss, "Lance et licio," *Zeitschrift der Savigny Stiftung für Rechtsgeschichte, Romanistische Abteilung* 43 (1922), p. 457.

6. Theodor Mommsen, *Römisches Strafrecht* (Leipzig, 1899), pp. 748–49 and notes.

7. See Jolowicz, *Historical Introduction to the Study of Roman Law,* pp. 171–72, for fuller discussion.

8. Nicholas, *Introduction to Roman Law,* p. 212 and n. 2. See also Francis de Zulueta, *Institutes of Gaius,* pt. 2 (Oxford: Clarendon Press, 1946–53), pp. 201–3, who suggests that the ceremonial search may have had magical elements.

9. Nelson B. Lasson, *The History and Development of the Fourth Amendment to the United States Constitution* (Baltimore: Johns Hopkins Press, 1937), pp. 15–17.

10. Cicero, *Second Verrine* 1.19.50.

11. Cicero, *Second Verrine* 2.74.182.

12. This is the view of Max Radin, *Handbook of Roman Law* (St. Paul: West Publishing Company, 1927), pp. 475–76.

CHAPTER 9

1. Patrick Devlin, *Trial by Jury* (London: Stevens & Sons, 1956), p. 9.

2. This last clause played an important role in the history of the Bill of Rights. It was the basis of *Barron v. Mayor & City Council,* 32 U.S. (7 Pet.) 243 (1833), decided by the Supreme Court of which John Marshall was chief justice, which concluded that the Bill of Rights applied only to the federal government and not to state or local governments. Barron claimed that the city's effective confiscation of his

property violated the Fifth Amendment prohibition. The Marshall court ruled that the intention of the Bill of Rights was to restrain the federal government only. "These amendments contain no expression indicating an intention to apply them to the state governments," the Court held. "This court cannot so apply them." The Fourteenth Amendment, ratified in 1868, stated that "No State shall make or enforce any law which shall abridge the privileges or immunities of citizens of the United States." But it was not until seventy years later that the Supreme Court held that the due process clause of the Fourteenth Amendment incorporated the rights protected by the Bill of Rights. This extended the provisions of the Bill of Rights to all levels of government, not only to the federal. The extent of the incorporation thesis, however, is still debated. Mr. Justice Black, in *Adamson v. California*, 322 U.S. 46, 80–90 (1947), argued unsuccessfully for "wholesale incorporation" of the protections of the Bill of Rights. The Court rejected this argument but achieved similar results through "selective incorporation." See Raoul Berger, *The Fourteenth Amendment and the Bill of Rights* (Norman: University of Oklahoma Press, 1989). Also Charles Fairman and Stanley Morrison, *The Fourteenth Amendment and the Bill of Rights: The Incorporation Theory* (New York: Da Capo Press, 1970).

3. A. H. M. Jones, *The Criminal Courts of the Roman Republic and Principate* (Oxford: Basil Blackwell, 1972; Totowa, New Jersey: Rowman and Littlefield, 1972), p. 63.

4. Jones, *Criminal Courts*, p. 45.

5. Jones, *Criminal Courts*, p. 79.

6. Jones, *Criminal Courts*, p. 79.

7. In a refinement of this principle, the Supreme Court in *Ashe v. Swenson*, 397 U.S. 436 (1970), ruled that all the charges against a person for related offenses must be brought and tried at the same time. This ruling, called collateral estoppel, was subsequently codified in the rules of the federal and most state courts. It arose from the prosecution of a man charged with robbing five other men in a poker game. The state prosecutors decided to try the accused of robbing only the first of the five men, with the intention of trying him subsequently for robbing the others if he was acquitted of the first charge.

8. Leonard W. Levy, *Origins of the Fifth Amendment* (Oxford: Oxford University Press, 1968), p. 431.

9. Callistratus (4 *de cognitionibus*) *Digest* 22.5.3.2.

10. See Edith Guild Henderson, "The Background of the Seventh Amendment," *Harvard Law Review* 80 (1966), p. 289. Henderson argues that the Seventh Amendment was never meant to codify a rigid form of jury practice, as there was no consistent pattern of juries in 1790 to be codified.

11. See Hansen, *Athenian Assembly*, pp. 104–5.

12. Aristotle, *The Athenian Constitution* 53.3, indicates that there was a jury of 201 for cases up to a 1,000 drachmae, 401 for those over 1,000 drachmae.

13. Robert J. Bonner and Gertrude Smith, *The Administration of Justice from Homer to Aristotle*, vol. 1 (Chicago: University of Chicago Press, 1938; reprint, New York: Greenwood Press, 1968), p. 226.

14. Aristotle, *The Athenian Constitution* 27.4.

15. A. R. W. Harrison, *The Law of Athens*, vol. 2 (Oxford: Clarendon Press, 1968–71), p. 49.

16. Gagarin, *Early Greek Law*, pp. 64, 78–79, 87, 112–15.

17. By Max Fränkel, "Der Attische Heliasteneid," *Hermes* 13 (1878), p. 464.

18. James Farley Cronin, "The Athenian Juror and His Oath" (Ph.D. diss., University of Chicago, 1934), p. 36.

19. Robert J. Bonner, *Lawyers and Litigants in Ancient Athens* (Chicago: University of Chicago Press, 1927), p. 37.

20. John H. Kroll, *Athenian Bronze Allotment Plates* (Cambridge, Massachusetts: Harvard University Press, 1972), p. 2.

21. In actual Athenian law, a tie vote of a jury is considered acquittal for the defendant.

22. Aeschylus, *Eumenides* 927–931 (tr. Lattimore).

23. David Luban, "Some Greek Trials: Order and Justice in Homer, Hesiod, Aeschylus and Plato," *Tennessee Law Review* 54 (1987), pp. 279, 313.

24. Callistratus (4 *de cognitionibus*), *Digest* 22.5.3 pr.

25. Callistratus (4 *de cognitionibus*), *Digest* 22.5.3.6.

26. Jones, *Criminal Courts*, p. 6. For the Roman juries, see also Bruce W. Frier, *The Rise of the Roman Jurists: Studies in Cicero's Pro Caecina* (Princeton: Princeton University Press, 1985).

27. Devlin, *Trial by Jury*, pp. 4–5, 163.

28. Barnaby C. Keeney, *Judgment by Peers* (Cambridge, Massachusetts: Harvard University Press, 1949), pp. 35–36.

29. Keeney, *Judgment by Peers*, p. 7.

30. Ferdinand Lot, "Quelques mots sur l'origine des pairs de France," *Revue historique*, 54 (1894), pp. 34–57.

31. That Vergil's great Roman epic the *Aeneid* was written in twelve books might have been an influence.

32. Keeney, *Judgment by Peers*, p. 20.

33. Keeney, *Judgment by Peers*, pp. 33–34.

34. Levy, *Origins of the Fifth Amendment*, p. 9.

35. Devlin, *Trial by Jury*, p. 8.

36. *Williams v. Florida*, 399 U.S. 78 (1970).

37. Thayer, "The Jury and Its Development," *Harvard Law Review* 5 (1892), p. 295.

38. Citing Charles L. Wells, "The Origin of the Petty Jury," *Law Quarterly Review* 27 (1911), pp. 347, 357.

39. Quoting John Proffatt, *Trial by Jury* 11, no. 2 (1877).

40. *Williams*, at 102.

41. *Duncan v. Louisiana*, 391 U.S. 145 (1968).

42. *Duncan*, at 155–56.

43. Quoted in *Jury Duty, Twentieth Judicial District, Davidson County, Tennessee* (Nashville: Metro Center Printing, 1989), p. 2.

44. Thomas L. Tedford, *Freedom of Speech in the United States* (Carbondale: Southern Illinois University Press, 1985), p. 36.

45. See Dan T. Carter, *Scottsboro: A Tragedy of the American South* (Baton Rouge: Louisiana State University Press, 1979 rev.), p. 273. Judge Horton never regretted his decision. Thirty-two years after the trial he referred to the family tradition he had learned as a child, *fiat justitia ruat coelum*: "Let justice be done though the heavens may fall."

46. Judges in the federal system can grant a new trial if they do not agree with the verdict. *Federal Rules of Criminal Procedure*, p. 33. Judges *must* dismiss a criminal conviction if they believe that no "reasonable" juror could have found the defendant guilty by proof beyond a reasonable doubt. *Federal Rules of Criminal Procedure*, p. 29(c). These remedies, however, are not used lightly by a judge; they are available only in those rare circumstances in which the judge believes that the jury verdict represents a gross injustice.

47. Devlin, *Trial by Jury*, p. 165.

48. Alexis de Tocqueville, "Trial by Jury in the United States Considered As a Political Institution," in *Democracy in America*, edited by J. P. Meyer and Max Lerner (New York: Harpter & Row, 1966), p. 297.

49. Antiphon 5.17–18.

50. See Elsa de Haas, *Antiquities of Bail* (New York: Columbia University Press, 1940), pp. 3–29.

51. Jones, *Criminal Courts*, pp. 114, 115.

52. Ulpian (9 *de officio proconsulis*), *Digest* 48.19.8.9.

53. Jurors have only been drawn from the entire adult population in America in the later years of the twentieth century.

CHAPTER 10

1. The last four words of the Tenth Amendment, "and of the people," were not included in Madison's proposals but were added by the Senate, perhaps to bring the meaning into conformity with the Ninth Amendment and to explicate the intent of both, that with regard to the federal government there are rights retained by the people. This is the view of Norman Redlich in his essay "Are There 'Certain Rights . . . ' Retained by the People?," in Randy E. Barnett, ed., *The Rights Retained by the People: The History and Meaning of the Ninth Amendment* (Fairfax, Virginia: George Mason University Press, 1989), p. 141.

2. James Wilson, *Of the Natural Rights of Individuals*, in *The Works of James Wilson*, ed. James DeWitt Andrews, vol. 2 (Chicago: Callahan, 1896), p. 307.

3. Jonathan Elliot, ed., *Debates in the Several State Conventions on*

the Adoption of the Federal Constitution, 2d ed., vol. 2 (Washington: Printed for the editor, 1836), p. 454 (remarks of James Wilson).

4. I Annals of Cong. 456 (1834), reprinted in Bernard Schwartz, *The Bill of Rights: A Documentary History,* vol. 2 (New York: Chelsea House Publishers, 1971), p. 1042.

5. Randy E. Barnett, "James Madison's Ninth Amendment," in Barnett, *Rights Retained by the People,* pp. 31–32.

6. Barnett, "James Madison's Ninth Amendment," pp. 32–33.

7. Barnett, "James Madison's Ninth Amendment," p. 40.

8. James Madison to Thomas Jefferson (October 17, 1788), reprinted in Schwartz, *Bill of Rights,* vol. 1, p. 616.

9. At the time of the greatest threat to the U.S. Constitution seventy years after the Bill of Rights was adopted, the Constitution of the Confederate States of America included almost identical language: "The enumeration, in the Constitution, of certain rights, shall not be construed to deny or disparage others retained by the people of the several States."

10. Barnett, "James Madison's Ninth Amendment," p. 17.

11. Brennan, Justice William, "Construing the Constitution," *U.C. Davis Law Review* 19 (1985), pp. 1, 9.

12. For a complete list, see Walter F. Murphy, James E. Fleming, and William F. Harris, *American Constitutional Interpretation* vol. 2 (Mineola, New York: Foundation Press, 1986), pp. 1083–84.

13. Barnett, "James Madison's Ninth Amendment," p. 41.

14. Barnett, "James Madison's Ninth Amendment," pp. 43–49.

15. Bennett B. Patterson, *The Forgotten Ninth Amendment* (Indianapolis: Bobbs-Merrill, 1955), p. 109. Redlich, "Are There Certain Rights Retained by the People?," p. 146, takes an intermediate approach, suggesting that the Ninth Amendment should be seen as dealing not with absolute but with "preferred" rights. Eugene M. Van Loan III, in "Natural Rights and the Ninth Amendment," in Barnett, *Rights Retained by the People,* pp. 165–66, argues that Madison saw the protected rights as substantive rather than procedural. Simeon C. R. McIntosh, "On Reading the Ninth Amendment: A Reply to Raoul Berger," in Barnett, *Rights Retained by the People,* p. 228, takes a political construction rather than natural law view of rights: "When I use the term 'rights,' I am speaking in the narrow sense of a claim created by a civil authority as opposed to other rights, such as natural rights, said to derive from man's rational nature."

16. *Griswold v. Connecticut,* 381 U.S. 479, 484 (1965).

17. *Griswold,* at 488. Raoul Berger, "The Ninth Amendment," in Barnett, *Rights Retained by the People,* pp. 218 and 192, takes severe exception to what he calls Goldberg's "legal legerdemain," which would take away the people's right to self-government and give it to the justices of the Supreme Court: "Who is to protect undescribed rights? Justice Goldberg would transform the ninth amendment into a bottomless well in which the judiciary can dip for the formation of

undreamed of 'rights' in their limitless discretion, a possibility the Founders would have rejected out of hand."

18. The cases respectively are *Freeman v. Flake*, 405 U.S. 1032 (1972); *Williams v. Board of Education*, 388 F. Supp. 93 (S.D.W.Va. 1975); *Burns v. Swenson*, 430 F.2d 771 (8th Cir. 1970); and *Tanner v. Armco Steel Corp.* 340 F. Supp. 532 (S.D. Tex. 1972).

19. *Roe v. Wade*, 314 F. Supp. 1217 (N.D.Tex. 1970), affirmed in part, 410 U.S. 113 (1973).

20. *Roe*, 410 U.S., at 153.

21. *Richmond Newspapers v. Virginia*, 448 U.S. 555 (1980) (plurality opinion).

22. *Richmond Newspapers*, at 579.

23. *Bowers v. Hardwick*, 478 U.S. 186 (1986).

24. *Bowers*, at 199 J. Blackmun, dissenting.

25. *Webster v. Reproductive Health Services*, 492 U.S. 490 (1989).

26. Still a fine discussion of the references to the Greek leagues during the debates over the Constitution is that of Richard M. Gummere, *The American Colonial Mind and the Classical Tradition* (Cambridge, Massachusetts: Harvard University Press, 1963), pp. 179–184.

27. Paul Petit, *Pax Romana*, tr. James Willis (Berkeley: University of California Press, 1976), p. 54.

28. In this discussion I follow Theodor Mommsen, *The Provinces of the Roman Empire*, ed. T. R. S. Broughton (Chicago: University of Chicago Press, 1968), pp. 82–122 (from Mommsen's *History of Rome*, vol. 5, book 8).

29. Mommsen, *Provinces of the Roman Empire*, p. 85.

30. Josephus, *Jewish War* 2.(xvi.4) 364.

31. *Hammer v. Dagenhart*, 247 U.S. 251 (1918), overruled in *United States v. Darby*, 312 U.S. 100 (1941).

32. *Hammer*, at 276.

33. *Darby*, at 100.

34. *National League of Cities v. Usery*, 426 U.S. 833 (1976), overruled in *Garcia v. San Antonio Metropolitan Transit Authority*, 469 U.S. 528 (1985).

35. *National League of Cities*, at 845.

36. *Garcia*, at 528.

37. My discussion of court cases related to the Ninth and Tenth Amendments largely follows that of Ellen Alderman and Caroline Kennedy, *In Our Defense: The Bill of Rights in Action* (New York: William Morrow, 1991), pp. 313–35.

38. Edward Dumbauld, *The Bill of Rights and What It Means Today* (Norman: University of Oklahoma Press, 1957), pp. 63, 65.

CONCLUSION

1. Sanford Levinson, *Constitutional Faith* (Princeton: Princeton University Press, 1988), p. 4.

2. This is the view of Robert N. Bellah, et al., *Habits of the Heart: Individualism and Commitment in American Life* (Berkeley: University of California Press, 1985). See especially the appendix, "Social Science as Public Philosophy," pp. 297–307.

Sources Cited

Abrams, Philip, ed. *John Locke: Two Tracts on Government.* Cambridge: Cambridge University Press, 1967.

Aeschines. *Prosecution of Timarchus.*

Aeschylus. *Eumenides.*

Alderman, Ellen, and Caroline Kennedy. *In Our Defense: The Bill of Rights in Action.* New York: William Morrow, 1991.

Ambrose. *De fuga saeculi.*

Aquinas, Thomas. *Summa theologica.*

Aristotle [attributed]. *The Athenian Constitution.*

———. *Nichomachean Ethics.*

———. *Politics.*

Athenaeus, *Deipnosophistae.*

Augustine. *The City of God.*

Augustus. *Res gestae.*

Babington, Anthony. *The Rule of Law in Britain from the Roman Occupation to the Present Day.* Chichester and London: Barry Rose Publishers, 1978.

Barker, Sir Ernest. *Traditions of Civility: Eight Essays.* Cambridge: Cambridge University Press, 1948.

Bellah, Robert N. et al. *Habits of the Heart: Individualism and Commitment in American Life.* Berkeley: University of California Press, 1985. Appendix: "Social Science As Public Philosophy," pp. 297–307.

Berger, Raoul. *The Fourteenth Amendment and the Bill of Rights.* Norman: University of Oklahoma Press, 1989.

Bible. Revised Standard Version.

Bietz, Charles R. *Political Equality: An Essay in Democratic Theory.* Princeton: Princeton University Press, 1989.

Boardman, John, Jasper Griffin, and Oswyn Murray, eds. *The Oxford History of the Classical World.* Oxford: Oxford University Press, 1986.

Bonner, Robert J. *Lawyers and Litigants in Ancient Athens.* Chicago: University of Chicago Press, 1927.

Bonner, Robert J., and Gertrude Smith. *The Administration of Justice from Homer to Aristotle.* Chicago: University of Chicago Press, 1938; repr. New York: Greenwood Press, 1968.

Boyd, Julian P., et al., eds. *The Papers of Thomas Jefferson.* Princeton: Princeton University Press, 1950.

Brant, Irving. *James Madison: Father of the Constitution.* Indianapolis: Bobbs-Merrill, 1950.

Breen, Quirinus. *Christianity and Humanism: Studies in the History of Ideas.* Edited by Nelson Peter Ross. Grand Rapids: William B. Eerdmans, 1968.

Brennan, William J., Jr. "Symposium: The Emergence of State Constitutional Law." *Texas Law Review* 63, nos. 6, 7 (March–April 1985), pp. 959–1318.

Burke, Edmund. Vol. 5, *Reflections on the Revolution in France.*

Burns, Alfred. "Athenian Literacy in the Fifth Century B.C." *Journal of the History of Ideas* 42 (1981), pp. 371–87.

Carey, George W. "The Separation of Powers" In *Founding Principles of American Government*, edited by George J. Graham, Jr., and Scarlett G. Graham, pp. 98–134. Chatham, New Jersey: Chatham House Publishers, 1977, 1984.

Carter, Dan T. *Scottsboro: A Tragedy of the American South.* Rev. ed. Baton Rouge: Louisiana State University Press, 1979.

Cassirer, Ernst. *The Individual and the Cosmos in Renaissance Philosophy.* Translated by Mario Domandi. New York: Harper and Row, 1963.

Casson, Lionel. "Imagine, if you will, . . . " *Smithsonian* 18 (October 1987), pp. 122–30.

Catullus. *Carmina.*

Chrysostom, John. *In epistolam ad Romanos* homil. 23 (*Patrologia Graeca* lx. 615).

Cicero. *Catilinarian.*

———. *De legibus.*

———. *De natura deorum.*

———. *De re publica.*

———. *In Vatinium.*

———. *Letters to Atticus.*

———. *Pro Caelio.*

———. *Pro Flacco.*

———. *Pro lege Manilia.*

———. *Pro Milone.*

———. *Pro Sestio.*

———. *Second Verrine.*

Clapp, James Gordon. "John Locke." *Encyclopedia of Philosophy,* edited by P. Edwards, Vol. 4, pp. 487–503. New York: Macmillan, 1967.

Cloud, Duncan. "Lex Iulia de vi: Part 1." *Athenaeum* 66 (1988), pp. 579–95.

———. *"Lex Iulia de vi: Part 2." Athenaeum* 67 (1989), pp. 427–65.

Cobbett, William. *The Parliamentary History of England from the Earliest Period to the Year 1803.* London: T. C. Hansard, etc., 1806–1820.

Codex Theodosianus.

Cohen, Edward E. *Ancient Athenian Maritime Courts.* Princeton: Princeton University Press, 1973.

Colish, Marcia L. *The Stoic Tradition from Antiquity to the Early Middle Ages.* 2 vols. Leiden: E. J. Brill, 1985.

Corpus inscriptionum Latinarum.

Corpus scriptorum ecclesiasticorum Latinorum.

Creasy, E. S. *The Rise and Progress of the English Constitution.* London: Richard Bentley and Son, 1892.

Cronin, James Farley. "The Athenian Juror and His Oath." Ph.D. diss., University of Chicago, 1934.

Cumont, Franz. *Les mystères de Mithra.* Bruxelles: H. Lamertin, 1913.

Dante, *De monarchia.*

Declareuil, Joseph. *Rome the Law-Giver.* London: Kegan Paul, Trench, Trubner; New York: A. A. Knopf, 1927.

de Haas, Elsa. *Antiquities of Bail.* New York: Columbia University Press, 1940.

Demosthenes 3; 9; 20.

D'Entrèves. A. P. *Natural Law: An Introduction to Legal Philosophy.* 2d ed. London: Hutchinson, 1970.

de Ste Croix, G. E. M. "Why Were the Early Christians Persecuted?" In *Studies in Ancient Society: Past and Present Series,* edited by M. I. Finley, pp. 210–49 and response by A. N. Sherwin-White following. London: Routledge and Kegan Paul, 1974.

de Tocqueville, Alexis. "Trial by Jury in the United States

Considered As a Political Institution." In *Democracy in America*. Edited by J. P. Mayer and Max Lerner. New York: Harper & Row, 1966.

Devlin, Patrick. *Trial by Jury*. London: Stevens & Sons, 1956.

de Zulueta, Francis. *Institutes of Gaius*. Oxford: Clarendon Press, 1946–1953.

Dialogues of Alfred North Whitehead, As Recorded by Lucien Price. Boston: Little, Brown and Company, 1954.

Digest.

Dio Cassius. *Epitome.*

Dionysius of Halicarnassus. *Roman Antiquities.*

Diósdi, György. *Ownership in Ancient and Preclassical Roman Law*. Budapest: Akadémiai Kiadó, 1970.

Domat, Jean. *The Civil War in Its Natural Order: Together with the Public Law*. 1722.

Douglas, Charles G., III. "The Clash over Constitutions: The Reassertion of State Authority." *The Judge's Journal* (Summer 1987), pp. 36–61.

Dover, K. J. *Greek Homosexuality*. London: Duckworth, 1978.

Dumbauld, Edward. *The Bill of Rights and What It Means Today*. Norman: University of Oklahoma Press, 1957.

Dunn, John. "The Politics of Locke in England and America in the Eighteenth Century." In *Problems and Perspectives*, edited by John W. Yolton, pp. 45–80. Cambridge: Cambridge University Press, 1969.

―――. *The Political Thought of John Locke*. Cambridge: Cambridge University Press, 1969; repr. 1975.

Dunne, Gerald T. *Hugo Black and the Judicial Revolution*. New York: Simon and Schuster, 1977.

Elliot, Jonathan, ed. *Debates in the Several State Conventions on the Adoption of the Federal Constitution*. 2d ed. Washington, D.C.: Printed for the editor, 1836.

Elshtain, Jean Bethke. *Women and War*. New York: Basic Books, 1987.

Erim, Kenan T. *Aphrodisias, City of Venus Aphrodite*. London: Muller, Blond & White, 1986.

Erskine, Thomas. *The Trial of Thomas Hardy for High Treason . . . Taken Down in Shorthand*. London, 1794.

Fairman, Charles, and Stanley Morrison. *The Fourteenth Amendment and the Bill of Rights: The Incorporation Theory*. New York: De Capo Press, 1970.

Farrand, Max,. ed. *Records of the Federal Convention of 1787*. Rev. ed. New Haven: Yale University Press, 1966.

Fears, J. Rufus. *Princeps a Diis Electus: The Divine Election of the Emperor As a Political Concept at Rome*. Rome: American Academy, 1977.

Feighan, Edward F. "A Way to Control Handguns." *New York Times*, April 15, 1987, p. A27.

Finley, M. I. "Athenian Demagogues." *Past and Present* 21 (1962).

Fitzgerald, Thomas R. "Limitations on Freedom of Speech in the Athenian Assembly." Ph.D. diss., University of Chicago, 1957.

Ford, Paul Leicester, ed. *Pamphlets on the Constitution of the United States*. New York: Da Capo Press, 1968; originally published Brooklyn, 1888.

Fox, Robin Lane. *Pagans and Christians*. San Francisco: Harper and Row, 1986.

Fränkel, Max. "Der Attische Heliasteneid." *Hermes* 13 (1878), p. 464.

Freedman, Warren. *The Privilege to Keep and Bear Arms: The Second Amendment and its Interpretation*. New York: Quorum Books, 1989.

Frier, Bruce W. *The Rise of the Roman Jurists: Studies in Cicero's Pro Caecina*. Princeton: Princeton University Press, 1985.

Fronto, Marcus Cornelius. *Ad M. Antoninum de Eloquentia*.

Gagarin, Michael. *Early Greek Law*. Berkeley: University of California Press, 1986.

Galie, Peter J. "State Supreme Courts, Judicial Federalism and the Other Constitutions." *Judicature* 71, no. 2 (August–September 1987), pp. 100–110.

Gibbon, Edward. *The Decline and Fall of the Roman Empire*.

Gomme, A. W., A. Andrewes, and K. J. Dover. *A Historical Commentary on Thucydides*. Oxford: Clarendon Press, 1970.

Gough, J. W. *Fundamental Law in English Constitutional History*. Oxford: Clarendon Press, 1955.

Green, Frederick. *The United Nations and Human Rights*. Washington, D.C.: Brookings Institution, 1956.

Gregory, I. *Moralia* xxi. 15.22 (*Patrologia Latina* lxxvi 203).

Griffith, G. T. "Isegoria in the Assembly at Athens." In *Ancient Society and Institutions (Studies Presented to Victor Ehrenberg)*. New York: Barnes and Noble, 1967.

Grote, George. *A History of Greece*. 2d ed. rev. London: John Murray, 1888.

Grotius, Hugo. *Laws of War and Peace*.

Gummere, Richard M. *The American Colonial Mind and the Classical Tradition.* Cambridge, Massachusetts: Harvard University Press, 1963.

Guterman, Simeon L. *Religious Toleration and Persecution in Ancient Rome.* London: Aiglon Press, 1951.

Guthrie, W. K. C. *The Sophists.* Cambridge: Cambridge University Press, 1971.

Hagendahl, Harald. *Augustine and the Latin Classics.* Stockholm: Almqvist & Wiksell, 1967.

Hahm, David E. *The Origins of Stoic Cosmology.* Columbus: Ohio State University Press, 1977.

Hand, Learned. *The Bill of Rights: The Oliver Wendell Holmes Lectures, 1958.* Cambridge, Massachusetts: Harvard University Press, 1958.

Handlin, Oscar. "Learned Books and Revolutionary Action, 1776." *Harvard Library Bulletin* 34 (1986), pp 362–79.

Hansen, Mogens Herman. *The Athenian Assembly in the Age of Demosthenes.* Oxford: Basil Blackwell, 1987.

Harris, William V. *Ancient Literarcy.* Cambridge, Massachusetts and London: Harvard University Press, 1989.

Harrison, A. R. W. *The Law of Athens.* Oxford: Clarendon Press, 1968–1971.

Havelock, Eric A. *The Greek Concept of Justice.* Cambridge, Massachusetts: Harvard University Press, 1978.

Herodotus. *Histories.*

Hicks, Robert Drew. *Stoic and Epicurean.* New York: Charles Scribner's Sons, 1910.

Hobbes, Thomas. *Leviathan.* London and Toronto: J. M. Dent & Sons; New York: E. P. Dutton, 1914, repr. 1934.

Holt, J. C. *Magna Carta.* Cambridge: Cambridge University Press, 1965.

Honoré, Tony. *Emperors and Lawyers.* London: Gerald Duckworth, 1981.

Howard, A. E. Dick. *The Road from Runnymede: Magna Carta and Constitutionalism in America.* Charlottesville: University Press of Virginia, 1968.

Hunt, Gaillard, ed. *The Writings of James Madison.* New York: G. P. Putnam's Sons, 1900–1910.

Institutes.

Inwood, Brad. *Ethics and Human Action in Early Stoicism.* Oxford: Clarendon Press, 1985.

Isidore. *Decretum Gratiani.*

Jolowicz, Herbert Felix. *Historical Introduction to the Study of Roman Law.* Cambridge: University Press, 1932.

———. *Roman Foundations of Modern Law.* Oxford: Clarendon Press, 1957.

Jones, A. H. M. *The Criminal Courts of the Roman Republic and Principate.* Oxford: Basil Blackwell, 1972; Totowa, New Jersey: Rowan and Littlefield, 1972.

Josephus. *Jewish War.*

Jury Duty, Twentieth Judicial District, Davidson County, Tennessee. Nashville: Metro Center Printing, 1989.

Keeney, Barnaby C. *Judgment by Peers.* Cambridge, Massachusetts: Harvard University Press, 1949.

Kidd, I. G. "Moral Actions and Rules in Stoic Ethics." In *The Stoics,* edited by John M. Rist, pp. 247–58. Berkeley: University of California Press, 1978.

Kirk, G. S., and J. E. Raven. *The Presocratic Philosophers.* Cambridge: Cambridge University Press, 1971.

Klibansky, Raymond. *The Continuity of the Platonic Tradition during the Middle Ages.* London: Warburg Institute, 1950.

Knappen, M. M. *Constitutional and Legal History of England.* Hamden, Connecticut: Archon Books, 1964.

Kroll, John H. *Athenian Bronze Allotment Plates.* Cambridge, Massachusetts: Harvard University Press, 1972.

Kunkel, Wolfgang. *An Introduction to Roman Legal and Constitutional History.* Translated by J. M. Kelley. 2d ed. Oxford: Clarendon Press, 1973.

Larsen, J. A. O. "The Judgment of Antiquity on Democracy." *Classical Philology* 49 (1954).

Lasson, Nelson B. *The History and Development of the Fourth Amendment to the United States Constitution.* Baltimore: Johns Hopkins Press, 1937.

Leges Henrici Primi.

Levinson, Sanford. *Constitutional Faith.* Princeton: Princeton University Press, 1988.

Levy, Leonard W. *Origins of the Fifth Amendment.* Oxford: Oxford University Press, 1968.

Lewis, J. D. "Isegoria at Athens: When Did It Begin?" *Historia* 20 (1971), pp. 129–40.

Lewis, Naphtali, and Meyer Reinhold, eds. *Roman Civilization.* 3d ed. New York: Columbia University Press, 1990.

Liebeschuetz, J. H. W. G. *Continuity and Change in Roman Religion.* Oxford: Clarendon Press, 1979.

Lintott, A. W. *Violence in Republican Rome.* Oxford: Clarendon Press, 1968.

Livy. *History of Rome.*

Locke, John. *An Essay concerning Human Understanding.*

——. *Two Treatises of Government.*

——. *Essays on the Law of Nature.* Edited by Wolfgang von Leyden. Oxford: Clarendon Press, 1954.

——. *The Educational Writings.* Edited by James Axtell. Cambridge: Cambridge University Press, 1968.

Long, A. A. *Hellenistic Philosophy: Stoics, Epicureans, Sceptics.* London: Gerald Duckworth & Company, 1974.

Lorimer, James. *The Institutes of Law, a Treatise of the Principles of Jurisprudence as Determined by Nature.* Edinburgh, T. & T. Clark, 1872.

Lot, Ferdinand. "Quelques mots sur l'origine des pairs de France." *Revue Historique* 54 (1894), pp. 34–57.

Luban, David. "Some Greek Trials: Order and Justice in Homer, Hesoid, Aeschylus and Plato." *Tennessee Law Review* 54 (1987).

Lucan. *Pharsalia.*

Lutz, Donald S. *The Origins of American Constitutionalism.* Baton Rouge: Louisiana State University Press, 1988.

MacKendrick, Paul (with the collaboration of Karen Lee Singh). *The Philosophical Books of Cicero.* New York: St. Martin's Press, 1989.

Mackintosh, James. *Vindiciae Gallicae: Defense of the French Revolution and Its English Admirers.* Dublin: Printed by W. W. Corbet for R. Cross et al., 1791.

MacPherson, C. B. *The Political Theory of Possessive Individualism.* Oxford: Clarendon Press, 1962.

Maine, Henry Sumner. *Dissertations on Early Law and Custom.* New York: H. Holt, 1886.

McDonnell, Kilian. "Does William of Ockham Have a Theory of Natural Law?" *Franciscan Studies* 34 (1974), pp. 383–92.

McIlwain, Charles H. *Constitutionalism Ancient and Modern.* Ithaca: Cornell University Press, 1947; repr. 1958.

Millar, Fergus. *The Emperor in the Roman World (31 BC–AD 337).* Ithaca: Cornell University Press, 1977.

Momigliano, Arnaldo. *On Pagans, Jews, and Christians.* Middletown, Connecticut: Wesleyan University Press, 1987.

Mommsen, Theodor. *Römisches Strafrecht.* Leipzig, 1899.

——. *The Provinces of the Roman Empire.* Edited with an introduction by T. R. S. Broughton. Chicago: University of Chicago Press, 1968.

Monumenta Germaniae historiae.

Murphy, Walter F., James E. Fleming, and William F. Harris. *American Constitutional Interpretation.* Mineola, New York: Foundation Press, 1986.

Nicholas, Barry. *An Introduction to Roman Law*. Oxford: Clarendon Press, 1962.

O'Connor, D. J. *Aquinas and Natural Law*. London: Macmillan, 1967.

Ogilvie, R. M. *The Romans and Their Gods*. London, 1969.

Ostwald, Martin. *From Popular Sovereignty to the Sovereignty of Law: Law, Society, and Politics in Fifth-Century Athens*. Berkeley: University of California Press, 1986.

Painter, Sidney. *Feudalism and Liberty*. Edited by Fred A. Cazel, Jr. Baltimore: Johns Hopkins Press, 1961.

Pallister, Anne. *Magna Carta: The Heritage of Liberty*. Oxford: Clarendon Press, 1971.

Parker, Henry. *Animadversions Animadverted*. 1642.

———. *Contra Replicant*. 1643.

Patterson, Bennett. B. *The Forgotten Ninth Amendment*. Indianapolis: Bobbs-Merrill, 1955.

Peterson, Merrill D., ed. *The Portable Thomas Jefferson*. New York: Viking Press, 1975.

Petit, Paul. *Pax Romana*. Translated by James Willis. Berkeley: University of California Press, 1976.

Plato. *Laws*.

———. *Republic*.

Pliny. *Natural History*.

Plutarch. *De Alexandri magni fortuna aut virtute*.

Polybius. *Histories*.

Pomeroy, Sarah. *Goddesses, Whores, Wives, and Slaves: Women in Classical Antiquity*. New York: Schocken Books, 1975.

Pound, Roscoe. *The Lawyer from Antiquity to Modern Times*. St. Paul: West Publishing, 1953.

———. *The Development of Constitutional Guarantees of Liberty*. New Haven: Yale University Press, 1957.

Powell, Justice Lewis, quoted in "Powell: What Right to Own Guns?" *American Bar Association Journal*, October 1, 1988. p. 30.

Proffatt, John. *Trials by Jury* 11, no. 2 (1877).

Radin, Max. *Handbook of Roman Law*. St. Paul: West Publishing Company, 1927.

Rapaczynski, Andrzej. *Nature and Politics: Liberalism in the Philosophies of Hobbes, Locke, and Rousseau*. Ithaca and London: Cornell University Press, 1987.

Redlich, Norman. "Are there 'Certain Rights . . . Retained by the People'?" In *The Rights Retained by the People: The History and Meaning of the Ninth Amendment*, edited by

Randy E. Barnett, p. 141. Fairfax, Virginia: George Mason University Press, 1989.

Reesor, Margaret. *The Nature of Man in Early Stoic Philosophy.* New York: St. Martin's Press, 1989.

Reinhold, Meyer. *Classica Americana: The Greek and Roman Heritage in the United States.* Detroit: Wayne State University Press, 1984.

Reynolds, J. M. *Aphrodisias and Rome. Journal of Roman Studies,* Monograph 1. London, 1982.

Rhodes, P. J. *The Athenian Boule.* Oxford: Clarendon Press, 1972.

Riccobono, Salvatore, et al., eds. *Fontes iuris Romani antejustiniani.* 2d ed. Vol. 1. Florence: S. a. G. Barbera, 1940–1943.

Riesenberg, Peter N. *Inalienability of Sovereignty in Medieval Political Thought.* New York: Columbia University Press, 1956.

Roberts, Jennifer Tolbert. *Accountability in Athenian Government.* Madison: University of Wisconsin Press, 1982.

Rommen, H. A. *The Natural Law: A Study in Legal and Social History and Philosophy.* Translated by Thomas R. Hanley. St. Louis and London: B. Herder Book Co., 1947.

Rosen, Edward. "The Invention of Eye Glasses." *Journal of the History of Medicine and Allied Sciences* 11 (1956), pp. 12–46, 183–218.

Rutland, Robert Allen. *The Birth of the Bill of Rights.* Chapel Hill: University of North Carolina Press, 1955.

———. *The Ordeal of the Constitution.* Boston: Northeastern University Press, 1983; originally published Norman: University of Oklahoma Press, 1966.

Sallust. *Catilinarian War.*

Samuel, Geoffrey. "Epistemology, Propaganda, and Roman Law: Some Reflections on the History of Subjective Right." *Journal of Legal History* 10 (September 1989), pp. 161–79.

Schroeder, D. N. "Aristotle on Law." *Polis* 4 (1981), pp. 17–31.

Schwartz, Bernard. *The Bill of Rights: A Documentary History.* New York: Chelsea House Publishers, 1971.

———. *The Great Rights of Mankind: A History of the American Bill of Rights.* New York: Oxford University Press, 1977.

Segre, Mario. "Due lettere di Silla." *Rivista di filologia* 66 (1938), pp. 253–63.

Seneca. *De clementia.*

———. *De ira.*

Sherwin-White, A. N. *The Roman Citizenship.* 2d ed. Oxford: Clarendon Press, 1973.

Sigmund, Paul E. *Natural Law in Political Thought.* Cambridge, Massachusetts: Winthrop Publishers, 1971.

Sinclair, R. K. *Democracy and Participation in Athens.* Cambridge: Cambridge University Press, 1988.

Skinner, Quentin. *The Foundations of Modern Political Thought.* Cambridge: Cambridge University Press, 1978.

Smallwood, E. Mary. *The Jews under Roman Rule.* Leiden: Brill, 1976.

Sophocles. *Antigone.*

Stanlis, Peter J. *Edmund Burke and the Natural Law.* Ann Arbor: University of Michigan Press, 1965.

Starr, Chester G. *The Birth of Athenian Democracy: The Assembly in the Fifth Century B.C.* New York: Oxford University Press, 1990.

Stein, Peter. *The Character and Influence of Roman Civil Law: Historical Essays.* London and Ronceverte: Hambledon Press, 1988.

Strauss, Leo. *Natural Right and History.* Chicago: University of Chicago Press, 1953.

Suetonius. *Lives of the Caesars.*

———. *Marcus Antoninus.*

Swindler, William F. *Magna Carta: Legend and Legacy.* Indianapolis: Bobbs-Merrill, 1965.

Sylloge inscriptionum Graecorum.

Syme, Sir Ronald. *The Roman Revolution.* Oxford: Oxford University Press, 1960.

———. *Tacitus.* Oxford: Clarendon Press, 1958.

Syrett, Harold C., ed. *The Papers of Alexander Hamilton.* New York: Columbia University Press, 1962.

Tacitus. *Annals.*

Tarter, Brent. "Virginians and the Bill of Rights." In *The Bill of Rights: A Lively Heritage,* edited by John Kukla, pp. 3–17. Richmond: Virginia State Library and Archives, 1987.

Taylor, Lily Ross. *The Divinity of the Roman Emperor.* Middletown, Connecticut: American Philological Association, 1931.

———. *Roman Voting Assemblies.* Ann Arbor: University of Michigan Press, 1966.

Tedford, Thomas L. *Freedom of Speech in the United States.* Carbondale: Southern Illinois University Press, 1985.

Tertullian. *Apologeticus.*

———. *De praescriptione hereticorum.*

Thomsen, Rudi. *The Origin of Ostracism.* Copehagen: Gyldendal, 1972.

Thucydides. *History of the Peloponnesian War.*
Tierney, Brian. *The Crisis of Church and State: 1050–1300.* Englewood Cliffs, New Jersey: Prentice Hall, 1964.
———, "Villey, Ockham and the Origin of Individual Rights." In *The Weightier Matters of the Law: Essays on Law and Religion,* edited by John Witte, Jr., and Frank S. Alexander. Atlanta: Scholars Press, 1988.
Troeltsch, Ernst. *The Social Teaching of the Christian Church.* Translated by O. Wyon. 2 vols. London: Allen & Unwin, 1931; repr. 1950.
———. "The Ideas of Natural Law and Humanity in Western Politics." Appendix I in *Natural Law and the Theory of Society, 1500, with a Lecture on the Ideas of Natural Law and Humanity by Ernst Troeltsch,* by Otto Friedrich von Gierke, translated with an introduction by Ernest Barker. Cambridge: Cambridge University Press, 1934.
Tuck, Richard. *Natural Rights Theories: Their Origin and Development.* Cambridge: Cambridge University Press, 1979.
Tully, James. *A Discourse on Property: John Locke and His Adversaries.* Cambridge: Cambridge University Press, 1980.
———. *The Individual and Society in the Middle Ages.* Baltimore: John Hopkins Press, 1966.
———. *Law and Politics in the Middle Ages: An Introduction to the Sources of Medieval Political Ideals.* Ithaca: Cornell University Press, 1975.
Ullmann, Walter. *The Medieval Idea of Law.* New York: Barnes and Noble; London: Methuen, 1946; repr. 1969.
Van Zyl, D. H. *Cicero's Legal Philosophy.* Roodepoort: Digma Publications, 1986.
Verbeke, Gerard. *The Presence of Stoicism in Medieval Thought.* Washington, D.C.: Catholic University of America Press, 1983.
Vickers, Brian. *In Defence of Rhetoric.* Oxford: Clarendon Press, 1988.
Villey, Michel. "La genèse du droit subjectif chez Guillame d'Occam." *Archives de philosophie du droit* 9 (1964), pp. 97–127.
———. *La formation de la pensée juridique moderne.* Paris: Montchrestien, 1968.
Vinogradoff, Paul. *Roman Law in Medieval Europe.* Oxford: Clarendon Press, 1929.
von Ivanka, Endre. *Plato Christianus: Übernahme und Umgestaltung des Platonismus durch die Väter.* Einsiedeln: Johannes Verlag, 1964.

von Leyden, Wolfgang. *Aristotle on Equality and Justice: His Political Argument*. New York: St. Martin's Press, 1985.

Watson, Gerard. "The Natural Law and Stoicism." In *Problems in Stoicism*, edited by A. A. Long. London: Athlone Press, 1971.

Wenley, Robert Mark. *Stoicism and Its Influence*. New York: Longmans, Green, 1927.

Wiess, Egon. "Lance et licio." *Zeitschrift der Savigny Stiftung für Rechtsgeschichte, Romanistische Abteilung* 43 (1922), p. 457.

Wilkin, Robert N. *Eternal Lawyer: A Legal Biography of Cicero*. New York: Macmillan, 1947.

Wills, Garry. *Cincinnatus: George Washington and the Enlightenment*. Garden City, New York: Doubleday, 1984.

Wilson, James. *Of the Natural Rights of Individuals*. In *The Works of James Wilson*, edited by James DeWitt Andrews. Chicago: Callahan, 1896.

Wirszubski, Chaim. *Libertas as a Political Idea at Rome during the Late Republic and Early Principate*. Cambridge: Cambridge University Press, 1950.

Wolff, Christian. *Ius naturae methodo scientifica pertractatum*. 1741.

Wolff, Hans Julius. *Roman Law: An Historical Introduction*. Norman: University of Oklahoma Press, 1951.

Woodhead, A. G. "*Isegoria* and the Council of 500." *Historia* 16 (1967), pp. 140ff.

Wright, Benjamin Fletcher, Jr. *American Interpretations of Natural Law: A Study in the History of Political Thought*. Cambridge, Massachusetts: Harvard University Press, 1931.

Xenephon. *Hellenica*.

Yavetz, Zvi. *Plebs and Princeps*. Oxford: Oxford University Press, 1969.

LEGAL CITATIONS

Adamson v. California, 332 U.S. 46 (1947).

Ashe v. Swenson, 397 U.S. 436 (1970).

Barron v. Mayor & City Council, 32 U.S. (7 Pet.) 243 (1833).

Bowers v. Hardwick, 478 U.S. 186 (1986).

Burns v. Swenson, 430 F.2d 771 (8th Cir. 1970).

Duncan v. Louisiana, 391 U.S. 145 (1968).

Freeman v. Flake, 405 U.S. 1032 (1972).

Griswold v. Connecticut, 381 U.S. 479 (1965).

Hammer v. Dagenhart, 247 U.S. 251 (1918), overruled in *United States v. Darby*, 312 U.S. 100 (1941).

Lopez v. United States, 373 U.S. 427 (1963).

National League of Cities v. Usery, 426 U.S. 833 (1976), overruled in *Garcia v. San Antonio Metropolitan Transit Authority*, 469 U.S. 528 (1985).

Republic Steel Corp. v. Maddox, 379 U.S. 650 (1965).

Richmond Newspapers v. Virginia, 448 U.S. 555 (1980) (plurality opinion).

Roe v. Wade, 314 F. Supp. 1217 (N.D.Tex. 1970), affirmed in part, 410 U.S. 113 (1973).

Sandidge v. United States, 520 A.2d 1057 (D.C. Cir. 1986), certiorari denied, 484 U.S. 868 (1987).

United States v. Cruikshank, 92 U.S. 542 (1875).

Tanner v. Armco Steel Corp. 340 F. Supp. 532 (S.D. Tex. 1972).

Webster v. Reproductive Health Services, 492 U.S. 490 (1989).

Williams v. Board of Education, 388 F. Supp., 93 (S.D.W.Va. 1975).

Williams v. Florida, 399 U.S. 78 (1970).

Brennan, Justice William. "Construing the Constitution." *U.C. Davis Law Review* 19 (1985).

Henderson, Edith Guild. "The Background of the Seventh Amendment." *Harvard Law Review* 80, no. 289 (1966).

Luban, David. "Some Greek Trials: Order and Justice in Homer, Hesiod, Aeschylus and Plato." *Tennessee Law Review* 80, no. 279 (1987).

Thayer, James B. "The Jury and Its Development." *Harvard Law Review* 5, no. 295 (1892).

Wells, Charles. "The Origin of the Petty Jury." *Law Quarterly Review* 27, no. 347 (1911).

American Political Thought and the Classics: A Bibliography

For further bibliographies on the classical tradition in America, see Meyer Reinhold, *Classica Americana* (Detroit: Wayne State University Press, 1984), pp. 352–64, and the bibliographies published annually since 1985 in *Classical and Modern Literature.*

Adair, Douglass. *Fame and the Founding Fathers*, edited by H. Trevor Colbourn. New York: W. W. Norton, 1974.

Aldridge, A. Owen. "Thomas Paine and the Classics." *Eighteenth Century Studies* 1 (1968), pp. 370–80.

Ames, R. A., and H. C. Montgomery. "The Influence of Rome on the American Constitution." *Classical Journal* 30 (1934–1935), pp. 19–27.

Andrews, Stuart. "Classicism and the American Revolution." *History Today* 37 (January 1987), pp. 37–42.

Appleby, Joyce O. *Capitalism and a New Social Order: The Republican Vision of the 1790's.* New York: New York University Press, 1984.

Bailyn, Bernard. *The Ideological Origins of the American Revolution.* Cambridge, Massachusetts: Harvard University Press, 1967.

———, "A Dialogue between an American and a European Englishman, by Thomas Hutchinson." *Perspectives in American History* 9 (1975), pp. 343–410.

———, ed. *Pamphlets of the American Revolution.* 4 vols. Cambridge, Massachusetts: Harvard University Press, 1965.

Banning, Lance. "Jeffersonian Ideology Revisited: Liberal and

Classical Ideas in the New American Republic." *William and Mary Quarterly* 43 (1986), pp. 3–19.

Barone, Dennis. "James Logan and Gilbert Tennent: Enlightened Classicist versus Awakened Evangelist." *Early American Literature* 21 (1986), pp. 103–17.

Becker, Carl. "The Spirit of '76." In *The Spirit of 1776 and Other Essays*, edited by Carl Becker, J. M. Clark, and William E. Dodds. Washington, D.C.: Brookings Institution, 1927.

Benario, Herbert W. "The Classics in Southern Higher Education." *Southern Humanities Review*, special issue (1977), pp. 15–20.

Berrigan, Joseph R. "The Impact of the Classics upon the South." *Classical Journal* 64 (1964), pp. 18–20.

Bietz, Charles R. *Political Equality: An Essay in Democratic Theory.* Princeton: Princeton University Press, 1989.

Botein, Stephen. "Cicero As Role Model for Early American Lawyers: A Case Study in Classical 'Influence.'" *Classical Journal* 73 (1978), pp. 313–21.

Boyd, Julian P., et al., eds. *The Papers of Thomas Jefferson.* Princeton: Princeton University Press, 1950.

Bradford, M. E. "A Teaching for Republicans: Roman History and the Nation's First Identity." *Intercollegiate Review* 11 (1976), pp. 67–81.

———. "A 'Better Guide than Reason': The Politics of John Dickinson." *Modern Age* 2 (1977), pp. 39–49.

———. "That Other Republic: Romanitas in Southern Literature." *Southern Humanities Review*, special issue (1977), pp. 4–13.

Bruce, D. D., Jr. "The Conservative Use of History in Early National Virginia." *Southern Studies* 19 (1980), pp. 128–46.

Bryson, W. Hamilton. "The Use of Roman Law in Virginia Courts." *American Journal of Legal History* 23 (1984), pp. 135–46.

Burns, Edward M. "The Philosophy of History of the Founding Fathers." *The Historian* 16 (1954), pp. 142–61.

Cappon, Lester J., ed. *The Adams-Jefferson Letters: The Complete Correspondence between Thomas Jefferson and Abigail and John Adams.* 2 vols. Chapel Hill: University of North Carolina Press, 1959.

Chinard, Gilbert. "Polybius and the American Constitution." *Journal of the History of Ideas* 1 (1940), pp. 38–58.

———. *The Literary Bible of Thomas Jefferson: His Commonplace Book of Philosophers and Poets.* New York: Greenwood Press, 1969.

Clough, Wilson O., ed. *Intellectual Origins of American National Thought: Pages from the Books Our Founding Fathers Read.* 2d ed. New York: Corinth Books, 1961.

Cohn-Haft, Louis. "The Founding Fathers and Antiquity: A Selective Passion." *Smith College Studies in History* 66 (1980), pp. 137–53.

Colbourn, H. Trevor. "Thomas Jefferson's Use of the Past." *William and Mary Quarterly* (3d ser.) 15 (1958), pp. 56–70.

———. *The Lamp of Experience: Whig History and the Intellectual Origins of the American Revolution.* Chapel Hill: University of North Carolina Press, 1965.

Commager, Henry Steele. "Leadership in Eighteenth-Century America and Today." *Daedalus* 90 (Fall 1961), pp. 652–73.

———. "The American Enlightenment and the Ancient World. A Study in Paradox." *Proceedings of the Massachusetts Historical Society* 83 (1971), pp. 3–15.

Corwin, Edward S. "The 'Higher Law' Background of the American Constitution." *Harvard Law Review* 42 (1928–1929), pp. 149–85, 365–409.

Cremin, Lawrence A. *American Education: The Colonial Experience, 1607–1783.* New York: Harper & Row, 1970.

Cunliffe, Marcus. "Thomas Jefferson and the Dangers of the Past." *Wilson Quarterly* 6, no. 1 (1982), pp. 96–107.

Curti, Merle. *The Growth of American Thought.* New York and London: Harper and Brothers, 1943.

Davis, Richard Beale. *Intellectual Life in Jefferson's Virginia, 1790–1830.* Chapel Hill: University of North Carolina Press, 1964.

Documentary History of the Ratification of the Constitution, ed. Merrill Jensen. 7 vols. Madison: State Historical Society of Wisconsin, 1976.

Douglass, Elisha P. "Fisher Ames, Spokesman for New England Federalism." *Proceedings of the American Philosophical Society* 103 (1959), pp. 693–715.

Dunn, John. "The Politics of Locke in England and America in the Eighteenth Century." In *John Locke: Problems and Perspectives,* edited by John W. Yolton, pp. 45–80. Cambridge: Cambridge University Press, 1969.

Eadie, John W., ed. *Classical Traditions in Early America.* Ann Arbor: Center for Coordination of Ancient and Modern Studies, University of Michigan, 1976.

Eaton, Clement. *The Mind of the Old South.* Baton Rouge: Louisiana State University Press, 1964.

Elliot, Jonathan, ed. *Debates in the Several State Conventions on the Adoption of the Federal Constitution.* 4 vols. Philadelphia: Lippincott, 1888; New York: Burt Franklin Reprints, 1974.

Else, Gerald F. "The Classics in the New World." *Newsletter, American Council of Learned Societies* 16, no. 5 (May 1965), pp. 5–15.

Elshtain, Jean Bethke. *Women and War.* New York: Basic Books, 1987.

Farrand, Max, Ed. *The Records of the Federal Convention of 1787.* 3d ed. 4 vols. New Haven: Yale University Press, 1966.

Farrell, James M. "John Adams and the Ciceronian Paradigm." Ph.D. diss., University of Wisconsin, 1988.

Finley, M. I. *Democracy Ancient and Modern.* New Brunswick, New Jersey: Rutgers University Press, 1985.

Fitzgerald, Thomas R. "Limitations on Freedom of Speech in the Athenian Assembly." Ph.D. diss., University of Chicago, 1957.

Fitzhugh, George. "The Politics and Economics of Aristotle and Mr. Calhoun." *DeBow's Review* 23 (1857), pp. 163–72.

Ford, Paul Leicester, ed. *Pamphlets on the Constitution of the United States: Published during Its Discussion by the People.* New York: Lenox Hill Publishing, 1888; New York: Burt Franklin Reprints, 1971.

Freedman, Warren. *The Privilege to Keep and Bear Arms: The Second Amendment and Its Interpretation.* New York: Quorum Books, 1989.

Goodman, Paul. "Elbridge Gerry: The Founding Father, and the Republic of Virtue." *Reviews in American History* 5 (1977), pp. 496–502.

Govan, Thomas F. "Alexander Hamilton and Julius Caesar: A Note on the Use of Historical Evidence." *William and Mary Quarterly* (3d ser.) 32 (July 1975), pp. 475–80.

Gribbin, William. "Rollin's Histories and American Republicanism." *William and Mary Quarterly* (3d ser.) 29 (October 1972), pp. 611–22.

Griswold, Charles L. "Rights and Wrongs: Jefferson, Slavery, and Philosophical Quandries." In *A Culture of Rights: The Bill of Rights in Philosophy, Politics, and Law, 1791 and 1991,* edited by Michael J. Lacey and Knud Haakonssen, pp. 144–214. Cambridge: Woodrow Wilson International Center for Scholars and Cambridge University Press, 1991.

Gummere, Richard M. "Socrates at the Printing Press: Benjamin Franklin and the Classics." *Classical Weekly* 26 (1932), 57–59.

———. "John Adams, Togatus." *Philological Quarterly* 13 (1934), pp. 203–10.

———. "The Heritage of the Classics in Colonial North America." *Proceedings of the American Philosophical Society* 99 (1955), pp. 68–78.

———. "John Dickinson, Classical Penman of the Revolution." *Classical Journal* 52 (November 1956), pp. 81–88.

———. "The Classical Politics of John Adams." *Boston Public Library Quarterly* 9, no. 4 (1957), pp. 167–82.

———. "The Classics in a Brave New World." *Harvard Studies in Classical Philology* 62 (1957), pp. 119–39.

———. "The Classical Ancestry of the United States Constitution." *American Quarterly* 14 (1962), pp. 3–18.

———. *The American Colonial Mind and the Classical Tradition.* Cambridge, Massachusetts: Harvard University Press, 1963.

———. *Seven Wise Men of Colonial America.* Cambridge, Massachusetts: Harvard University Press, 1967.

Haines, Charles Grove. *The Revival of Natural Law Concepts.* New York: Russell and Russell, 1965.

Hamilton, Alexander, John Jay, and James Madison. *The Federalist: A Commentary on the Constitution of the United States.* Edited by Benjamin Fletcher Wright. Cambridge, Massachusetts: Harvard University Press, 1965.

Handlin, Oscar. "Learned Books and Revolutionary Action, 1776." *Harvard Library Bulletin* 34 (1986), pp. 362–79.

Hansen, Mogens Herman. *Was Athens a Democracy?: Popular Rule, Liberty and Equality in Ancient and Modern Political Thought.* Copenhagen: Royal Danish Academy of Science and Letters, 1989.

Harrington, J. Drew. "Henry Clay and the Classics." *Filson Club History Quarterly* 61 (1987), pp. 234–46.

Hartfield, Mariane. "New Thoughts on the Proslavery Natural Law Theory: The Importance of History and the Study of Ancient Slavery." *Southern Studies* 22 (1983), pp. 244–59.

Hatch, Orrin G. "Civic Virtue: Wellspring of Liberty." *National Forum* 64, no. 4 (Fall 1989), pp. 34–38.

Henderson, Edith Guild. "The Background of the Seventh Amendment." *Harvard Law Review* 80, no. 2 (December 1966), pp. 289–387.

Higonnet, Patrice L. R. *Sister Republics: The Origins of French and American Republicanism.* Cambridge, Massachusetts: Harvard University Press, 1988.

Hoeflich, M. H. "Roman and Civil Law in American Legal

Education and Research Prior to 1930: A Preliminary Survey." *University of Illinois Law Review,* no. 3 (1984), pp. 719–37.

Hoffman, Richard J. "Classics in the Courts of the United States, 1790–1800." *American Journal of Legal History* 22 (1978), pp. 55–84.

Hunt, Edmund B. "The Rebels and the Ancients: The Use of Ancient Classics in American Polemical Literature, 1763–1776." Ph.D. diss., Ohio State University, 1974.

Hutson, James H. "John Dickinson at the Federal Constitutional Convention." *William and Mary Quarterly* (3d ser.) 40 (1983), pp. 256–82.

Imholtz, August A., Jr. "Jefferson and Anacreon." *Classical Bulletin* 61 (1985), p. 21.

Johnson, Richard R. "Hellas in Hesperia: Ancient Greece and Early America." In *Paths from Ancient Greece,* edited by Carol G. Thomas, pp. 140–67. Leiden: Brill, 1988.

Jones, Howard Mumford. *Revolution and Romanticism.* Cambridge, Massachusetts: Belknap Press of Harvard University Press, 1974.

———. *O Strange New World. American Culture: The Formative Years.* New York: Viking Press, 1964.

Kaiser, Leo M. "Latin Quotations in John Quincy Adams." *Classical Bulletin* 57 (1980), pp. 20–21.

———. "Robert Proud, Horace, and the Revolution." *Classical Bulletin* 56 (1980), pp. 76–77.

Kennedy, George. "Classical Influences on *The Federalist.*" In *Classical Traditions in Early America,* edited by John W. Eadie. Ann Arbor, 1976, pp. 119–38.

———. "A Southerner in the Peloponnesian War." *Southern Humanities Review,* special issue (1977), pp. 21–25.

———. "*Fin-de-Siecle* Classicism: Henry Adams and Thorstein Veblen; Lew Wallace and W. D. Howells." *Classical and Modern Literature* 8, (1987), pp. 15–21.

Kerber, Linda K. *Federalists in Dissent: Imagery and Ideology in Jeffersonian America.* Ithaca: Cornell University Press, 1970.

———. *Women of the Republic: Intellect and Ideology in Revolutionary America.* Chapel Hill: University of North Carolina Press, 1980.

Ketcham, Ralph. *From Colony to Country: The Revolution in American Thought, 1750–1820.* New York: Macmillan, 1974.

Knox, Bernard. "The Enduring Myths of Ancient Greece." *Classical Outlook* 62 (1985), pp. 118–21.

Koch, Adrienne. *The Philosophy of Thomas Jefferson.* New York: Columbia University Press, 1943.

Lasson, Nelson B. *The History and Development of the Fourth Amendment to the United States Constitution.* Baltimore: Johns Hopkins Press, 1937.

LeBoutillier, Cornelia Geer. *American Democracy and Natural Law.* New York: Columbia University Press, 1950.

Lehmann, Karl. *Thomas Jefferson, American Humanist.* Chicago: University of Chicago Press, 1964.

Levy, Leonard, W. *Origins of the Fifth Amendment.* Oxford: Oxford University Press, 1968.

Litto, Frederick W. "Addison's *Cato* in the Colonies." *William and Mary Quarterly* (3d ser.) 23 (July 1966), pp. 431–49.

Lounsbury, Richard. "*Ludibria Rerum Mortalium*: Charlestonian Intellectuals and Their Classics." In *Intellectual Life in Antebellum Charleston*, edited by Michael O'Brien and David Moltke-Hansen, pp. 325–69. Knoxville: University of Tennessee Press, 1986.

MacKendrick, Paul. "This Rich Source of Delight: The Classics and the Founding Fathers." *Classical Journal* 72 (1976–1977), pp. 97–106.

Malsberger, John W. "The Political Thought of Fisher Ames." *Journal of the Early Republic* 2 (1982), pp. 1–20.

May, Henry F. *The Enlightment in America.* New York: Oxford University Press, 1976.

McDonald, Forrest. *Alexander Hamilton: A Biography.* New York: Oxford University Press, 1976.

———. "A Founding Father's Library." *Library of Liberty* 1 (1978), pp. 4–15.

———. *Novus Ordo Seclorum: The Intellectual Origins of the Constitution.* Lawrence: University of Kansas Press, 1985.

Meyers, Marvin, ed. *The Mind of the Founder: Sources of the Political Thought of James Madison* New York: Bobbs-Merrill, 1973.

Middlekauff, Robert. *Ancients and Axioms: Seconary Education in Eighteenth-Century New England.* New Haven: Yale University Press, 1963.

Miles, Edwin A. "The Whig Party and the Menace of Caesar." *Tennessee Historical Quarterly* 27 (1968), pp. 361–79.

———. "The Old South and the Classical World." *North Carolina Historical Review* 48 (1971), pp. 258–75.

———. "The Young American Nation and the Classical World." *Journal of the History of Ideas* 35 (1974), pp. 259–74.

Miller, John C. *The Wolf by the Ears: Thomas Jefferson and Slavery.* New York: Free Press, 1977.

Morison, Samuel Eliot. *The Puritan Pronaos: Studies in the Intellectual Life of New England in the Seventeenth Century.* New York: New York University Press, 1936.

Mullett, Charles F. "Classical Influences on the American Revolution." *Classical Journal* 35 (1939–1940), pp. 92–104.

———. "Ancient Historians and 'Enlightened' Reviewers." *Review of Politics* 21 (1959), pp. 550–65.

———. *Fundamental Law and the American Revolution, 1760–1776.* New York: Octagon Books, 1966.

Murphy, John P. "Rome at the Constitutional Convention." *Classical Outlook* 51 (1974), pp. 112–14.

O'Connor, Joseph F. "Thomas Jefferson's Reading List: The Classics and the Development of the 'Whole Man.' " *Chronicle of Higher Education*, February 3, 1988, p. A48.

Pangle, T. "Federalists and the Idea of Virtue." *This Constitution* 5 (Winter 1984), pp. 19–26.

Pound, Roscoe. *The Lawyer from Antiquity to Modern Times.* St. Paul: West Publishing, 1953.

Reid, John Philip. *The concept of Liberty in the Age of the American Revolution.* Chicago: Chicago University Press, 1988.

Reinhold, Meyer. *Classica Americana: The Greek and Roman Heritage in the United States.* Detroit: Wayne State University Press, 1984.

———. *The Classick Pages: Classical Reading of Eighteenth-Century Americans.* University Park, Pennsylvania: American Philological Association, 1975.

———. "The American Interpretation of Classical Virtue." *Humanities* 8, no. 1 (1987), pp. 4–7.

———. "The Latin Tradition in the United States." *Helios* 14 (1987), pp. 123–39.

Reinhold, Meyer, and John W. Eadie. "Research on the Classical Influences on Early America." *Classical World* 67 (1973), pp. 1–3.

Rexine, John E. "Classical Political Theory and the U.S. Constitution." *Greek Orthodox Theological Review* 21 (1976), pp. 321–40.

Richard, Carl J. *The Founding Fathers and the Classics.* Ph.D. diss., Vanderbilt University, 1988.

Robathan, Dorothy M. "John Adams and the Classics." *New England Quarterly* 19 (1946), pp. 91–98.

Schleiner, Winfried. "The Infant Hercules: Franklin's Design for a Medal Commemorating American Liberty." *Eighteenth Century Studies* 10 (1976–1977), pp. 236–44.

Stein, Peter. "The Attraction of the Civil Law in Post-Revolutionary America." *Virginia Law Review* 52 (1966), pp. 403–34.

Storing, Herbert J., ed. *The Complete Antifederalist.* 7 vols. Chicago: University of Chicago Press, 1981.

Stourzh, Gerald. *Alexander Hamilton and the Idea of Republican Government.* Palo Alto: Stanford University Press, 1970.

Tolles, Frederick B. "Quaker Humanist: James Logan As a Classical Scholar." *Pennsylvania Magazine of History and Biography* 79 (1955), pp. 415–38.

Turk, Milton H. "Without Classical Studies." *Journal of Higher Education* 4 (1933), pp. 339–46.

Van Cromphout, Gustaaf. "Cotton Mather As Plutarchan Biographer." *American Literature* 46 (1974–1975), pp. 465–81.

———. "*Manductio ad Ministerium*: Cotton Mather As Neoclassicist." *American Literature* 53 (1981), pp. 361–79.

von Leyden, Wolfgang. *Aristotle on Equality and Justice: His Political Argument.* New York: St. Martin's Press, 1985.

Wieacker, Franz. "The Importance of Roman Law for Western Civilization and Western Legal Thought." *Boston College International and Comparative Law Review* 4, no. 2 (1981), pp. 257–81.

Wiesen, David S. "Herodotus and the Modern Debate over Race and Slavery." *The Ancient World* 3 (1980), pp. 3–16.

Wills, Garry. *Explaining America: The Federalist.* New York: Penguin Books, 1981.

———. *Cincinnatus: George Washington and the Enlightenment.* Garden City, New York: Doubleday, 1984.

Wilson, Douglas L. "The American *Agricola*: Jefferson's Agrarianism and the Classical Tradition." *South Atlantic Quarterly* 80 (1981), pp. 339–54.

———, *Jefferson's Literary Commonplace Book.* Princeton: Princeton University Press, 1989.

Wiltshire, Susan Ford. "Thomas Jefferson and John Adams on the Classics." *Arion* 6 (Spring 1967), pp. 116–32.

———. "Sam Houston and the *Iliad*." *Tennessee Historical Quarterly* 32, no. 3 (Fall 1973), pp. 249–54.

———. "Jefferson, Calhoun and the Slavery Debate: The Classics and the Two Minds of the South." *Southern Humanities Review*, special issue (1977), pp. 33–40.

———. "Aristotle in America." *Humanities* 8, no. 1 (1987), pp. 8–11.

———. "The Greek Origin of Public Life and the Constitutional Separation of Powers." *Touchstone* 11 (1987), pp. 10–12.

———. *The Usefulness of Classical Learning in the Eighteenth Century.* University Park, Pennsylvania: American Philological Association, 1977.

Wish, Harvey. "Aristotle, Plato, and the Mason-Dixon Line." *Journal of the History of Ideas* 10 (1949), pp. 254–266.

Wood, Gordon S. *The Creation of the American Republic, 1776–1787.* Chapel Hill: University of North Carolina Press, 1969.

———. "The Intellectual Origins of the American Constitution." *National Forum* 64, no. 4 (Fall 1989), pp. 5–11.

Wright, Benjamin Fletcher, Jr. *American Interpretations of Natural Law.* Cambridge, Massachusetts: Harvard University Press, 1931.

Wright, Louis B. "The Purposeful Reaading of Our Colonial Ancestors." *Journal of English Literary History* 4 (1937), pp. 85–111.

———. "The Classical Tradition in Colonial Virginia." *Papers of the Bibliographical Society of America* 33 (1939), pp. 85–97.

———. "Thomas Jefferson and the Classics." *Proceedings of the American Philosophical Society* 87 (1943–1944), pp. 223–33.

———. *The First Gentlemen of Virginia: Intellectual Qualities of the Early Colonial Ruling Class.* San Marino, California, 1940.

———. *Tradition and the Founding Fathers.* Charlottesville: University Press at Virginia, 1975.

Index

Abrams, Philip, 85
Abstractions: dangers of, 87; Roman aversion to, 18
Accountability, of public officials, 40, 115, 156
Actium, battle of, 106
Adams, John, 91
Adamson v. California, 97
Aemilius Paulus, L., 141
Aeschines, 112
Aeschylus, *Oresteia* of, 156–57
Agora (Athenian), 122
Agrippa, Marcus, 178
Alcibiades, 114
Alexander the Great, 13, 19
Alphabet, Greek, invention of, 10
Ambrose, 23, 32, 34
American Revolution, 59, 88, 132, 187n.4; illegal search and seizure as cause of, 146; and quartering of soldiers, 142
Amphictyonic leagues, 99, 176, 213n.26
Anabaptists, 197n.52
Androcles, 114
Anglicans, opposition to religious liberty clause by, 90
Anselm, 45
Antifederalists, 91, 95
Antigone, 25
Antipatros, 121
Antiphon, 166
Antonius, Marcus, 106, 117
Aphrodisias (Asia Minor), 143
Aphrodite, 106

Apollo, temple of, on Palatine, 106
Aquae Sextae (Aix), 177
Aquinas, Thomas, 27, 32, 60, 65, 79, 97; accommodation of Greek philosophy to Christianity by, 36; "double ordering" of, 67; fluidity of thought of, 37; invention of term for "political science" by, 38; knowledge of Roman law of, 38; lack of thoroughgoing rationalism in thought of, 39; reconciliation of Christianity and Aristotelianism by, 35–39; reliance on divine revelation of, 12; *Summa contra Gentiles* of, 36; *Summa theologica* of, 36
Areopagus, Council of, 114, 120
Ares, 106
Argentinus, 106
Aristophanes, and enfranchisement of women, 203n.91
Aristotelianism, in Middle Ages, 64
Aristotle, 4, 12, 17, 26, 27, 42, 66, 67, 70, 80, 81, 135; and Christianity, 35; idea of state of, 87; organic theory of society of, 41; politics of, rooted in city-state, 13; preference for arms-bearers in mixed polity of, 136–37; quoted by John

Locke, 13; recommendation of, by Locke to students, 188n.18; revival of "natural man" of, in England, 52; as source of natural law theory, 13; view of state as natural unit of, 66; world view of, 73
Arles, Roman amphitheater at, 180
Armsbearing: classical antecedents to, 134–42; in Greece, 134–38; individualistic interpretation of, consistent with cowboy ethic, 135; at Rome, 138–42; state constitutions with collective right, 134; state constitutions with individual right of armsbearing, 134
Army: professionalization of, at Rome, 138–39; standing, in peacetime, in English Bill of Rights, 85; in Virginia Declaration of Rights, 132–33
Articles of Confederation, 91, 176
Ascending theme of government, 39, 40, 52, 87
Ashe v. Swenson, 209n.7
Assemblies, Roman, 123–29; given no power, 124; membership in, determined by wealth, 125–26; standing rather than seated, 127; for voting, 126–27. *See also* Ecclesia

239